Fathers Paulist

Five-minute sermons for low masses on all Sundays of the year by priest of the Congregation of St. Paul

Vol. 1

Fathers Paulist

Five-minute sermons for low masses on all Sundays of the year by priest of the Congregation of St. Paul
Vol. 1

ISBN/EAN: 9783337265021

Printed in Europe, USA, Canada, Australia, Japan

Cover: Foto ©Lupo / pixelio.de

More available books at **www.hansebooks.com**

Five-Minute Sermons

For Low Masses on all Sundays of the Year by Priests of the Congregation of St. Paul

VOLUME I.

Frederick Pustet & Co.,
Printers to the Holy Apostolic See and The Sacred Congregation of Rites.
Ratisbon   Rome   New York   Cincinnati

PREFACE.

THESE short sermons were commenced in St. Paul's Church, New York, toward the close of the year 1876. The motive for doing this was that the great number of persons who generally attend only a Low Mass on Sundays might enjoy the advantage of hearing the word of God preached, without being delayed too long for their convenience. For this reason they were limited in time to five minutes, while the effort was made to condense within this brief compass a sufficient amount of matter at once instructive and hortatory, in plain and simple language, to answer the practical purposes of a popular discourse. In order to secure this twofold object of making the sermons so short that they would not overrun the limit of five minutes, and at the same time so solid and pungent that they would furnish a real nutriment and stimulus to the minds and hearts of the audience, it was obviously necessary that they should be carefully written out. For each priest to write and commit to memory his own sermon would be undertaking too much; and therefore the plan was adopted of assigning to one the task of writing all the sermons, to be read by each priest celebrating a Low Mass for the people. The sermons have been published every week in the *Catholic Review,* and an advanced sheet of the printed copy, pasted on a tablet, has been furnished, to be used in preaching the sermon at each one of the Low Masses on the Sunday. The utility of these sermons, the satisfaction they give to the people who hear them, and the advantage which can be derived by reading them after they have been published, are too obvious to need explanation. This advantage we hope to make more extensive by now publishing the greater part of the sermons which have been thus far preached, and printed in a weekly newspaper, in the more convenient and permanent form of a volume. It is hoped that they will be practically useful to many priests who may read them, or use them in preparing similar short sermons of their own for those occasions when it is not practicable to give longer and more elaborate discourses to their congregations. Many of them will be found, besides, to furnish a nucleus for the composition of sermons of the usual length and rhetorical completeness. To the faithful they afford matter for spiritual reading and profitable meditation which is all the better for being put into a brief and simple shape.

The merit of devising and first carrying into execution this excellent plan of preaching the Five-Minute

Preface. v

Sermons at Low Mass belongs to the late Rev. Algernon A. Brown, C.S.P. It is quite proper to praise the works of one who has departed this life, even though he was one of our own society. Many of the sermons written by Father Brown and contained in the present volume are masterpieces in the art of miniature discourse. They are not fragments or sections of sermons, reading like pages taken from longer discourses or meditations, but genuine sermonettes, each one complete and perfect in itself. They are marked, also, by a grave and solemn earnestness remarkable in the utterances of so very young a priest, and seeming to be like a shadow from a very near proximity to the eternal world, cast over his spirit as he rapidly drew near to the goal of his appointed course. It will surely be deemed appropriate, and prove agreeable to the readers of this volume of sermons, that a few lines should be consecrated to the memory of the one who may justly be called its author, although the greater portion of its actual contents came from others who succeeded to him in the task from which he was called away at so early a period of his sacerdotal life.

Father Algernon Brown, the son of a respectable physician who is still living and resides in the Isle of Wight, was born at Cobham, Surrey, England, May 30, 1848. He was bred in the Established Church of England, and during his early youth was educated at a ritualistic school in Brighton. His tastes and predilections were ecclesiastical, and he entered warmly into the study and practice of the doctrinal, moral, and liturgical views and ways of the Anglican ritualists. At the age of eighteen he was received into the Catholic Church by Father Knox, of the Oratory, and went first to St. Edmund's College, afterwards to Prior Park, in order to prepare himself for the priesthood.

After nearly completing his course, and having already received minor orders, he came in 1871, with two younger brothers, both converts, and one of the two an ecclesiastical student, to the United States, and was ordained priest by the Most Rev. Archbishop Purcell in the Archdiocese of Cincinnati, May 25, 1872.

In the year 1874 he was received as a member of the Congregation of Paulists after a year's novitiate. During the four years which elapsed between this period and that of his death Father Brown suffered continually, and often severely, from ill health, yet nevertheless continued to labor bravely and cheerfully, beyond his strength, until he was actually overpowered by fatal disease. His special department of work lay in the direction of the sacristy and of the ceremonies at the public offices of divine worship, and the management of the devout confraternities established in the parish. His accurate knowledge of the rubrics, ceremonial, and sacred chant, his ardent zeal for the order and decorum of the divine service, and his untiring assiduity in the work assigned him, were equally valuable to the religious community of which he was a member, and edifying to the people.

After the Easter of 1877 his failing health obliged him to make a visit to his native England and his paternal home as the last hope of prolonging his life. In the following autumn he returned, enjoying a considerable but only temporary amelioration in his physical condition, which soon after began to grow sensibly worse. On the Feast of the Immaculate Conception he attempted for the last time by a heroic effort to say Mass, but was prevented by a fainting-fit which prostrated him at the foot of the altar as he was commencing the Introit. From this day forward he was slowly dying, until at last, after long and careful preparation, he closed his eyes peacefully under the icy hand of death. His death occurred on Monday in Passion Week, the 8th of April, 1878, at the age of twenty-nine years and eleven months, and his solemn obsequies were celebrated on the following Wednesday. All the sermons in this volume which can be identified with certainty as his are marked with his initial letter, B. May they long remain unfaded, a bouquet of immortelles

IN MEMORIAM!

ST. PAUL'S CHURCH,
  NINTH AVENUE AND FIFTY-NINTH STREET, NEW YORK.
    FEAST OF ALL SAINTS, 1879.

FIVE MINUTE SERMONS
VOLUME I.

CONTENTS.

	PAGE
First Sunday of Advent:	
Sermon I.,	18
Sermon II.,	20
Sermon III.,	22
Second Sunday of Advent:	
Sermon IV.,	27
Sermon V.,	30
Sermon VI.,	32
Third Sunday of Advent:	
Sermon VII.,	37
Sermon VIII.,	39
Sermon IX.,	42
Fourth Sunday of Advent:	
Sermon X.,	47
Sermon XI.,	49
Sermon XII.,	52
Sunday within the Octave of Christmas:	
Sermon XIII.,	56
Sermon XIV.,	59
Sermon XV.,	62
The Epiphany:	
Sermon XVI.,	66
Sermon XVII.,	68

Contents.

                                              PAGE

First Sunday after Epiphany:
    Sermon XVIII., ... 73
    Sermon XIX., ... 75

Second Sunday after Epiphany:
    Sermon XX., ... 80
    Sermon XXI., ... 83
    Sermon XXII., ... 86

Third Sunday after Epiphany:
    Sermon XXIII., ... 91
    Sermon XXIV., ... 93

Fourth Sunday after Epiphany:
    Sermon XXV., ... 97
    Sermon XXVI., ... 100
    Sermon XXVII., ... 103

Fifth Sunday after Epiphany:
    Sermon XXVIII., ... 108
    Sermon XXIX., ... 111

Sixth Sunday after Epiphany:
    Sermon XXX., ... 115
    Sermon XXXI., ... 118

Septuagesima Sunday:
    Sermon XXXII., ... 122
    Sermon XXXIII., ... 125
    Sermon XXXIV., ... 127

Sexagesima Sunday:
    Sermon XXXV., ... 133
    Sermon XXXVI., ... 136
    Sermon XXXVII., ... 138

Quinquagesima Sunday:
- Sermon XXXVIII., ... 142
- Sermon XXXIX., ... 145
- Sermon XL., ... 147

First Sunday of Lent:
- Sermon XLI., ... 152
- Sermon XLII., ... 154
- Sermon XLIII., ... 157

Second Sunday of Lent:
- Sermon XLIV., ... 161
- Sermon XLV., ... 164
- Sermon XLVI., ... 166

Third Sunday of Lent:
- Sermon XLVII., ... 170
- Sermon XLVIII., ... 173
- Sermon XLIX., ... 175

Fourth Sunday of Lent:
- Sermon L., ... 179
- Sermon LI., ... 182

Passion Sunday:
- Sermon LII., ... 186
- Sermon LIII., ... 188
- Sermon LIV., ... 192

Palm Sunday:
- Sermon LV., ... 196
- Sermon LVI., ... 198
- Sermon LVII., ... 200

Contents.

Easter Sunday:

	PAGE
Sermon LVIII.,	204
Sermon LIX.,	207
Sermon LX.,	210

Low Sunday:

Sermon LXI.,	214
Sermon LXII.,	217
Sermon LXIII.,	219

Second Sunday after Easter:

Sermon LXIV.,	223
Sermon LXV.,	225
Sermon LXVI.,	227

Third Sunday after Easter:

Sermon LXVII.,	233
Sermon LXVIII.,	235
Sermon LXIX.,	238

Fourth Sunday after Easter:

Sermon LXX.,	243
Sermon LXXI.,	245
Sermon LXXII.,	248

Fifth Sunday after Easter:

Sermon LXXIII.,	252
Sermon LXXIV.,	254
Sermon LXXV.,	257

Sunday within the Octave of the Ascension:

Sermon LXXVI.,	260
Sermon LXXVII.,	263
Sermon LXXVIII.,	265

Contents.

Feast of Pentecost, or Whit-Sunday:

	PAGE
Sermon LXXIX.,	269
Sermon LXXX.,	272
Sermon LXXXI.,	274

Trinity Sunday:

Sermon LXXXII.,	279
Sermon LXXXIII.,	282
Sermon LXXXIV.,	284

Second Sunday after Pentecost:

Sermon LXXXV.,	289
Sermon LXXXVI.,	292
Sermon LXXXVII.,	295

Third Sunday after Pentecost:

Sermon LXXXVIII.,	299
Sermon LXXXIX.,	301
Sermon XC.,	304

Fourth Sunday after Pentecost:

Sermon XCI.,	308
Sermon XCII.,	311

Fifth Sunday after Pentecost:

Sermon XCIII.,	315
Sermon XCIV.,	317

Sixth Sunday after Pentecost:

Sermon XCV.,	321
Sermon XCVI.,	323
Sermon XCVII.,	326

Contents.

Seventh Sunday after Pentecost:

	PAGE
Sermon XCVIII.,	330
Sermon XCIX.,	332
Sermon C.,	335

Eighth Sunday after Pentecost:

Sermon CI.,	339
Sermon CII.,	342
Sermon CIII.,	344

Ninth Sunday after Pentecost:

Sermon CIV.,	349
Sermon CV.,	352

Tenth Sunday after Pentecost:

Sermon CVI.,	356
Sermon CVII.,	359
Sermon CVIII.,	361

Eleventh Sunday after Pentecost:

Sermon CIX.,	366
Sermon CX.,	369
Sermon CXI.,	371

Twelfth Sunday after Pentecost:

Sermon CXII.,	376
Sermon CXIII.,	378
Sermon CXIV.,	381

Thirteenth Sunday after Pentecost:

Sermon CXV.,	385
Sermon CXVI.,	388
Sermon CXVII.,	390

Contents.

Fourteenth Sunday after Pentecost:
- Sermon CXVIII., ... 394
- Sermon CXIX., ... 397
- Sermon CXX., ... 400

Fifteenth Sunday after Pentecost:
- Sermon CXXI., ... 404
- Sermon CXXII., ... 406
- Sermon CXXIII., ... 409

Sixteenth Sunday after Pentecost:
- Sermon CXXIV., ... 413
- Sermon CXXV., ... 416

Seventeenth Sunday after Pentecost:
- Sermon CXXVI., ... 420
- Sermon CXXVII., ... 422

Eighteenth Sunday after Pentecost:
- Sermon CXXVIII., ... 426
- Sermon CXXIX., ... 428

Nineteenth Sunday after Pentecost:
- Sermon CXXX., ... 433
- Sermon CXXXI., ... 436

Twentieth Sunday after Pentecost:
- Sermon CXXXII., ... 440
- Sermon CXXXIII., ... 442

Twenty-first Sunday after Pentecost:
- Sermon CXXXIV., ... 447

Twenty-second Sunday after Pentecost:
    Sermon CXXXV., ...
    Sermon CXXXVI., ...

Twenty-third Sunday after Pentecost:
    Sermon CXXXVII., ...
    Sermon CXXXVIII., ...
    Sermon CXXXIX., ...

Twenty-fourth or Last Sunday after Pentecost:
    Sermon CXL., ...
    Sermon CXLI., ...
    Sermon CXLII., ...

First Sunday of Advent.

Epistle. *Romans xiii.* 11–14. Brethren: Know that it is now the hour for us to rise from sleep. For now our salvation is nearer than when we believed. The night is passed, and the day is at hand. Let us therefore cast off the works of darkness, and put on the armor of light; let us walk honestly as in the day; not in rioting and drunkenness, not in chambering and impurities, not in contention and envy; but put ye on the Lord Jesus Christ.

Gospel. *St. Luke xxi.* 25–33. At that time Jesus said to his disciples: There shall be signs in the sun, and in the moon, and in the stars: and upon the earth distress of nations, by reason of the confusion of the roaring of the sea and of the waves, men withering away for fear, and expectation of what shall come upon the whole world. For the powers of heaven shall be moved: and then they shall see the Son of Man coming in a cloud with great power and majesty. But when these things begin to come to pass, look up and lift up your heads: because your redemption is at hand. And he spoke to them a similitude. See the fig-tree, and all the trees: when they now shoot forth their fruit, you know that summer is nigh; so you also when you shall see these things come to pass, know that the kingdom of God is at hand. Amen I say to you. this generation shall not pass away, till all things be fulfilled. Heaven and earth shall pass away, but my words shall not pass away.

SERMON I.

Heaven and earth shall pass away.—St. Luke xxi. 33.

Ah! my friend, how are you? How do you do? Where are you going? These are every-day expressions, dear brethren. Probably some neighbor spoke to you thus as you were coming to Mass. This is the first Sunday in Advent, the Sunday of judgment, and I am going to put the same questions to you. I begin with the last one. Where are you going? Young men, old men, women, girls, children, people, priests, rich and poor, where are all of you going? Are you going to church or for a walk? No, we have a trial at court and are summoned to appear. Whose trial? Our own. Yes, we are all going to judgment, the trial of eternity before the all-seeing Judge. We are all formed in a great procession. No matter whether we are good or bad, in a state of grace or of mortal sin, no matter whether our case is a good one or a bad one, no matter if our cause be just or unjust, we are all going to judgment—all going to the great trial, in which every living soul, each man and woman and child, shall be the prisoners at the bar, and God, the judge of all, shall sit upon the great white Throne. When will that trial-day come? No one knows, not even the angels, our Lord says. Judgment will come suddenly. Time has been given you. You have been told "beforehand." The *actual* coming will be sudden. "Behold, I come as a thief in the night." "Behold, I come quickly." "Behold, I come as the lightning." Such are the terms in which our Lord speaks of his second advent. When men are eating and drinking, marrying, buying, and selling, burying the dead, laboring, praying, waking or sleeping, *then* there will be a cry heard, "Behold, the Bridegroom cometh; go ye forth to meet Him." Go forth just as you are; just as the moment finds you; without a moment more to prepare, without an instant in which to say, "God help me!" Where are you going, then? Going to judgment. Going to a *sudden* judgment. Going to meet accusers who will rise out of the graves of earth and from the pit of hell to bear witness against sinners for all the commandments they have broken, all the duties they have neglected, all the scandal and bad example they have given. Woe to bad parents in that day! Woe to disobedient children in that day! Woe to the drunken, the impure, the thieves, the liars, the false witnesses, the apostates in that day! Ah! then, how do *you* do, Christian, Catholic? How are you, baptized of God? How is your health, the health of your soul? Are you in the fever of sin? Do you see upon your souls great livid plague-spots of mortal offences against the Almighty? Then tremble, for you have to face the God "whose eyes are brighter than the noonday sun"! He will ask: "How are you? What mean these stains upon your soul? Where is the white garment that I gave you? Where is my image and likeness?" Woe to every one who cannot answer these questions; for to be unable to answer means to be unable to go to heaven, means that you will be found guilty by the Eternal Judge and condemned to everlasting death. Let, then, these two questions ring in your ears: Where are you going? How are you in God's sight? You are going to judgment. Are you in a fit state to appear there? Brethren, it will be an awful day, that day of judgment, even for the just. "Where, then, shall the unjust and the sinner appear?" Look up to the heavens as you leave this church. The clouds are not yet riven. The sun is not yet darkened. Oh! then there is yet time. There is a moment's lull before the storm breaks; a second's pause before the trumpet sounds. But the day of judgment *will come*, for Jesus Christ has told us so, and, as he says: "Heaven and earth shall pass away, but my words shall not pass away." B.

SERMON II.

Brethren: Know that it is now the hour for us to rise from sleep.—Rom. xiii. 11.

To-day, my dear brethren, is the New Year's Day of the Catholic Church. To-day she begins again that round of seasons and festivals which will never cease to be repeated till that day comes of which this season of Advent reminds us—that day in which, as St. Peter tells us, "the heavens shall pass away with great violence, and the elements shall be melted with heat, and the earth and the works which are in it shall be burnt up"; that day when He who died for us on the cross shall come to judge the living and the dead.

The church begins her year with Advent, because this season represents principally, not that last coming of our Lord of which I have just spoken, but rather that time which went before his first coming —that long period of several thousand years, answering to the four weeks of this season, with which the world's history began, and in which it was waiting for the promise of redemption to be fulfilled. But there is another very good reason for each one of us to begin our own new year now, and it is one of the reasons why the second advent of Christ is presented to our minds by the church, as well as his first, at this time.

It is that we may now make that serious examination of our past life, and those firm resolutions for the future, that we can best make at the beginning of a new year, when we feel most strongly that one more of those short cycles by which our life is measured has gone for ever beyond our reach, and brought us so much nearer not only to the day of general judgment, but also to that more imminent one in which each one of us shall stand alone before the throne of God to give an account of the use which we have made of these precious years which he has given us, and which are passing so rapidly away.

This new year's day of the church is a time, then, above all others in which we should make those resolutions without which we cannot be saved.

It is said that hell is paved with good intentions; it may with equal truth be said that heaven is paved with good resolutions. What is the difference between the two? An intention is a purpose the carrying out of which is put off till some other time; a resolution is one which is carried out now. So, as the putting off of our good purposes is the sure way to lose our souls, the carrying them out at once is the means absolutely necessary to salvation and certain to secure it.

No one ever saved his soul without some time or other making a resolution to keep the law of God, and going to work at once to carry it out, and persevering in it to the end of life. Such a resolution has got to be made at some time, and now is the time to make it.

Look back, then, my brethren, on this first day of the new year, at the one which has just gone never to return, and see if you are satisfied with the way you have spent it. Ask yourselves if you have not been trifling away enough of the short time which was given you to be spent in the service of God, and if there is any too much left to make some recompense to him for all that he has done for you; and say, with the church in the Epistle of this Sunday, that now it is indeed the hour to rise from sleep, from this fatal sleep of indifference and ingratitude, and go to work in real earnest on the business of your salvation, and not rest again till the time for rest has come. God will surely give that eternal rest to those who labor during life, but he has not promised it to sluggards and traitors, as those certainly are who care only for themselves and not for him, and who expect their reward without doing anything to deserve such a favor at his hands.

SERMON III.

Heaven and earth shall pass away.—St. Luke xxi. 33.

By the word "heaven" our Lord does not mean that heaven to which we shall be admitted if we are faithful, for that, as we know, is eternal. No; he means some part of the visible heavens with which our earth is immediately connected. The earth, and to some extent the visible heaven also, we do not know how, will pass away as to their present state—they will be so changed that it may be said that the old earth and the old heaven have been destroyed.

It is to remind us of this second coming, or advent, of our Lord, when the world and all that it contains shall pass away, as well as of his first coming, which we are to celebrate at Christmas, that the church keeps this season on which we have just entered, and calls it by this name of Advent.

This truth, that the heavens and earth which we see shall pass away, or be destroyed, is a matter of faith. We cannot, probably, prove by science that this must take place, certainly not that such a change is so near as the Scriptures seem to indicate; but we do not need the light of faith to show us that they shall pass away from *us*, and that, perhaps, very soon. In a few years—perhaps in a few months or days—we shall close our eyes in death, and the heavens and earth which we now see shall disappear from our sight for ever. There are two lessons which we may learn from this evident and certain truth, and which the church wishes us to consider at this time.

The first is that the pleasures of this world are so fleeting and uncertain that it is not worth while for us to take any pains to secure them. We can only hold them for a little while at the most; they are like the treasures which one sometimes possesses in a dream and which melt away in the hands on waking. A moment after death it will make no difference to us whether we have had them or not; they will seem to have been possessed only as in a dream when we wake to the reality of the next world. "They have slept their sleep," says the Psalmist, "and all the men of riches have found nothing in their hands." The life of one who makes pleasure his object is like a sleep; and, as St. Paul warns us in the Epistle of to-day, "it is now the hour for us to rise from sleep. For now our salvation is nearer than when we believed."

Our real salvation, the only life which is really worth enjoying, is coming very soon. This life is only a season of Advent to prepare for that eternal festival to which we have been invited by the King of kings.

So, as our first conclusion is that it is not worth while to seek for the pleasures of this life, our second is that it is not a matter for great grief if we have pain and affliction in it. One would not mind suffering for a day, or even for a week, if the rest of only this short mortal life was to be passed in uninterrupted enjoyment. So, if it be the will of God, perhaps we can manage to pass a few years in pain and sorrow, with the promise, which will not fail us, of a happiness that shall be eternal.

Especially when we remember that pain and sorrow in this life make that promise all the more sure. "Blessed are ye poor," says our Lord, "for yours is the kingdom of God. Blessed are ye that hunger now, for ye shall be filled. Blessed are ye that weep now, for ye shall laugh. . . . Blessed are they that mourn, for they shall be comforted." "Behold," he says, "I come quickly, and my reward is with me, to render to every man according to his works." Let this, then, be our care, not to seek pleasure nor to avoid pain which shall soon pass away, but so to live that we shall be anxious to meet him and have a well-grounded hope of receiving that reward; that when he says, "Surely I come quickly," we may be able to answer with the apostle, "Amen. Come, Lord Jesus." For that life is the best in which one is most willing and ready to die; in which one hears most gladly that this heaven and this earth shall pass away.

Second Sunday of Advent.

EPISTLE. *Romans xv.* 4–13. Brethren: What things soever were written, were written for our instruction; that through patience and the comfort of the Scriptures, we might have hope. Now the God of patience and of comfort grant you to be of one mind one towards another, according to Jesus Christ: that with one mind, and with one mouth, you may glorify God and the Father of our Lord Jesus Christ. Wherefore receive one another, as Christ also hath received you unto the honor of God. For I say that Christ Jesus was minister of the circumcision for the truth of God, to confirm the promises made to the fathers. But that the Gentiles are to glorify God for his mercy, as it is written: Therefore will I confess to thee, O Lord, among the Gentiles, and will sing to thy name. And again he saith: Rejoice, ye Gentiles, with his people. And again: Praise the Lord, all ye Gentiles; and magnify him, all ye people. And again Isaias saith: There shall be a root of Jesse; and he that shall rise up to rule the Gentiles, in him the Gentiles shall hope. Now the God of hope fill you with all joy and peace in believing: that you may abound in hope, and in the power of the Holy Ghost.

GOSPEL. *St. Matt. xi.* 2–10. At that time: When John had heard in prison the works of Christ, sending two of his disciples he said to him: Art thou he that art to come, or look we for another? And Jesus making answer said to them: Go and relate to John what you have heard and seen. The blind see, the lame walk, the lepers are cleansed, the deaf hear, the dead rise again, the poor have the gospel preached to them. And blessed is he that shall not be scandalized in me. And when they went their way, Jesus began to say to the multitudes concerning John: What went you out into the desert to see? a reed shaken with the wind? But what went you out to see? a man clothed in soft garments? Behold they that are clothed in soft garments are in the houses of kings. But what went you out to see? a prophet? yea, I tell you, and more than a prophet. For this is he of whom it is written: Behold, I send my Angel before thy face, who shall prepare thy way before thee.

SERMON IV.

Behold, I send my Angel before thy face.—ST. MATT. xi. 10.

I SUPPOSE, brethren, among the first things you remember hearing of in your childhood were "*the angels of God*" or, as people often say, "*the angels of God in heaven.*" You remember, I am sure, how pleased you were to look at their pictures, with sweet faces and large, outstretched wings, and how glad you were when you were told that one of those guardian spirits was always by your side. But this morning I want to speak to you, not of the "angels of God in heaven," but of the *angels of God on earth.* And who are *they?* you will ask. Are they spirits? Have they wings like the angels we saw years ago in the picture-book? No, they have not wings; they are not pure spirits; they are men, women, and children just like ourselves. The word "angel" means a messenger, one who is sent with tidings. Thus St. John Baptist (who was sent to tell the world that Jesus Christ was coming) is called in to-day's Gospel "an angel"—that is, a messenger from God. Now, brethren, all of us ought to be messengers of God to our neighbor and to the world. We are all Catholics, have all been called to know the true faith, and we have all been taught how to observe God's moral law. First, then, we Catholics ought to be the *angels of God on earth* to those who are not Catholics. We ought to do our best in our own little circle to spread the knowledge of our holy religion. By our lives we ought to show the world that the Catholic religion makes us better citizens, better and more honest men of business, and truer lovers of our neighbors and mankind. Many of you "live out" at service in Protestant or infidel families; many of you are working for non-Catholic employers; many are employed in factories, surrounded by those who belong to false religions or who have no religion at all. Oh! what chances such have to be *angels of God on earth.* You can show by your fidelity to work, by your strict honesty, by your modest behavior, that you belong to a religion which comes from God. By a seasonable word, by the loan of a book, by showing your horror of cursing and swearing and of bad talk, you would be doing God's work, and showing to those outside the church that there is *something* in your belief which makes you good. Have you done this? Have you not, on the contrary, often scandalized our non-Catholic friends by your bad example, your dishonesty, your exhibitions of temper, your outbursts of blasphemy, and your consent to what was impure? Ah! when you do these things you are the *angels of the devil on earth.* You are doing his work and bearing his message. Again, to your own Catholic brethren and to your own family you can be *angels of God on earth!* Have you got a scandalous neighbor, a negligent father or mother, a wicked child, a profligate husband or son? Oh! be angels of God to these unfortunate ones. By your good example, your patience in affliction, by your charity and forbearance, your strict attention to your religious duties, and, in short, by a really good life, you will be able to "prepare the way of the Lord." You will "go before his face" to prepare the way for his graces. Don't let it be said by those who are not good Catholics, "I don't see that those who go to their duties are any better than I am." Show them that you *are* better, and that it is *religion* that makes you so. "Example is better than precept." Actions speak louder than words. Oh! then be angels of God to those outside the church, be angels of God to your children, to your parents, to your friends and neighbors. Once there was a child who had been very badly brought up by his parents. He went to church by chance one day, and heard an instruction on the laws of the church. When he came home, although it was Friday, there was meat for dinner. The boy would not eat it. Furious at this, his bad parents beat him; but the child remained firm, till at last, touched by his example, the parents converted themselves and lived as good Catholics. That boy was an angel of God on earth. "Go ye and do in like manner," and then our Lord Jesus Christ, the "Angel of the great covenant," will summon you at death to take your place among his holy angels, with whom you shall be glorified and chant his praises for ever and ever. **B.**

SERMON V.

He that is not with me is against me.—St. Matt. xii. 30.

There are many Christians who do not seem to know that they are Christians. They do not seem to realize what the word Christian means; or, if they do, they do not act as if they did. They do not understand, if we are to judge them by their actions, that it is the name of one of the two great parties in this world—the party of Christ and that of Antichrist.

The issues between these two parties are more important than those between any others that ever have been or ever will be; for they are questions not only of time but of eternity. And the principles of these parties are so different that no compromise between them is possible. They are fighting with each other for the possession of the world, and neither will be satisfied till complete victory is gained—that is, till the other ceases to be. Every one has got to belong to one of these parties. It is impossible for any one to remain neutral in this contest and a mere spectator of it. Every one has got to be on one side or the other. This is what our Lord himself says: "He that is not with me is against me."

Every one, then, that does not wish to be on the devil's side has got to be on that of Christ. But this is just what a great many of you, my dear friends, do not, I am afraid, see so clearly as you should. You often try, I fear, to stand off and be on neither side when duty requires you to come out boldly on the side to which you belong.

Perhaps, for instance, you are compelled to associate daily with persons—either infidels, Protestants, or bad Catholics—whose mouths are full of impious or impure talk, which they expect you to agree with or join in. They enjoy this filth and profanity, and pretend to think their foul and blasphemous jests very funny, which they very seldom are; and they expect you to laugh at them, as they themselves do.

Now, I do not say that you are bound each and every time to reprove these sins, but I do say that you are sometimes. You cannot expect not to be counted among these people, and justly so counted, too, unless you say or do enough in some way to show plainly on what side you are. Do not, then, keep your faith and piety shut up in your prayer-books, only to be brought out when you are on your knees before God and no one by who will not admire you for them. No; bring them out plainly in the sight of his enemies, and let them see that you are really in earnest—that you really and truly believe that you have got a soul to save, and that your professions are not at all a pretence.

For, if you do not do this, you will be carried over to the other side in spite of yourself. If you do not reprove and separate yourself from what is sinful, you will join in it. Your own experience ought to show you that. Your effort to be neither the one thing nor the other, neither God's servant nor the devil's, always has been in vain and always will be. For the Eternal Truth has said, "He that is not with me is against me."

Yes, my brethren, it is certain that if you will not confess Christ boldly and openly before men; if you will not acknowledge that his faith and his morals are yours also; if you will not bravely and generously take his part in the great battle which he is fighting in this world, and in which he has enlisted you to fight under him; but if, on the other hand, you sneak off into a corner and stay there as long as his enemies are in sight, he will not count you as his servants or friends, and you will not be so, either in this world or in the world to come. "He that shall deny me before men, I will also deny him before my Father who is in heaven." And if you will not confess him, you must deny him; there is no middle course.

Be not, then, runaways, but brave soldiers in the conflict to which you are called. The enemies of Christ are not afraid to let their principles be known; if you would imitate their example the tables would be turned. They would be ashamed of themselves, if you would not be; and it is they who ought to be ashamed, not you. Moreover, God would get the glory which belongs to him, and if you will not give it to him you cannot expect him to save your mean and cowardly souls.

SERMON VI.

What went you out into the desert to see ? a reed shaken with the wind ?—St. Matt. xi. 8.

In these words, my dear brethren, our Lord holds up the character of his great precursor, St. John Baptist, as a model for the imitation of his disciples, and also for our imitation. "St. John is not like a reed shaken with the wind; see that you follow his example"—that is the meaning and the lesson of this question asked by our Lord.

St. John, indeed, was not like a reed shaken with

the wind. He was rather like a massive column of stone, which is not moved a hair's-breadth from its place by the most furious storms. He was firm and unyielding to all the assaults of temptation. Born free from original sin, he persevered without actual sin through the whole of his glorious life.

He has set us a magnificent example of firmness and fortitude—virtues in which Christians of the present day are wofully wanting. There is a great deal of piety nowadays, but it seems often to be of a very superficial kind. It looks well, but it does not wear well. Its outside is very promising, but there is something wanting inside, and that is a backbone. It does very well in the sheltered atmosphere of the church, but it breaks down when it is taken out of doors into the world.

The assaults it seems to be weakest against are those which come from without. It stands well against interior temptations, on the whole, but it quails before even a word spoken against it. It is dreadfully afraid of what people will say. It is very much under the power of false shame and what is called human respect. It is a most lamentable sight to see people who are really in their hearts and principles thoroughly good Christians, and who might be the instruments in God's hands of a great deal of good both for his glory and the salvation of others, so terribly under the influence of human respect that their example counts almost for nothing, or perhaps is even a scandal and a discouragement to those around them. They have a great deal of faith, and they really want to avoid sin, but they do not seem to want anybody to know that such is the case. One would, perhaps, think they were very humble and did not want anybody to know how good they are—and I have no doubt that they do not want some people, at any rate, to think that they are good; but it is not on account of humility, but on account of fear. They are afraid of what these people will say; they tremble at the slightest breath. They are very different from St. John, and very much like reeds shaken by the wind; and it requires only a very light wind to shake them, considering the strength they ought to have.

There are Catholics, for instance—and plenty of them, to the glory of our faith be it said!—who have a great horror of the dreadful sin of impurity, and would by no means of their own accord commit any offence of this kind. But their daily occupations lead them among others who have very different ideas and habits, or who, perhaps, are sinning wilfully against the clearest light. These wretched people are continually bandying jests or telling stories which show the corruption of their minds. Out of the abundance of their hearts their mouths are always speaking; they are bad trees, and all the time bringing forth bad fruit. Well, do our good Christians show any disgust for these things? Oh! no; they will say they cannot help laughing at them. I am afraid they are deceiving themselves; they could help it, if they dared to help it. They would seldom or never laugh if such foul things occurred to their own mind; they would be too much afraid of God. But now their fear of God disappears before their fear of man.

Or these good Christians meet with people who, either through ignorance or malice, ridicule and blaspheme the Catholic Church and the true faith.

Perhaps these people only need to find some Catholic who will stand up boldly for his religion. If any one would only confess Christ before them it might be the beginning of their conversion. But, instead of coming out fearlessly for the truth, our good Christians are afraid of being thought foolish or priest-ridden; and if they acknowledge that they are Catholics at all, it is only to compromise or deny what they in their hearts believe, so that people may think that they are pretty good Protestants after all.

These instances will suffice to show what I mean. You can find plenty of others yourselves. Do so, and resolve, for the sake of God our Saviour and for the glory of his name, to put an end to this despicable cowardice, if you have been guilty of it. Catholic faith and morals are things to glory in, not to be ashamed of. And, besides, there is really nothing to fear. What you are afraid of is only like the wind which passes by; in their hearts even the wicked will honor and hold in everlasting remembrance the true and faithful servants of God.

Third Sunday of Advent.

EPISTLE. *Phil. iv.* 4–7. Rejoice in the Lord always: again, I say, rejoice. Let your modesty be known to all men: The Lord is nigh. Be not solicitous about anything: but in everything by prayer and supplication with thanksgiving let your petitions be made known to God. And the peace of God which surpasseth all understanding, keep your hearts and minds in Christ Jesus.

GOSPEL. *St. John i.* 19–28. At that time: The Jews sent from Jerusalem priests and levites to John, to ask him: Who art thou? And he confessed, and did not deny: and he confessed: I am not the Christ. And they asked him: What then? Art thou Elias? And he said: I am not. Art thou the prophet? And he answered: No. They said therefore unto him: Who art thou, that we may give an answer to them that sent us? what sayest thou of thyself? He said: I am the voice of one crying in the wilderness, Make straight the way of the Lord, as said the prophet Isaias. And they that were sent, were of the Pharisees. And they asked him, and said to him: Why then dost thou baptize, if thou be not Christ, nor Elias, nor the prophet? John answered them, saying: I baptize with water; but there hath stood one in the midst of you, whom you know not. The same is he that shall come after me, who is preferred before me: the latchet of whose shoe I am not worthy to loose. These things were done in Bethania beyond the Jordan, where John was baptizing.

SERMON VII.

Let your modesty be known to all men.—PHIL iv. 5.

TO-DAY, brethren, is called *Gaudete*, or Rejoicing Sunday, and is intended by the church as a little *let-up*, as the people say, on the solemn season of Advent. To-day flowers deck the altars; at the High Mass the dalmatic, the deacon's vestment of joy, which has not been used for two Sundays, is again assumed. Where possible, and where the church is rich enough to buy them, rose-colored vestments should be worn. The first words of the Mass are, "Rejoice in the Lord always; again I say, rejoice." It is just as if the church said to you all: "Be glad and joyful; make yourselves as happy as you can." "Ah!" some of you will say, "that is just the doctrine for us; that is just what we like." Do not be too fast, my friends. Listen to what comes next. "Rejoice," says the church; but in that rejoicing, in that striving to live happily, "let your modesty be known to all men." So, then, the Christian is to be a happy man, but he is also to be a modest man—a man of simple or moderate habits. My friends, does not the shoe pinch you a little? Do you not see the cap gradually taking a form that will fit some of your heads? You men, when you are together on some festive occasion—when you have a gala-day of one kind or another—you rejoice then, it is true, but is your modesty known to all men? Have you not often aped the manners and swagger of the worldly-minded? Have you not listened to indecent stories? Have you not told some such? Oh! what scandal you give when you do these things. Then your *immodesty* is known to all men. You are going with the crowd. You are following the multitude to do evil. You are walking in the wide path that leadeth unto perdition. You unfortunate drunkards that totter as you walk, who fall in the gutter and by the wayside, is your modesty known to all men? No, your shame is known to all men, and the shame of all who belong to you. Again, what think you of the woman who, because it is the fashion, goes out to balls indecently and improperly dressed—who is not covered as becomes a Christian matron or maiden, but is so clad as to bring the blush of lust to the face of the brazen, and of shame to that of the pure in heart; or of those who go to all sort of plays and spectacles, who encourage the most questionable of dances and ballets, and bring up their children in the same spirit? Is their modesty known to all men? My friends, to find the modesty of such people would be like searching for a needle in a bundle of hay. You would never find it. You, too, who spend every cent you have upon your backs, who have almost all your hard earnings invested in dry goods and millinery, who come to church tricked out in finery which belongs neither to your state nor calling, offend also against Christian moderation and modesty. Once there was an old jackdaw who dressed himself up in peacock's feathers; then off he went among the peacocks and tried to pass for one of them. But these splendid birds soon found him out and pecked him almost to death. My friends, when you deck yourselves out in clothing, in fashions which are beyond your means, unsuited to your calling as a Christian, unfit for your state in life, and fit, indeed, for none but the vain people of the world, what are you? Nothing but jackdaws in peacock's feathers. Oh!

then don't make yourself ridiculous. Follow the advice of St. Paul : " Let your modesty be known to all men." These are the days of immodesty, of wasteful extravagance, of extreme vanity. Oh! then set your faces against this running tide of worldliness. Be modest, speak modestly, dress modestly, enjoy yourselves modestly. Don't dress up your children luxuriously, instilling into their minds even in childhood the spirit of vanity. Don't put on too much style or too many airs. Be happy, rejoice always, but be modest, be simple. " Let your modesty be known to all men. The Lord is nigh. For the rest, brethren, whatsoever things are true, whatsoever modest, whatsoever holy, whatsoever lovely, whatsoever of good fame, if there be any virtue, if any praise of discipline, think on these things. The grace of our Lord Jesus Christ be with your spirit."

B.

SERMON VIII.

There hath stood One in the midst of you, whom you know not.—St. John i. 26.

St. John spoke these words, as the Gospel tells us, not to his disciples, but to those who had been sent from Jerusalem to question him on his mission, to ask him what business he had to preach and to baptize. It may be that both those who were sent and those who sent them had no real desire to know if he were indeed a prophet, but were merely trying to make him say something which could be used against him—to set a trap for him, like those which they afterward tried to set for our Divine Lord—since his language to them certainly seems like a rebuke.

For who was this One who had stood in their midst, and whom they had not known? It was our Lord Jesus Christ. It was the Son of God, the Word made flesh. He had been living in their midst since his childhood, but they had not known him. Even those in his own town of Nazareth, who had often met him in their streets, who had often seen him and spoken to him, had passed him by as if he was no more than one of themselves, as if he were only a poor carpenter's boy.

Now, we, my dear brethren, are something like these Jews at that time. For during our lives there has stood One also in the midst of us, whom we have not known. And it is the same One whom the thoughtless and the sinful passed in the streets of Nazareth, and whom they afterward crucified in Jerusalem. The King of Glory is in our midst at this moment; he who dwells in the tabernacle of the altar is indeed God made man.

It is true for us as well as for them that we cannot see that it is he with our bodily eyes; but there is much more to point him out to us than there was to them. The church has taken care that we shall not pass him by unnoticed; all the worship of the sanctuary is directed to his throne—that poor throne in our midst which he has come down from heaven to occupy. It is because of him that the altar blazes with candles and is adorned with flowers, and that the clouds of incense rise; it is to him that we bend the knee; all the splendid ceremonial of the Catholic religion is only our poor effort to worthily honor Him who has condescended to dwell among us under the sacramental veils.

And yet, in spite of all the care which his church

has taken, do we not too often behave as the Jews of his own time had a better excuse for behaving? A better excuse, I say, for they needed a special light to recognize him; but all we need is faith, and that we all have. But one would think that his people had no faith, to see the way in which they sometimes conduct themselves in his most holy presence.

It would seem as if a Christian had not faith in that Real Presence when you see him pretend, as it were, to reverence the altar by a sort of half-genuflection, very quickly made, which looks more like a sign of disrespect than of adoration. What would you think if you should see the priest, when saying Mass, making his genuflections in this way? Well, you ought to do the same as he. Our Lord is as really before you as before him; and you are not more exalted in your station than the priest, that you can afford to treat God more familiarly. Bring the knee to the floor slowly and reverently when you pass the high altar, or any other altar, while the Blessed Sacrament is on it. And when our Lord passes in procession, or in any other way, through the church, kneel down and pray; do not stand or sit and stare about.

And remember, too, that he is as really present when he goes outside the church as when he remains in it. The state of things in this country requires us to carry him to the sick without the solemnity which should be observed; but he is as truly in your houses when he comes to give himself to you there as if the priest brought him with lights and sacred vestments, with the sound of the bell, and with a train of attendants to do him honor. Imagine what you would do if he should come visibly at the side of the priest, with that Face with which you are so familiar, with glory shining round him, and with the prints of the nails in his hands and feet; and do the same now. Do not stand around and talk to the priest as if he had come for a social visit; kneel down as soon as he enters the room, if the Blessed Sacrament is with him. And do not kneel leaning on a chair, with your backs to our Lord; that is a strange way to show respect for him.

If you will only think who it is that stands in the midst of you, you will find out many other things which I have not time to suggest. It is not really so much want of faith as want of thought that makes people behave to our Lord in the irreverent and almost insulting way that they sometimes do. Think, then, about this matter, and you will need no rubrics to teach you what to do in the presence of Him whom you really know and love.

SERMON IX.

I am the voice of one crying in the wilderness, Make straight the way of the Lord.—St. John i. 23.

WHENEVER, my dear brethren, men are going to a place they always ask the way. They also make up their minds as to which is the long way, which the short way, which the most convenient and easiest way. They do this with reference to the places to which they go in this world. Now, we are all going to heaven; at least, each one of us will say, I hope I am going there. We know there are many places to which we can go in this world, and many different ways by which we can get to them. There are also many places in heaven, but there is but *one* way of getting to any one, even to the least of them.

Which is that way? Some will say it is the good way, or the way of the good man. Another will say it is attending to your duties, to your church. Yet another will say it is by keeping away from mortal sin. Each answer is a good one, but neither one brings out the important point. The true answer, and the first one to be given, is that it is God's way —the way of the Lord. Yes, my dear brethren, it is the very way, the one and only way, that our Lord Jesus Christ has travelled before us. Every step he took along this path was marked by the precious Blood from his own veins. It is the way of the cross, of sacrifice, of penance and mortification.

Are we all going this way? Is each one of us now here present moving daily and hourly on this path? It is almost useless to ask this question, for I know many, very many indeed, will answer, No! It is indeed a sad truth that most people, most even of our Catholic people, are not going this way.

But why is this? One reason is because they do not try, sincerely and earnestly, to fix in the mind that this is the only condition upon which any soul can be saved. For our Lord himself declares that unless a man take up his cross *daily* and follow him he cannot be his disciple. They do not realize that there is an absolute necessity, an unchangeable law in this assertion. God has said it, and will not unsay it. Yet how quickly will men stop a business or a transaction that will surely cause them to lose their money! How quickly will they turn from a road that is sure to lead to death! They realize the necessity when property and life are to be lost; but they will not see or feel the same necessity when their souls and eternal life are most certainly to be for ever lost.

Again, they are discouraged because the way is hard and difficult. Show me any way in life not hard and difficult. Ask the father, the mother, the single man, the married man. Ask the rich and the poor, the old and the young, the active business man, the idle and slothful man, as well as the common tramp. All have the same answer—that life is a hard road any way you may take it.

Man, then, is reduced to the necessity of suffering and mortification. The secret of this is that all men are under sin, all poisoned by it. The only remedy is to cure ourselves, to get rid of this poison. The way of the Lord is the way given us to go in order to find this cure. All along this way we find the remedy at every turn. It is found in a good confession, in true penance and mortification, in the sacrament of the altar, the Body and Blood of our Lord Jesus Christ, which is intended to nourish our souls and to act against this terrible poison.

Make straight, then, the way of the Lord. Do not be terrified by trouble, pain, and difficulties of any kind. Do not permit the devil to make you think it will always last, always be the same. These difficulties become less and less by degrees. They wear away, as it were, or God so fills the soul with strength and patience that it is the same in the end. We then bear easily by the grace of God that which was so troublesome at first.

Set to work, then, at once. Let your souls be ready for the holy Feast of Christmas. Remember that we must celebrate that as Christians ought to do.

Gratitude, love, Christian manliness, and honor require that all shall celebrate the birthday of a suffering God in such a manner as to make him feel he is truly remembered and honored. The least one can do, then, is to begin to make straight the way of the Lord by cleansing the soul of all mortal sin and by making a good Christmas communion. That feast, you know, is a time when great graces are given to the sincere soul. Do not, then, for the sake of your own soul, fail to keep Christmas day as a true Catholic should keep it.

Fourth Sunday of Advent.

Epistle. 1 *Cor. iv.* 1–5. Brethren: Let a man so look upon us as the ministers of Christ, and the dispensers of the mysteries of God. Here now it is required among the dispensers, that a man be found faithful. But as to me it is a thing of the least account to be judged by you, or by human judgment: but neither do I judge my own self. For I am not conscious to myself of anything, yet in this am I not justified: but he that judgeth me, is the Lord. Therefore judge not before the time; until the Lord come, who both will bring to light the hidden things of darkness, and will make manifest the counsels of the hearts: and then shall every man have praise from God.

Gospel. *St. Luke iii.* 1–6. Now in the fifteenth year of the reign of Tiberius Cæsar, Pontius Pilate being governor of Judea, and Herod being tetrarch of Galilee, and Philip his brother tetrarch of Iturea and the country of Trachonitis, and Lysanias tetrarch of Abilina, under the high-priests Annas and Caiphas: the word of the Lord came to John, the son of Zachary, in the desert. And he came into all the country about the Jordan, preaching the baptism of penance for the remission of sins: as it is written in the book of the words of Isaias the prophet: A voice of one crying in the wilderness: Prepare ye the way of the Lord, make his paths straight. Every valley shall be filled: and every mountain and hill shall be brought low: and the crooked shall be made straight, and the rough ways plain. And all flesh shall see the salvation of God.

SERMON X.

CHRISTMAS EVE.

For he shall save his people from their sins.—St. Matt. i. 21.

To be *saved*, dear brethren, always supposes a previous danger. Thus, we say saved from drowning, saved from a fire, saved from a terrible accident. Also it supposes a person or thing that saves. Now, dear friends, we are met together here to-day, and it is Christmas Eve. The church tells us in the holy Gospel that Jesus Christ came to save his people. Let us think, then, for a few moments what danger it was that he came to save us from, and who he was who came to act the part of Saviour. The danger from which we were to be saved was the danger of sin. Sin is dangerous in the extreme. It is more dangerous than the most terrible disease, more perilous than the cholera or the plague. These things only kill the body; mortal sin kills the soul. If Jesus Christ had not redeemed us sin would have destroyed us. Adam and Eve brought sin into the world. Sin spread with the awful swiftness of an epidemic. It threatened to descend upon mankind and to bury everything beneath the ruins of everlasting death. Then, when poor human nature seemed about to be overwhelmed, Jesus came and saved it, washed us in his precious Blood, and snatched the uplifted sword from the hand of the enemy. Yes, the danger was great, but we were saved from it. But a little while ago we read in the papers of an awful calamity—the burning of the Brooklyn Theatre. We can imagine how frightful was the scene of hundreds of human creatures fighting for life—the all too narrow door before them, the crushing multitude around them, the scathing, ruthless flames behind them. What would we think of one who, saved from such a place, should afterwards make light of the danger and care nothing for the one who saved him? O brethren! it was not from the danger of earthly fire, from the peril of blazing rafters, falling beams, and a trampling multitude, that Christ saved you and me. 'Twas from the fire of hell that he snatched us. 'Twas from the danger, the all-surrounding danger, of sin. And what have we done, many of us? We have turned back, let go the hand that held us, and gone back into the appalling peril. Because men do not see a *material* danger they will not believe there is *any*. Dear friends, there is danger. You that have gone back into the ways of sin, you that are in mortal sin now, at this moment—you are in an awful danger. Save your lives, then; take the hand held out to you or you are lost! Brethren, some of those poor creatures who perished in the Brooklyn fire were so charred, so burnt that they could not be recognized. Take care that you do not become so disfigured by sin that at the last day God will say to you: "I know ye not."

Who saved us from the awful peril? It was Jesus Christ, Jesus the Son of God, Jesus the Babe of Bethlehem. In the morning it will be Christmas day. The church will bid you come to the crib. Will you still persist in rejecting the Saviour? You know who he is. You know he is God. You know he is full of love and full of power—full of love for your souls, full of power to rescue you from the danger in which you stand. Come to him, then, and no matter how black or how many your sins may be, you will know that "he shall save his people from their sins." Brethren, I doubt not that many of you mourn the loss of some dear ones. Within the last few years some one has gone from the fireside, some sweet voice has been stilled for ever. Perhaps a father or a tender, beloved mother has gone home to rest with God—gone in the peace of Christ to their reward. 'Tis Christmas Eve in heaven to-day, and oh! don't you think they are waiting for you—praying for you that you may be there with them? Don't disappoint them. Don't let them wait in vain. Flee from sin, the danger that threatens to separate you from them for ever. Do not disappoint Jesus and Mary and Joseph. Do not spend this holy time in sin. Don't go back into the danger. Keep Christmas like a Christian. Then, brethren, in the morning, the bright morning of eternity, the Christmas morning of heaven, we shall see His glory. We shall be united to Jesus and our dear ones who have gone before. We shall hear them and the white-winged angels who circle around the throne, singing aloud: "Glory be to Jesus Christ the Babe of Bethlehem, for he hath saved his people from their sins!"

B.

SERMON XI.

Preaching the baptism of penance for the remission of sins.— St. Luke iii. 3.

ST. JOHN BAPTIST certainly seems, from what we read about him in the Gospels, to have been quite a stern and uncompromising preacher. He did not come with a coach and four to take people to heaven.

He had but one message for every one, high and low, rich and poor; and that message was: "Repent of your sins; do penance for them, and bring forth fruits worthy of penance. Cease to do evil, learn to do good; get rid of your bad habits, and put good ones in their place. If you have wronged any one, make restitution for it; and, moreover, practise charity even to those whom you have not wronged. These things you must do; there is no other way possible in which you can flee from the wrath to come."

This was St. John's doctrine, everybody must acknowledge. But some people seem to think that our Lord, when he came, offered salvation to sinners on somewhat easier terms than these. This, however, is a great mistake. There never has been, is not, and never will be any way for a sinner to be saved except by doing penance. Our Saviour did, indeed, by his coming make salvation easier; but how was it that he did so? It was not by offering it on any other terms than these, but by making it easier for men to comply with these terms. He did not free us from the obligation of doing penance, but gave us more abundant grace that we might be better able to do penance. That is plain enough to every one who will stop and think.

And yet some Christians seem to imagine that it is enough to be a Catholic, to be quite sure of one's salvation. Practically, at least, they hold the heresy which the devil brought in at the time of the so-called Reformation, and which before that time hardly any one had dared to put in words—that a man may be justified by faith without good works. They say to themselves the very thing which St. John warned the Jews not to say: "We have Abraham for our father." They say to themselves: "We are Catholics; we are children of the holy church; all we have to do is to remain so (and, thank God! we have not the least idea of being anything else), and then to receive the rites of our church when we come to die, and we will be as sure of going to heaven as a child which has just been baptized."

But, my friends, this is a fatal delusion. Depend upon it, the devil is glad when he sees men or women with this notion in their heads, for he has got good hopes of having them with him in hell. He knows well what such people do not seem to know: that it is not enough to be a Catholic, but that one must also be a good Catholic, if he is to be saved. He knows as well as St. John that penance is necessary now, as it always has been; but he takes good care not to preach what he knows.

And what is penance? Is it a mere confession that we are sinners? No, by no means. If it were, every one would be a penitent who was not a fool, for every one who has common sense must acknowledge that he has sinned. Nor is it a mere acknowledgment that sin is a bad thing, and a wish that we had not committed it, and that God had given us more grace that we might not have done so. No, it is a real and hearty sorrow for it, with a conviction that we might have avoided it, and that the fault was not with God, who gave us plenty of grace to avoid it, but with ourselves, who did not make use of the grace which he gave. And following from this, as a matter of course, is a firm conviction that we can avoid it for the future, and a firm determination to do so. And following from this, also as a matter of course, is a real change in our lives, a real giving up of sin. That is the only certain mark of a true repentance and of a good confession—that a man stops committing mortal sin. The priest may indeed give absolution to one who continues to fall; but it is with the gravest fears that the sentence which he pronounces is not confirmed by Him who alone has power to forgive.

I said in the beginning that salvation was easier than before our Lord came, because we have now more grace to help our weakness. But that only makes penance the more necessary. "A man making void the law of Moses," says St. Paul, "died, without any mercy, under two or three witnesses; how much more, do you think, he deserveth worse punishments, who hath trodden under foot the Son of God, and hath esteemed the blood of the testament unclean, by which he was sanctified, and hath offered an affront to the Spirit of grace?" Be warned, then, in time; repent indeed, and change your lives. Make not only a confession but a good confession at this holy time, and cease, for the love of God, to offend him any more.

SERMON XII.

Prepare ye the way of the Lord.—St. Luke iii. 4.

Before our Blessed Lord came into public notice his missionary, St. John Baptist, appeared in the wilderness preaching penance, and good works worthy of penance, to the people, who were in the darkness and bondage of sin. He cried out in a loud, thrilling voice: "Prepare ye the way of the Lord." So the church on the last Sunday of Advent, the first before Christmas, cries out to those who expect to meet our Lord on Christmas and worship him on that glorious feast : "Prepare ye the way of the Lord." To the tepid and lukewarm she cries out : "Come away from your darling venial sins ; fill up your empty hearts to the brim with the overflowing love and grace of God ; be more generous in his worship and service." To the young : "Prepare ye the way of the Lord." Give me your heart while you are young and tender ; do not be allured by the empty joys and false pleasures of the world ; avoid those dangerous occasions of sin that are about to entice you, and keep your youth innocent and pure, that you may see the evening of your life in joy, and not in bitter remorse.

To the old : Forget the past ; if it has been bad, ask pardon and do penance ; if good, preserve it and live in grace and fervor, so that when you are near the end of your pilgrimage here you may attain to the great destiny for which you have been created.

To the sinner—to the one in mortal sin ; the one who has not had a happy Christmas for many a year, for the sinner has no chance to have part in the real joy of Christmas ; to the sinner who has been exalted with pride and worldly pleasure, who has been in the valley of impurity, and wilful neglect, and cold indifference—oh ! to you there is a voice terrible and irresistible : "Prepare ye the way of the Lord." Prepare it by prayer for grace; warm your heart by gratitude and love ; fall on your knees at the foot of the cross in the confessional ; have your heart purified by the bitter waters of penance, and you will indeed have a happy Christmas.

Then the promise: All flesh shall see the salvation of God. Yes, to know and to feel and see the pardon and peace and love of God—to have the consciousness that he is our friend, and that we have no enmity against him—is the way to see on this earth the fruits of salvation.

The poor shall see the salvation of God. O ye poor men and women who have nothing in this world but sorrow, tears, and bitter suffering! to you this coming feast of Christmas is a foretaste of the great reward that is prepared for you. God loves you. He spurned the palaces and royal robes of the Cæsars when he came on the earth, and chose a poor Virgin for his mother and a hovel for his birthplace. The poor shepherds were the first to see him, and they will be near to him in his glory. "Blessed are ye poor, for yours is the kingdom of heaven." For He who was rich, for your sakes became poor.

The poor shall see the salvation of God; for He who was rich, for their sakes became poor.

The rich shall see the salvation of God; for they will be taught humility by looking into the crib at Bethlehem, and learning a lesson that they can learn nowhere else, and that will dazzle them more than their jewels, diamonds, dresses, or palaces.

So if we prepare the way of the Lord we shall finally see the salvation of God in eternity, where we shall rejoice evermore in the thought that all our preparation here to please God, by keeping the commandments, suffering, and toiling, will be rewarded by the vision of the Redeemer of all nations who washed their robes and made them white in the Blood of the Lamb.

Sunday within the Octave of Christmas.

EPISTLE. *Gal. iv.* 1-7. Brethren: As long as the heir is a child, he differeth nothing from a servant, though he be lord of all: but is under tutors and governors until the time appointed by the father: even so we, when we were children, were in bondage under the elements of the world. But when the fulness of the time was come, God sent his Son, made of a woman, made under the law: that he might redeem those who were under the law; that we might receive the adoption of sons. And because you are sons, God hath sent the Spirit of his Son into your hearts, crying: Abba, Father Therefore now he is no more a servant, but a son. And if a son, an heir also through God.

GOSPEL. *St. Luke ii.* 33-40. At that time: Joseph, and Mary the mother of Jesus, were wondering at these things, which were spoken concerning him. And Simeon blessed them, and said to Mary his mother: Behold this child is set for the ruin, and for the resurrection of many in Israel, and for a sign which shall be contradicted. And thy own soul a sword shall pierce, that out of many hearts thoughts may be revealed. And there was a prophetess, called Anna, the daughter of Phanuel, of the tribe of Aser; she was far advanced in years, and had lived with her husband seven years from her virginity. And she was a widow until fourscore and four years; who departed not from the temple, by fastings and prayers serving night and day. Now she at the same hour coming in, gave praise to the Lord; and spoke of him to all that looked for the redemption of Israel. And after they had performed all things according to the law of the Lord, they returned into Galilee, to their own city, Nazareth. And the child grew, and waxed strong, full of wisdom: and the grace of God was in him.

SERMON XIII.

And the Child grew, and waxed strong, full of wisdom: and the grace of God was in him.—ST. LUKE ii. 40.

JESUS CHRIST is our model in all things, and in the verse above quoted we see him presented as the model of youth. Your children, brethren, ought to be strong in body, wise in mind, and to have the grace of God in their hearts. Now, who is to form them after the model of Jesus Christ? It is the duty of parents. First, then, you ought to take care of the bodily wants of your children, in order that they may grow and wax strong. How often parents offend against this duty! There are some who let their children eat just what they please, who pamper their appetites, who give them all kinds of unwholesome food. Such children will never be healthy. There are others who spend all their money in drink—who leave their poor little ones at home, moaning and starving with hunger; who, through their imprudence, leave their children without food for a whole day, having squandered their earnings in all sorts of foolish and wicked pleasures. Then, too, there are those who allow their children to sit up till all hours of the night, who let them go off to heated ball-rooms, who dress them either too much or too little—who either coddle them up so that they can hardly stand a whiff of air, or else send them out to shiver with cold. No wonder that our city children are unhealthy; no wonder death sweeps them away as it does. Is it not because parents are neglectful? Look to it, then; see to the diet, the clothing, the habits of your children. Do not over-task their feeble strength by sending them too soon to work. Never permit them to form luxurious appetites. Watch over their daily lives, see that they take proper exercise; then, like the child Jesus, they will " grow and wax strong." Neglect the duty of corporal education, and we shall have a generation of sickly children and adult invalids. And if it be so necessary for parents to watch over the bodies of their children, what shall I say of the duty of watching over their minds and souls? Your children should be full of wisdom, and the grace of God should be in their hearts. Oh! when I think of the neglect of many Catholic parents in this respect I am tempted to take up the Gospel's most awful tone, and cry, Woe to you, careless parents! woe, eternal woe to you guilty fathers and mothers, who are letting your little ones run to destruction!

You make your home uncomfortable by your crossness, by your curses, by your slovenly, untidy habits. Your children, from their earliest infancy, take to the street. They hear impurity, blasphemy, and cursing. They hear words and see sights which are not fit to be mentioned here on God's altar. They keep what company they like. They learn infamous and immoral habits that destroy both body and soul. Oh! for God's sake beware, beware! Do you think they will ever be full of wisdom or have the grace of God in their hearts? Again, you are anxious enough that they shall learn to read and write, to keep books and be quick at figures, but are you sure they know their catechism or can tell a priest all they ought to know of Jesus Christ, their Saviour, or how many sacraments and commandments there are? Where are they on Sundays? Where are they when confession day comes around? Oh! these are vital questions, if you want them to be full of grace and wisdom. Some boys and girls of our day, brethren, have lost a great deal of their freshness. They smoke, they chew tobacco, they flirt, they act like little men and women. There is no innocence about them. They are revolting spectacles to men and angels. Wisdom, forsooth! They have none. Grace of God? It is destroyed. Their childhood is more like the childhood of an incarnate devil than of an incarnate God. Look, then, carefully to your children. Look to the little ones; correct them when they are babies. Don't wait till a child is in its teens; then it will be too late. Set them a good example. You know the story of the old crab, who said to her little ones, "Why do you walk sideways?" "Suppose, mother," they said, "*you* show us how to walk straight." Yes, if you are wicked, foolish, and sinful, your children will be like you. "Like father, like son," says the proverb. Oh! then you parents, be pure as Mary, be industrious, modest, patient like St. Joseph; then your children, like Jesus, will grow and wax strong, full of wisdom and of the grace of God. B.

SERMON XIV.

This Child is set for the fall, and for the resurrection of many in Israel.—St. Luke ii. 34.

These words of to-day's Gospel, my dear brethren, have, perhaps, a strange sound to us at this joyful Christmas season. It seems strange that holy Simeon should have said that the blessed Infant whom he held in his arms, and who had come to save the world, should have been set for the fall of many of even his own chosen people.

And yet we know that his coming was actually the occasion of the fall not merely of many but of far the greater part of that chosen people of Israel. However strange Simeon's prophecy may seem, we see that it was a true one. Up to that time the Jewish people were God's true church on earth; now almost all of them are wanderers outside of it, rejecting the true Messias whom their fathers crucified, and either vainly looking for one who will never come or ceasing in despair to look for any Messias at all. Instead of Christ's coming having been the means of salvation for them, it has really been the occasion of their fall from the grace which they had before.

But though we know that it has been so, it may still seem strange that it should have been so. One would think that the Saviour, who is our joy, our pride, and our glory, would have been theirs too, and even more theirs than ours, having been born of their own nation, a Jew of the royal line of David. But if we consider the matter a little we shall see that it was natural enough that it should turn out as it did; and we shall see, moreover, that there is a good deal of danger that, as they fell from grace when Christ was presented to them, so we may do the same.

For we shall, if we think, find out the reason why they fell, which is the reason why we may fall too. They were looking for a Saviour, indeed, but not for such a Saviour as actually came. They were looking for one who would redeem them from their subjection to the Roman Empire; who would make their nation what it had been in the days gone by; who would make them an independent and powerful people; who would give them the greatness and glory of this world. So when he did not fulfil their expectation, when he came not with earthly splendor but in poverty and suffering, they were scandalized. It was only his miracles which made them hesitate; and when he would work miracles no longer, when he would not save himself from the cruel and ignominious death of the cross, they rejected him with the horrible imprecation, "His Blood be upon us and upon our children."

Yes, my brethren, the cross was their scandal, and the cross is likely to be our scandal, too, for we have the same fallen human nature as they. "We preach Christ crucified," says St. Paul, "unto the Jews indeed a stumbling-block, and unto the Gentiles foolishness"; and it is a good deal the same with us Christians now.

We feel glad, indeed, when Christmas comes; but I am afraid that if we had been living at the time of the first Christmas we should not have been much more likely to rejoice at the birth of our Lord than his own people were at that time. Christmas now is very pleasant, with its festivity, its amusements, its giving and receiving of presents; but there is not much of the cross in this. The original Christmas, with its cold, its poverty, and its humiliation, was quite a different thing.

It is right for us to rejoice at Christmas; but perhaps we should not rejoice if we remembered that our Lord came to bring into the world the cross not only for himself but also for us too. That is the scandal for us now. We can see what the Jews could not, that it was right that he should suffer; but we cannot see that it is right that we should suffer too—that what holy Simeon said to his Blessed Mother is true for each one of us: "Thy own soul a sword shall pierce." So in this way, even now, "this Divine Child," with his cross in his hand for a Christmas present to us, "is set for the fall of many in Israel." We are too apt to shrink away when he urges us to accept it for his sake.

Indeed, we should always fall away when the cross is offered to us, had we only our own natural strength to depend upon. It is not in us, by any natural power, to bear the cross of Christ. But he offers with it the grace to bear it. And in this way he is set also for our resurrection. For it is only by the cross, by bearing the cross ourselves, that we can rise from sin, which is the only death which we really have to fear.

This Child, then, is set for our fall by our natural weakness, but for our resurrection by his supernatural grace. His will is that it should be for the latter; let his will, then, be done. Let us welcome him, then, at Christmas, but let us welcome his cross too; for it is only by bearing it ourselves that we can come to eternal life.

SERMON XV.

Behold, this Child is set . . . for a sign which shall be contradicted.—St. Luke ii. 34.

My brethren, can this be possible? It is not only possible but too true. Our Lord Jesus Christ, the sign of the love of God the Father to us, is contradicted, is resisted, by those whom he came to save.

And is it only those who are strangers to him that contradict him? No; it is those who know him well and who ought to be his friends—his own people, who call themselves Catholics, who claim to belong to his true church.

What does the word "contradict" mean? It means to speak against or in opposition to any one. It may mean, also, to act against any one, or even to reject inwardly what one says, though not a word of contradiction be spoken. Fervent gratitude would now exclaim: "Surely no Catholic can do any of these to Jesus Christ?" Yet such there are, though perhaps many of them do not realize what they do.

Who are they? They are those who speak against and resist the teachers he has sent them; who put themselves always in opposition to the authority of the church, and even to its head, the Vicar of Christ on earth; who believe no more than they are obliged to under pain of ceasing to be Catholic at all; and who never obey except when it suits their own convenience. "Well," you will say, "I am not that kind of a Catholic." I am glad you are not; still, there are many such. But there are many more who do not go quite so far as that, and yet have a good deal of the same spirit. Perhaps you are one of them.

Who are these that I speak of? They are those who are always opposing their pastors and confessors, finding fault with and criticising their words and their actions. They reject their counsel. They even make a jest of their opinions. They think them behind the times, and not up to the spirit of the present day. They even sometimes violate the sacred confidence of the confessional, and talk thus lightly even of what has been said to them there.

Or they oppose outwardly the plans and efforts of their parish priests. They think that they know more about everything than their pastors. Unwilling to unite with them in their work for our Lord, they are discontented because others are not as rebellious and disobedient as themselves. They do not rest until they succeed in making a party against those whom they should unite to support, which destroys a great deal of the good which they have done, and prevents much which they could otherwise do. In vain do they pretend to be friends of Christ when they thwart and spoil his work. The work of the parish is as much his work as that of any other part of the church. The church makes parishes wherever she sends her priests. If the people in them oppose her she cannot do God's work.

Or if they do not resist they despise their priests, or certainly act as if they did. They do not seem to remember that every priest, unworthy as he is, of course, still represents our Lord. If they respect him, it is as a man, not as a priest; that is, they do not respect the priest at all as such. They use him for their own convenience when their conscience requires them to hear Mass or approach the sacraments; but otherwise they treat him just as a Protestant might do. And by this bad example they lessen the respect of others for him, and weaken the authority and influence for good which he ought to have. This really is resisting and contradicting our Lord, whom he represents. Let all, then, examine themselves, and see if they are not in the habit of speaking, acting, or neglecting their duties in such a way as to oppose and contradict our divine Lord. Be humble as he was on the first Christmas day, and try to help, not to hinder, his agents in all they are obliged to do to carry out his work; for he has said to them: "He that heareth you heareth me; and he that despiseth you despiseth me."

The Epiphany.

EPISTLE. *Isaias lx.* 1–6. Arise, be enlightened, O Jerusalem: for thy light is come, and the glory of the Lord is risen upon thee. For behold darkness shall cover the earth, and a mist the people: but the Lord shall arise upon thee, and his glory shall be seen upon thee. And the Gentiles shall walk in thy light, and kings in the brightness of thy rising. Lift up thy eyes round about, and see: all these are gathered together, they are come to thee: thy sons shall come from afar, and thy daughters shall rise up at thy side. Then shalt thou see and abound, and thy heart shall wonder and be enlarged; when the multitude of the sea shall be converted to thee, the strength of the Gentiles shall come to thee. The multitude of camels shall cover thee, the dromedaries of Madian and Epha: all they from Saba shall come, bringing gold and frankincense: and showing forth praise to the Lord.

GOSPEL. *St. Matt. ii.* 1–12. When Jesus, therefore, was born in Bethlehem of Juda, in the days of King Herod, behold, there came wise men from the East to Jerusalem, saying: Where is he that is born King of the Jews? For we have seen his star in the East, and we are come to adore him. And Herod the King hearing this, was troubled, and all Jerusalem with him: and assembling together all the chief priests and Scribes of the people, he enquired of them where Christ should be born. But they said to him, In Bethlehem of Juda; for so it is written by the prophet: "And thou Bethlehem, the land of Juda, art not the least among the princes of Juda: for out of thee shall come forth the ruler who shall rule my people Israel." Then Herod, privately calling the wise men, enquired diligently of them the time of the star's appearing to them; and sending them into Bethlehem, said: Go and search diligently after the child, and when you have found him, bring me word again, that I also may come and adore him. And when they had heard the king, they went their way; and behold, the star which they had seen in the East went before them, until it came and stood over where the child was. And seeing the star, they rejoiced with exceeding great joy. And going into the house, they found the child with Mary his mother, and falling down, they adored him; and opening their treasures, they offered him gifts; gold, frankincense, and myrrh. And having received an answer in sleep that they should not return to Herod, they went back another way into their own country.

SERMON XVI.

Rise, and take the Child and his mother, and go into the land of Israel—ST. MATT. ii. 20.

AT this season of Christmas and Epiphany, in these days when the church brings us to the manger in which the infant Son of God was laid, it is impossible for any Christian to come to Jesus without coming to Mary also. He cannot see the one without seeing the other; and surely he will not adore the one without honoring the other also.

It is plain enough to us all at this time how inseparable Our Lady is from her Divine Son, and how we must go to her if we would gain admission to his presence. But we are apt enough to forget it at other seasons, even at times like the month of May, specially consecrated to her love and service.

We are apt to imagine devotion to her as a sort of thing apart by itself, beautiful and reasonable, it is true, but still having no necessary connection with the worship of God. We do not understand that it is impossible for us to love and adore him as he wishes unless we also honor his Blessed Mother—as impossible as it would be to have a true devotion to her and forget him. The two devotions must go hand-in-hand not only now but through all the year.

The forgetting of this is one great reason why there is so much sin in the world. One who has a true love for Mary can hardly fall into mortal sin; and that not only because she will specially pray for him and defend him, but also because he will love her Son too much to do so. And even if he should fall into mortal sin he will not stay in it long; not only because she will obtain his conversion, but also because love of God cannot be far away while that of his Blessed Mother remains.

This is also true, in its measure, of venial as well as of mortal sin, and of those imperfections which keep people from being saints. You will hear many complaining that they do not make any progress in the spiritual life; that they are always committing the same faults, and even just as often; and that they have no more piety now than they had years ago—perhaps not even so much.

Well, of course there may be many reasons for this; but one of them, perhaps, is that they do not cultivate a real, solid devotion to Our Blessed Lady. They say, no doubt, some prayers to her, and they believe fully and firmly everything about her which the church teaches; but they do not realize that **they cannot acquire the love of her Divine Son un-**

less they make his Mother theirs also; that they give themselves entirely to her as her loving children, with all their mind and strength, all their heart and soul.

What a pity it is to neglect so easy and so safe a way not only of salvation but of perfection! It will lead to everything else, and nothing else will lead anywhere without it.

Let us, then, my dear brethren, at the beginning of this new year make a good resolution—that is, to have more devotion to Our Lady than we have ever had before. Let us take, as St. Joseph did, the Child and his Mother, and set out with them from this place of our exile to the land of Israel, the true promised land above. Let us take them both, not only at Christmas but always, through our whole journey here below; not to guard and guide them, as he did—for we have not such a privilege—but that they may guard us, and guide us to the country which is waiting, not for one people only, but for the redeemed of all nations, for all the Israel of God.

SERMON XVII.

And opening their treasures, they offered him gifts; gold, frankincense, and myrrh.—St. Matt. ii. 11.

To-day, my brethren, is a great day for us. It is, in one way, a greater day than Christmas itself; a day, that is, in which we have more cause for rejoicing than we had even then. For what was it which we celebrated then, and what is it which we are celebrating now? Then it was the birth of our Lord into this world, and it was indeed a thing which we had cause to rejoice over; but to-day it is something even more joyous for us than that. It is not only that he was born into this world, but that he was born for us, for us Gentiles—to save us as well as his own chosen people, the Jews. The three wise men whom that wonderful star led to his crib were not of that people, but Gentiles like ourselves; and the star which appeared to them signified the appearance to them and to us of the true Light which was hereafter to enlighten in a more wonderful way than before not only a single nation, but every man coming into this world. Appearance or manifestation is what the Greek word "epiphany" means.

It was natural, then, that they should offer gifts to their newly-born Saviour, for they could not but do so in acknowledgment of the great gift which he had given to them. But let us see what was the meaning of the gifts which they did offer—of these gifts of gold, frankincense, and myrrh.

They may be, and have been, interpreted in a great many different ways, all of which may well be true. It is commonly said that the wise men offered gold to our Lord because he is the King of heaven and earth; frankincense, because he is Almighty God; and myrrh, because he is also man, and was to suffer death for the sins of the world—myrrh being used to embalm the dead, and hence being a symbol of death. But there is another signification of these gifts which is, perhaps, more practical for us, because it suggests more directly the three gifts which each one of us must offer to him who is our Saviour as well as theirs, if we would partake of the salvation which he came to bring to us.

These three gifts are, then, understood by some to represent the three duties of almsgiving, prayer, and fasting, by which we are redeemed from the tyranny of the world, the devil, and the flesh. These last three are the great enemies of our salvation, and they must be overcome if we are to be saved. The love of the world, and of the treasures which it offers us, can only be destroyed by sacrificing those treasures for the sake of God, of his church, and of his poor; the power of the devil, who sets himself up as the god whom we are to serve and obey, can only be resisted by constant prayer, by which we draw near to the true God, and devote ourselves over and over again to his service; and the control of the flesh, with its base and degrading appetites, over our immortal souls can only be shaken off by fasting—that is, by mortification of various kinds, by persistently refusing to our bodies all dangerous and sinful indulgences, and by sometimes depriving them of pleasures which are innocent in themselves.

These three duties are practised in their perfection by those whom God calls to the religious life by the three vows of poverty, obedience, and chastity. By the vow of poverty the religious sacrifices at once the goods of this world; by that of obedience he frees himself from the tyranny of the devil, subjecting himself entirely to God, whom his superiors represent; by that of chastity he renounces sensual pleasure.

But it is not religious alone who are called on to make these three gifts. The same obligation, in its due measure, rests upon each of you. Almsgiving, prayer, and mortification are duties for all Christians. It is hard to see how any one can be saved who gives no more to God and the poor than what is extorted from him, as it were, by force; who merely says prayers now and then because he is afraid to give up the practice, but who seldom or never really prays; and who indulges without scruple in everything which his flesh desires, intending to stop short of nothing but mortal sin.

Let such things, then, my brethren, not be said of us. As we kneel with the wise men this morning before the manger of our infant God, let us make with them these three gifts. Let us offer to him, as they did, with a full and willing heart, our possessions, our bodies, and our souls. This is the time for making presents, and these are the presents which he expects. Be generous, then, with him, and he will be generous with you. "Give to the Most High according to what he hath given to thee."

First Sunday after Epiphany.

EPISTLE. *Rom. xii.* 1–5. Brethren: I beseech you, by the mercy of God, that you present your bodies a living sacrifice, holy, pleasing to God, your reasonable service. And be not conformed to this world: but be reformed in the newness of your mind, that you may prove what is the good and the acceptable, and the perfect will of God. For I say, through the grace that is given me, to all that are among you, not to be more wise than it behooveth to be wise, but to be wise unto sobriety, and according as God hath divided to every one the measure of faith. For as in one body we have many members, but all the members have not the same office: so we being many are one body in Christ, and each one members one of another in Christ Jesus our Lord.

GOSPEL. *St. Luke ii.* 42–52. When Jesus was twelve years old, they went up to Jerusalem according to the custom of the feast, and after they had fulfilled the days, when they returned, the child Jesus remained in Jerusalem; and his parents knew it not. And thinking that he was in the company, they came a day's journey and sought him among their kinsfolks and acquaintance. And not finding him, they returned into Jerusalem, seeking him. And it came to pass, that after three days they found him in the temple sitting in the midst of the doctors, hearing them and asking them questions. And all that heard him were astonished at his wisdom and his answers. And seeing him, they wondered. And his mother said to him: Son, why hast thou done so to us? behold thy father and I have sought thee sorrowing. And he said to them: How is it that you sought me? did you not know that I must be about the things that are my Father's? And they understood not the word that he spoke unto them. And he went down with them, and came to Nazareth: and was subject to them. And his mother kept all these words in her heart. And Jesus increased in wisdom and age, and grace with God and men.

SERMON XVIII.

And he went down with them, and came to Nazareth, and was subject to them.—St. Luke ii. 51.

Such, my dear friends, is the brief record of our Lord's boyhood and youth. When we next hear of him he has begun his mission to the world. But brief as the record is, it teaches a great lesson—the lesson of obedience. First it proclaims this lesson to children and the young generally. They ought to be subject to their parents. Is this the case? Often, we know, it is not. There are proud, rebellious, and disobedient children in many families—girls and boys who will not do what they are told; who go to places forbidden by their parents; who speak of their parents as the "old man" and the "old woman"; children who do their best to make father and mother subject to *them;* who think they know better than their parents, and who despise those set over them by God. So glaring has this disrespect for parents become that a witty man has said that soon the sign and title of a firm will be "Jones and Father" instead of "Jones and Son." Disobedient, proud children, I point you this morning to the little home of Nazareth. Look in, conceited, self-sufficient boys and girls.

What do you see? God obedient to his creatures; Jesus with Joseph and his Mother; Jesus, "very God of very God," subject to them. There is your example. Woe to you if you do not follow it! Disobedience made hell for the devil and his angels, and disobedience, if persisted in, will make hell for you. Hell is the headquarters of disobedience, and will be the home of the disobedient and rebellious for evermore. So, then, you that are young, cut down your pride, bend the neck a little easier to the yoke. Be more like Jesus, who went home with his parents, stayed home with them, and was *subject* to them.

But not only to children and the young does this lesson come home; it strikes all of us. In one sense we are all children—children of holy church, whose chief pastor is called the Holy Father, and whose priests are called by all "fathers." Now, then, you "children of an older growth," how have you shown your obedience? Are you very particular to keep the laws of *mother* church? How about fasting and abstinence? What of hearing Mass on a Sunday and of abstaining from servile work? Was your last Easter duty made? Again, how about the advice of your *father* confessor? Have you followed it? How do you keep the minor laws and regulations which the pastor of each particular church sees fit to make for the better ordering of his services, etc., etc.? When the priest has to rebuke you, to reprove you, how do you take it? O my friends! these are the days of disobedience and false independence, and therefore these questions are of vital importance. You must *obey*, if you want to be good Catholics. You must turn a deaf ear to the suggestions of **worldly pride; you must be submissive to holy** mother church, to our Holy Father the Pope, to the pastors and fathers set over you in God's providence. Obedience! obedience!—that must be your watchword. You must not be scaling the mountains of pride hand-in-hand with infidel and heretic, and the devil's staff for a support. You must obey the church and follow *her* teachings, and submit to lawful authority. As St. Paul says: "Be not wise in your own conceits. For I say, by the grace that is given me, to all that are among you, not to be more wise than it behooveth to be wise, but be wise unto sobriety. Let every soul be subject to higher powers: they that resist purchase to themselves damnation." Finally, brethren, show yourselves law-loving, obedient citizens of the country in which you live. Let the Catholic always be found on the side of order and regularity. In a word, show to your pastors and superiors, show even to our worst enemies, that you have learnt well the lesson contained in these few words: "He went down with them, and came to Nazareth, and was subject to them." B.

SERMON XIX.

Behold the Lamb of God: behold, he who taketh away the sins of the world—St. John i. 29.

THERE are no words of the Gospel, my dear brethren, more frequently used in the church of God than these. You often hear them from the lips of the priest, but perhaps you do not remember when. They are more familiar to you in Latin than in English. The moment when they are said is that when the greatest of all gifts is about to be given to you. It is just before the giving of Holy Communion. The priest, turning to you with the ciborium in his hand, raises one of the sacred particles from it, and shows it to you, saying, *Ecce Agnus Dei*—which means, "Behold the Lamb of God"—*ecce qui tollit peccata mundi*. "Behold, he who taketh away the sins of the world."

The church has put the words in the mouth of the priest at this time, when he distributes Holy Communion, because he is then showing Christ to the faithful. And she puts them in the Gospel of to-day, because on this day, the octave of the great feast which we celebrated last Sunday, she commemorates what we may call our Lord's second Epiphany after his hidden life of thirty years, when St. John the Baptist, his great precursor, taking the place of the star which showed him to the wise men, showed him to those who were to become his disciples, and who were to accompany him in that ministry of three years upon which he was about to enter.

As St. John took the place of the star, so the Catholic priest now takes the place of St. John. He has now to show Christ to the world, and especially to the faithful. And St. John, in his humility and self-concealment, has set an example to him which he should try to copy, and which a good priest does try to copy. That is, he tries to show our Lord to the people and to keep himself in the background; he tries to bring the faithful to his Master and theirs, not to himself. He desires that they should see in all that he does not his own power or gifts, but the grace of God, by which alone he can do them any good; that they should not be drawn to him, but to the Lamb of God, who alone can take away their sins.

And what the good priest does you also, my brethren, should do. You should not think of the priest, but of Him whom the priest represents, and in whose power he acts. And especially should you take care to do this in those sacramental acts which the priest does more particularly in the name of God; that is, when he celebrates Holy Mass, baptizes, hears confessions, or gives Holy Communion. For, in truth, it is not he who does these things, but our Lord Jesus Christ. He, the Lamb of God, is the true priest. He who instituted the sacraments also is the one who confers them.

Remember this when you receive them. When you go to the altar-rail for Holy Communion, and when the priest holds up the sacred Host before you, saying, *Ecce Agnus Dei, ecce qui tollit peccata mundi*, think not of the priest, of his virtues or his faults, but of the immaculate Lamb of God, who is coming to you, a poor sinner.

And when the priest is baptizing think not of him, but of the Holy One who, by his own baptism in the Jordan, gave water the power to wash away sin. Look at him standing by the side of the priest with infinite love and compassion, and purifying the soul which he came from heaven to save.

When you bow your head to receive absolution in the Sacrament of Penance think not of the minister of the sacrament before whom you kneel, and who is, at the best, but a sinful man, but of Him against whom you have sinned, and who is now about to forgive you once more. Think only of that loving Saviour who is both your God and your **Judge**—your judge now not in justice but in mercy.

And, above all, at holy Mass remember who it is that is saying Mass; who it is that is there at that altar, offering himself in sacrifice for you. Do not be criticising the priest, and thinking whether he is devout or not; his dispositions do not c ncern you much more than those of your neighbor who is kneeling by your side. Say to yourself, as you look at the altar, *Ecce Agnus Dei ecce qui tollit peccata mundi.* Behold in the midst of that throne the Lamb standing as it were slain, and fall down with the angels in adoration before him.

Yes, my brethren, *Christus apparuit nobis; venite, adoremus*—" Christ has appeared to us; come, let us worship him." Such are the words of the church in the Divine Office at this time. Let us, then, seek him, find him, and adore him in this holy Catholic Church, and in all that is done in it by his power and in his name.

Second Sunday after Epiphany.

FEAST OF THE HOLY NAME OF JESUS.

EPISTLE. *Rom. xii.* 6-16. Having gifts different, according to the grace that is given us, whether prophecy, according to the proportion of faith, or ministry in ministering; or he that teacheth, in teaching: he that exhorteth in exhorting; he that giveth with simplicity; he that ruleth with solicitude; he that showeth mercy with cheerfulness. Love without dissimulation. Hating that which is evil, adhering to that which is good; loving one another with brotherly love; in honor preventing one another; in solicitude not slothful; in spirit fervent; serving the Lord: rejoicing in hope; patient in tribulation; instant in prayer; communicating to the necessities of the saints; pursuing hospitality. Bless them that persecute you; bless and curse not. Rejoice with them that rejoice, weep with them that weep; being of one mind one to another; not high-minded but condescending to the humble.

EPISTLE OF THE FEAST. *Acts iv.* 8-12. Then Peter, filled with the Holy Ghost, said to them: Ye rulers of the people and ancients, hear: If we this day are examined concerning the good deed done to the infirm man, by what means he hath been made whole; be it known to you all, and to all the people of Israel, that in the name of our Lord Jesus Christ of Nazareth, whom you crucified, whom God hath raised from the dead, even by him doth this man stand here before you whole. This is the stone which was rejected by you, builders; which is become the head of the corner; nor is there salvation in any other. For there is no other name under heaven given to men, whereby we must be saved.

GOSPEL. *St. John ii.* 1–11. At that time: There was a marriage in Cana of Galilee: and the mother of Jesus was there. And Jesus also was invited, and his disciples, to the marriage. And the wine failing, the mother of Jesus saith to him: They have no wine. And Jesus saith to her: Woman, what is that to me and to thee? my hour is not yet come. His mother said to the waiters: Whatsoever he shall say to you, do ye. Now, there were set there six water-pots of stone, according to the manner of the purifying of the Jews, containing two or three measures apiece. Jesus saith to them: Fill the water-pots with water. And they filled them up to the brim. And Jesus saith to them: Draw out now and carry to the chief steward of the feast. And they carried it. And when the chief steward had tasted the water made wine, and knew not whence it was, but the waiters knew who had drawn the water, the chief steward calleth the bridegroom, and saith to him: Every man at first setteth forth good wine, and when men have well drunk, then that which is worse: but thou hast kept the good wine until now. This beginning of miracles did Jesus in Cana of Galilee, and he manifested his glory, and his disciples believed in him.

GOSPEL OF THE FEAST. *St. Luke ii.* 21. At that time: After eight days were accomplished that the child should be circumcised, his name was called Jesus, which was called by the Angel, before he was conceived in the womb.

SERMON XX.

His name was called Jesus.—ST. LUKE ii. 21.

TO-DAY, dear friends, we keep the Feast of the Holy Name. Our dear Lord is known to us by many names—he is called the Word, the Christ, the Son of God, the Lamb of God, the Prince of Peace, and the like—but to day we are met together to honor his *real* name; the name by which he was called when on this earth; the name which belonged to him just as our names belong to us; the name by which we are to be saved—the holy name of JESUS! Brethren, this name is a holy name, because it is the name of a God made man. It is a precious name: Jesus shed his Blood for us for the first time as he received it. It is a great and noble name, for it belongs to the mightiest Warrior the world ever saw—to Him who fought with sin and death, and conquered in the fight. It is a terrible name, for when we invoke it hell trembles, earth fears, and even heaven bows the knee. Oh! then, dear brethren, if this name is holy—if precious, if great and noble, if terrible—how much it ought to be revered and respected. We are told by our dear patron, St. Paul, that our Lord "humbled himself, becoming obedient unto death, even the death of the cross. For which cause God also hath exalted him, and hath given him a name which is above all names: that in the name of Jesus every knee should bow of those that are in heaven, on earth, and under the earth." And yet, in spite of all this, although it is so plain that this name is holy, precious, mighty, and terrible, although it is clear that when it is uttered the faithful on earth, the white-winged angels in heaven, ay, and even the lost spirits in hell bow to do homage to it, nevertheless there is a creature who will not worship; there is a created being worse than the very demons; there is found one who will not reverence that name, holy and good and true—and that creature is the *blas-*

phemer. Yes, brethren, in our streets, in our factories, in our very homes that holy name is taken in vain. Jesus—that sweet name is mixed up with everything that is foul and disrespectful. Jesus' name, the name of our King, our Saviour, and our Judge, is used as an oath; and not only by men coarse and hardened, but by boys and girls, by women, and, O unheard of impiety! even by little children. Passing through the streets the other day, I heard a volley of curses in which the holy Name was mingled, and the curser was a boy who could not, I am sure, have been more than eight or nine years of age; and, alas! it is not the first time that I have heard such things. O brethren! I beseech you, by the wounds and cross of Jesus Christ, look to this great sin. When I hear these little baby blasphemers, who scarce, perhaps, know what they say, I know they have learned these oaths from the father, the elder brothers, and perhaps even from the mother, and I tremble to think how deep the evil has sunk into the hearts of men. Oh! then let us never again misuse the holy Name; let us cast out cursing and swearing from our midst, lest it drive us and our children into hell.

It belongs to us to be devout to the holy name of Jesus, for we are taught by holy church to ask for every blessing through it. Are we tempted? Let us call upon it, and He who bears it will come to our aid. Are we in sorrow? Let us whisper to ourselves, Jesus! Jesus! and he who knelt in the dark garden and sweat blood for us, he who faced the horrors of death, forsaken and heart-broken, will send us comfort and heal our wounds. Do our sins terrify us? Let us look up to the Cross of Calvary. There on the topmost beam is written the sweet **name of Jesus**; there beneath hangs the *Saviour* and the Comforter. Do we need strength for the battle of life, and courage in the struggle against the world, the flesh, and the devil? Jesus! Jesus! the Mighty One the Conqueror, the Lion of Juda, he who is called "Faithful and true, and with justice doth he judge and fight"—he will arm us for the battle and nerve our heart for the combat. Oh! let us reverence the dear, holy name of our sweet Saviour while we live; and when at last our death-cold lips can part no more to utter it, may the great God give us each a friend to whisper it in our ears, so that Jesus! Jesus! Jesus! may be the last name that we shall hear on earth, and the first which our enraptured spirits will hear in heaven. B.

SERMON XXI.

His name was called Jesus.—St. Luke ii. 21.

To-day we celebrate the Feast of the most Holy Name of our Lord and Saviour Jesus Christ. The church sets apart a special Sunday for the celebration of this feast, to bring before our minds the sacredness of this name—its preciousness, and the reverence due to it.

This name is the name of the God-Man who came into the world to save us from hell. It is the greatest of all names, because it is the name of the greatest of all beings. It was given to our Lord by the archangel when he announced to the Blessed Virgin that she was to be the mother of God. An angel first pronounced it; the Blessed Virgin and St. Joseph were the first to call the new-born Babe of Bethlehem by that name; and all holy men and women, from the time of the adoration of the poor shepherds and wise men down to this hour, have had the greatest veneration for that name.

The angel St. Gabriel said to the Blessed Virgin: "He shall be called Jesus, for he shall save his people from their sins." You see, then, how precious this name is: it is the name by which we are to be freed from our sins delivered from hell, and admitted among the blessed, the redeemed of all nations. It is the name by which we are the receivers of the supernatural graces of all the holy sacraments. And St. Paul says: God gave to his only-begotten Son "a name that is above every name, that at the name of *Jesus* every knee should bow of those that are in heaven, on earth, and in hell, and that every tongue should confess that the Lord Jesus Christ is in the glory of God the Father." It is the name not only of the Infant of Bethlehem, but it is the name of that One whom you see in the Stations and nailed to the cross, bleeding, and dying, and dead for you.

And yet how our blood runs cold, how we tremble with horror, when we see how little reverence is shown for this name! You need not go far or stay out very long before you hear that name used most irreverently by the child who has hardly learned his prayers, as well as by thieves, drunkards, and murderers, and the lowest rabble that tread the streets of this city; not only by bad men and women, but by people who profess to be respectable Catholics. How often we are made to wonder why Almighty God does not send a thunderbolt and strike dead the blasphemer, or cause the earth to open under those who so treat this holy name, and swallow them up quickly in punishment for their crime! A man who steals, or gets drunk, or gives way to lust sees a sensual temporary good in these sins; but what good, what use is there in blasphemy, in cursing, in swearing? None. It is a direct blow at Almighty God himself. If a man were to insult your mother your vengeance would be roused, and you would think no punishment too great for the offender. Shall God not be jealous of his name? Shall he not punish? Yes, he will. He says: "Thou shalt not take the name of the Lord thy God in vain; for the Lord will not hold him guiltless who taketh his name in vain."

If, then, you have not controlled your gift of speech, which was given you to edify your neighbor, to speak and sing the praises of God, but have given way to a habit of using God's holy name and that of his Son in vain, ask him to give you the grace to overcome the habit. If you hear people on the street or in company blaspheming, cursing, or swearing, lift up your heart to God and make reparation for the injury by saying the prayer, "Blessed be the name of the Lord." Never give scandal to others, and especially the little ones around your family hearth, by blaspheming, or even by carelessly using the name of God or his saints without due reverence. Many men and women have grown up with this old habit clinging to them—a habit that they contracted at home, and that they learned when young from their father and mother. Cursing and swearing are the language of hell. Blessing, prayer, and praise are the language of heaven. Do all in your power to learn the language of the saints—that is, the language of love and reverence for the holy name of Jesus. For ' his name is holy and terrible." Repeat the prayer which is sung and said in the holy Mass on this feast:

"O God, who hast made thy only-begotten Son to be the Saviour of mankind, and hast commanded that he should be called Jesus, mercifully grant that we may so venerate his holy name on earth that we may be favored with beholding his face for ever in heaven."

SERMON XXII.

There was a marriage in Cana, of Galilee; and the Mother of Jesus was there. And Jesus also was invited, and his disciples, to the marriage.—St. John ii. 1, 2.

As we read the story of this marriage, my dear brethren, it must certainly occur to all of us how singularly favored it was, above all that have ever been celebrated since the beginning of the world, in being honored with the presence of our Lord and Saviour Jesus Christ, of his Blessed Mother, and of his apostles, and in the fact that it witnessed the first of the miracles which he performed in his three years' ministry—the change of water into wine. But when we come to look at the matter more closely we shall see that, great as was the honor which this marriage received, every Christian marriage has the same. For every Christian marriage is honored really and truly, though not visibly, with the presence of our Lord, his Blessed Mother, and the apostles; and at every Christian marriage a miracle of grace is performed of which we may well believe the change of water into wine to have been only a shadow or type.

For what is marriage now in the church of Christ? It is one of the sacraments. And what does that mean? It means that whenever a marriage is contracted by those who are baptized there is a grace given with it by our Lord's infallible promise. This grace, moreover, is one which, like those given in the sacraments of Baptism, Confirmation, and Holy Orders, is to remain permanently in the soul, and to be a source or fountain from which new graces are continually to flow. So I am right in saying that our Lord is present at a Christian marriage; for it is only from him that this grace can come. And I am right in saying that Our Lady is present at it; because this grace, while it comes from him, comes through her. For she is the channel through which his grace comes to us; which is shown in this marriage at Cana, of which the Gospel tells us, by his working the miracle of the change of the water into wine at her intercession. And, lastly, I am right in saying the apostles are present at a Christian marriage; for such a marriage can only lawfully be celebrated in the presence of the priest, who represents them.

I said, furthermore, that at every Christian marriage a miracle is worked which was represented by our Lord's miracle at Cana. This miracle is the giving of this wonderful sacramental grace; and it is well represented by the conversion of water into wine. It is a miracle—that is to say, an extraordinary and supernatural work of God—because it is not naturally connected with marriage itself. Marriage, in itself, is nothing but a contract or agreement between two parties, having no special blessing or grace, except that which comes from its honorable nature and the good dispositions of the parties themselves. Such is marriage among the unbaptized. But among Christians it is, as I have said, elevated to the dignity of a great sacrament—the contract remaining, but the sacrament being added to it; and it cannot exist among Christians without both. Now, I think you will agree with me that this is well represented by the change of water into wine, in which water, indeed, remains, but is blended with the spirit in such a way that neither can be taken away without destroying the very substance of the wine.

Such, then, my brethren, is the dignity of Christian marriage, represented to us in this marriage at Cana, in Galilee. But is it honored among Christians according to its dignity?

How many are there who reverence this sacrament as they should? It is one of the sacraments of the living, as they are called; that is, one of those which require the soul, when receiving it, to be in the state of grace. The Catholic who comes to it in the state of mortal sin commits a horrible sacrilege as surely as he would if he should go to the altar-rail and receive Holy Communion without repentance for his sins. Do not forget this. Do not dare to come to receive the sacrament of matrimony without preparing your soul by a good confession; not only on account of the dreadful sacrilege of which you will be guilty in receiving it unprepared, but also for fear of losing the grace which it is meant to give you throughout life, and which grace may never return; for, like that offered to the soul in Holy Communion, if once **despised and rejected, it may be lost for ever.**

And, for the sake of Him who instituted this great sacrament, do not make it, as too many do, an occasion of mortal sin by making it a privileged time for drunkenness and immodes y. A wedding ought to be a time of joy, but for a joy of purity and sobriety. If you make it a time for opening the door to sin for yourselves and for others, tremble lest you bring down on yourselves for the rest of your lives the curse of God instead of his blessing.

Invite, then, like the couple at Cana, our Lord to be present at your marriage, and behave as you would if you were to see him there. So shall you receive his benediction, both for time and eternity

Third Sunday after Epiphany.

Epistle. *Rom. xii.* 16–21. Brethren: Be not wise in your own conceits. Render to no man evil for evil. Provide things good not only in the sight of God, but also in the sight of all men. If it be possible, as much as is in you, have peace with all men. Revenge not yourselves, my dearly beloved; but give place to wrath, for it is written: "Revenge is mine; I will repay, saith the Lord." But if thy enemy be hungry, give him to eat; if he thirst, give him drink; for doing this thou shalt heap coals of fire upon his head. Be not overcome by evil, but overcome evil by good.

Gospel. *St. Matt. viii.* 1–13. At that time: When Jesus was come down from the mountain, great multitudes followed him; and behold a leper coming, adored him, saying: Lord, if thou wilt, thou canst make me clean. And Jesus, stretching forth his hand, touched him, saying: I will; be thou made clean. And immediately his leprosy was cleansed. And Jesus said to him: See thou tell no man; but go show thyself to the priest, and offer the gift which Moses commanded for a testimony to them. And when he had entered into Capharnaum, there came to him a centurion, beseeching him and saying: Lord, my servant lieth at home sick of the palsy, and is grievously tormented. And Jesus said to him: I will come and heal him. And the centurion, making answer, said: Lord, I am not worthy that thou shouldst enter under my roof; but only say the word, and my servant shall be healed. For I also am a man under authority, having soldiers under me; and I say to this man, Go, and he goeth, and to another, Come, and he cometh, and to my servant, Do this, and he doeth it. And Jesus, hearing this, wondered, and said to those that followed him : Amen I say to you, I have not found so great faith in Israel. And I say unto you that many shall come from the east and the west, and shall sit down with Abraham, and Isaac, and Jacob, in the kingdom of heaven ; but the children of the kingdom shall be cast out into exterior darkness : there shall be weeping and gnashing of teeth. And Jesus said to the centurion : Go, and as thou hast believed, so be it done to thee. And the servant was healed at the same hour.

SERMON XXIII.

Only say the word, and my servant shall be healed.—St. Matt. viii. 8.

The centurion in to-day's Gospel, dear friends, is certainly a shining example to us of many virtues. Particularly is he an example to those among us who are rich and well off, or who have any servants or others employed under our authority. When any one is taken sick, what is the first cry ? Go for the priest. Run for the doctor. And instantly a messenger is sought out. Now, this man's servant was sick. What did he do ? Centurion, and high in station as he was, he went *himself* for One who was both doctor and priest. His servant, doubtless, had served him faithfully, had been obedient and trustworthy ; and now that this servant is sick, remembering the sublime virtue of charity, the master runs off to our Lord and begs of him to speak the word that would heal the servant. Now, many of you, dear brethren, have in your houses hired help, and the poor are around you who serve you in many useful ways; who do work which, did they not exist, would have to be left undone. How do you treat those fellow-Christians? Ah! I am afraid, often in a very different spirit to that displayed by the centurion. They are sick. You grumble at the inconvenience to which you are put, but what do you do to help them? Do you get the doctor? Do you offer them such nourishment as a sick person needs? Do you visit your servant's sick-bed, or the beds of the poor, to whom we are all indebted for so much service? I wish it were always so, but it is not. Often a servant is made to work when bed would be a more fitting place to be in than the kitchen. Often the poor suffer dreadfully because those whom they serve in health will not help them in sickness. Oh! then let us all follow the example of the good centurion, and if our servants in our house, or our servants out of the house, are sick, let us, moved by a divine charity, hasten at once to their relief.

And then in spiritual things how do we act? Catholic heads of families, employers, masters and mistresses, keepers of stores and workshops, how do you look after those that work for you? Do you see that they go to Mass? Do you give them time to get to confession? Do you look after the moral conduct of those you employ? When they are sick and suffering are you solicitous that they should have the comfort and help which the holy sacraments afford? Are you sensible of the responsibility which lies upon you to see that the priest is sent for, especially when they are in danger of death? Oh! I am much afraid that many are very neglectful in this respect. So long as their work is done they care very little for those they employ. Catholic employers often don't bestow a thought upon these things. But don't deceive yourselves: God will require all these souls at your hands. No Catholic man or woman ought to keep in their houses a servant who is negligent of his or her religious duties. You should give your help and your employees plenty of time to go to Mass and confession; and, more than that, it is your duty to *see* that they go. You should not employ by the side of innocent young men and women all sorts of roughs and blackguards. By so doing you put immortal souls in peril. You should remember that you are head of the family, and that the help and the employees are part of that family, and therefore you are bound in conscience to care for them. Imitate, then, the centurion. Love those you employ. Have a great charity for them. Cherish them, tend them in all their wants. Correct their faults, reward their fidelity; and by so doing you will advance Christ's kingdom on earth and people his kingdom in heaven. B.

SERMON XXIV.

If it be possible, as much as is in you, have peace with all men; revenge not yourselves, my dearly beloved.—ROMANS xii. 18-19.

THERE are a good many people who seem to find it very difficult to have peace with all men, or at any rate with all women; for, strange to say, it is, for some reason or other, what is known as the gentler sex that gives and has the most trouble in this respect.

Of course it is all the fault of some other party that they cannot live in peace; not their own at all. They themselves are perfectly innocent—lambs, in fact, among wolves. Other people are always persecuting and tormenting them, or at any rate belying them; this last is one of the favorite complaints of these poor, harmless, and much-abused creatures. They try to have peace as far as possible, but other people will not let them.

And of course they never revenge themselves on their cruel enemies. Oh! no. They never injure or belie them; they would not do such a thing for the world. They may, indeed, meekly complain of their troubles to the few friends they have got left; they tell how wicked these people are who give them so much annoyance. They try to lower other people's esteem of them; but, of course, that is not meant for injury—that is only that others may be duly warned of such dangerous characters. In their zeal they may draw on their imagination a little; but of course that is not belying. They, perhaps on some rare occasions will try to take it out of their persecutors in one way or another; but then that is not revenge—that is only standing up for their rights. They would like to have peace, and so they try to have it by making reconciliation as hard as possible.

It is plain what good Christians they are from their enjoyment of the words which follow those which I have quoted from the Epistle of to-day. These words are: "Revenge is mine, I will repay, saith the Lord." These are, indeed, a great consolation to them.

"Yes," they say to themselves, "I leave them to God. I cannot revenge myself on my enemies as I would like; I don't dare to, or my conscience won't let me; but I hope God will punish them as they deserve. Revenge belongs to him, I know, and I am glad to think that in his own good time he will lay it on to them well. I shall do all my duty if I wish patiently for the time when he will begin to do it; and meanwhile I will console myself by praying that he may convert them and make every one of them as good a Christian as I am."

The delusion under which these good Christians are laboring would be amusing, if it were not so dangerous. The danger is that the revenge of God, about which they like to think, is hanging as much over their own heads as over those of the ones with whom they are at variance. They are not really trying to have peace; their own revenge is what they want, though they are willing that Almighty God should be the instrument of it.

They do not care either to preserve peace or to regain it in the only way in which it can be preserved or regained—that is, by charity and humility. Their charity is all for themselves. They may tread on other people's corns, but nobody else must tread on theirs. Other people must be humble, and, if they give offence, even carelessly, must make an abject apology; but they themselves are too good to be obliged to do that.

Perhaps, however, my friends, some of you really do want to live in peace with all. If so, you can do it by following a very simple rule. It is this: Be careful what you say or do to others; they are sensitive as well as yourself—perhaps more so. You must not expect other people to be saints, even if you are one yourself. Do not flatter what is bad in them, but acknowledge what is good; stroke them the right way. If they really do you an injury see if you have not provoked it; examine your own actions. If you are sure you have not, put it down to ignorance or misapprehension; try to find out what the matter is, and set it right by an explanation, if you can. But if you have committed a fault do not be too proud to acknowledge it. If you cannot procure a reconciliation speak well of the other party, and believe him or her to be, on the whole, better than yourself. For one who has true humility this will not be very hard to do.

This is the real meaning of the counsel of St. Paul; if you follow it you will, indeed, live in peace as far as it is possible in this world.

Fourth Sunday after Epiphany.

EPISTLE. *Rom. xiii.* 8–10. Brethren: Owe no man anything, but that you love one another. For he that loveth his neighbor, hath fulfilled the law. For "Thou shalt not commit adultery. Thou shalt not kill. Thou shalt not steal. Thou shalt not bear false witness. Thou shalt not covet." And if there be any other commandment, it is comprised in this word: "Thou shalt love thy neighbor as thyself." The love of the neighbor worketh no evil. Love, therefore, is the fulfilling of the law.

GOSPEL. *St. Matt. viii.* 23–27. At that time: When Jesus entered into the ship, his disciples followed him; and behold a great tempest arose in the sea, so that the ship was covered with waves, but he was asleep. And his disciples came to him, and waked him, saying: Lord, save us, we perish. And Jesus saith to them: Why are you fearful, O ye of little faith? Then rising up he commanded the winds and the sea, and there came a great calm. But the men wondered, saying: Who is this, for even the winds and the sea obey him?

SERMON XXV.

And Jesus saith to them: Why are you fearful, O ye of little faith?—ST. MATT. viii. 26.

SOME people are always worrying. It would seem that they must enjoy it, for they always find something to worry about. If one good matter for worrying is settled they will be sure to rake up another to take its place. Some of them worry about temporal matters, some about spiritual; but whatever their taste may be in this respect, they are so fond of the amusement that, if they cannot get their favorite matter to worry about, they will take something else rather than not have any at all.

You would think that this taste for worrying would be a very uncommon one; but, strange to say, it is not so. In fact, the number of worriers is almost as great as the number of people in the world, and they are worrying about every conceivable thing, though generally only about one thing at a time; it may be about their sins or about somebody else's sins —their children's, for instance—or it may be, and is more likely to be, about some temporal matter, such as their health or the state of their worldly affairs.

Now, what do I mean by worrying? I do not mean thinking seriously about things either spiritual or temporal—for a great many, though not all, of the things people worry about are worthy of serious consideration, whereas nothing is worth a moment's worry—but I do mean thinking about them in a way that can do no good, and that only serves to turn the mind in on itself and away from God.

Here, for instance, is a case of worrying, to which I have just alluded: A good father and mother have children who are growing up, as so many children are growing up, especially in this city, in neglect of their duties and are acquiring various bad habits. Of course this is very painful to their parents, and there is very good reason that it should be. They would be unnatural or wicked parents if it were not so. They ought to be distressed about it; and I did not say that people should never be distressed, but only that they should not worry. But these parents probably do worry. They occupy their minds with all sorts of useless questions and imaginations. They say: "What have I done that these children of mine are so bad?" And perhaps, though they ask this question, they never really stop to examine themselves and find out if they have neglected their own duty in any way, so as to make an act of contrition for it, and make good resolutions, if it be not too late, for the future. What they mean rather by it is: "How can God allow this when I have done my duty?" And then they say: "Suppose these children get worse and disgrace my name, and even lose their souls—what shall I do then?" Or perhaps they say: "What shall I do now?" But that does not really mean anything, for either they do not set their wits to work to find out what they can do, or they have concluded with good reason that they cannot do anything except pray; and that they do not do, for their time of prayer is taken up with this same useless worrying.

Now, what does all this come from? It comes from a distrust in God's love and providence. It comes from a feeling like what the apostles had, as we read in to-day's Gospel, as if He who ought to take care of them were asleep; but they ought to have known, as their own psalms could have taught them, that "He shall neither slumber nor sleep that keepeth Israel." Even though they knew him not to be God, they should have known that God, who had sent him into the world, and on whom their faith in him rested, would not allow them to come to any harm; and they should have been willing, when they had done their own duty, to trust in his providence for the rest. They might, indeed, well have waked him to get his help and advice as to what to do; but he, who read their hearts, knew that their anxiety had its source, not in prudence, but in distrust, and so he deservedly rebuked them, saying: "Why are you fearful, O ye of little faith?"

That is the reason why we, like the apostles, are worrying. It is because we have little faith. We distrust God's providence and mercy, and spend our time in this distrust and complaining, instead of quietly finding out and doing our own duty, and then simply and confidently leaving the result to him. But we have less excuse for it than they, for we know more of him than they did then. Let us, then, be ashamed of our want of faith, and try to do better in this respect for the future.

SERMON XXVI.

And behold, a great tempest arose in the sea.—St. Matt. viii. 24.

Almost all of us, my dear brethren, have at some time of life been in a position like that of the apostles in their little boat on the Sea of Galilee. We have been out at sea in a storm, with the waves beating against our frail craft and threatening to swamp it every moment. So we do not need to draw on our imagination to realize what their feelings must have been.

Perhaps you may think I am exaggerating when I say this; most of you, I suppose, cannot remember ever having been in a storm at sea. But it is quite true, nevertheless. Only the sea and the storm were far more dangerous ones than those to which the apostles were exposed that night. For the sea over which you were, and still are, sailing is the sea of this mortal life; and the storm was the storm of temptation; and the danger was that of death, not to the body, but to the soul.

But perhaps you do not remember ever having met with any very violent storm, even of this kind. Well, it may be that God has singularly favored you, and given you a very quiet and smooth sea to sail over so far. If so, you are an exception to the common rule. It may be, however, that you escaped the storm in another way; that is, by going to the bottom at once. You know the most furious tempests do not reach very far below the surface of the ocean, so that one can always escape them by sinking. So you, perhaps, have escaped temptation by yielding to it at once; as soon as you were tempted to commit mortal sin you committed it, and sank into its horrible and fathomless abyss, continually deeper and deeper, till you were brought up again to the light and air of God's pardon and peace by some mission which he sent you, or by some other extraordinary grace from him.

But that was not what you were made for, any more than a ship is made to be continually sinking and being pulled up to the surface again. Ships are made to sail, not to sink. Their builders expect that they will battle with the elements, not be overcome by them; nay, more, they expect that the very winds which seem to threaten their safety shall be the means of sending them to the port which they are intended to reach. And what the builder expects of his ship is what God, who has made us, expects of us; especially of us Christians, with whom he has taken such great pains. He expects, and he has a right to expect, that we shall stay on the surface—that is, that we shall keep in the state of grace; that we shall battle with the winds and waves—that is, that we shall resist temptation; and, furthermore, he expects that the winds, even if they be ahead, shall help us on our course—that is, that they shall be the means, and even the principal means, of bringing us into the safe harbor of our eternal home.

Let us not, then, be surprised, nay, let us even rejoice, if we fall into temptation, so long as we do not seek it. "My brethren," says St. James, "count it all joy, when you shall fall into divers temptations." And why? First, because the fact that you are harassed by temptations is a sign that you have not given way to them. It shows that you are on the surface, that you have not foundered yet when you feel the winds and the waves.

And, secondly, because it is a sign that our Lord puts confidence in you. The builder of a ship, if he could do it, would proportion the wind to the size and strength of his vessel; and that is what our Maker actually does. He has let his saints have temptations compared with which yours are as nothing at all. Such as he allows you to have are meant for your salvation and perfection; the more he thinks you worthy of, the better.

But do not seek them. A prudent captain keeps out of the track of storms. Be content with those which you cannot avoid, for those are the only ones which God means you to have.

When you cannot avoid them meet them courageously. Do not get frightened, as the apostles did, for God is with you as he was with them, though he may seem to be asleep. He has not forgotten you, and with his help you will conquer them, every one.

But you must ask him to do so. You must go to him as the apostles did, saying: "Lord, save us, we perish." He did not blame them for that, but for their terror and want of trust in his providence. You must work when you are in the storm of temptation as if the result all depended on yourself; you must pray as if it all depended on him. If you do this you will not sink in the tempest; nay, when it is over you will find that it has driven you nearer to the harbor where storms never come.

SERMON XXVII.

CANDLEMAS-DAY.

A light to the revelation of the Gentiles, and the glory of thy people of Israel.—St. Luke ii. 32.

THE blessing of candles, and the esteem which Catholics have for candles when they are blessed, is one of the things which Protestants find it very hard to understand. They have no idea of a candle, except that it is a very old-fashioned article, useful enough, perhaps, if you want to grope in some dark corner of the house, but, on the whole, a very poor affair in these days of gas and the electric light. They cannot see why any one who can get a good kerosene lamp should use a candle instead; unless, perhaps, it might be because the candle will not explode.

The reason for their perplexity is pretty plain. It is because they do not, or it may be will not, understand that we honor and prize candles, as we do the images of the saints and many other things, not for what they are, but for what they represent; and also on account of the sanctification and real use, not to our bodies so much as to our souls, that the blessing of the church is able to give to anything to which it is attached.

Protestants, I say, do not or will not understand these things; but Catholics do. It is not superstition which makes a Catholic prize a blessed candle. He knows, first, that it has been selected by the church to represent our Blessed Lord himself; that its feeble light is a sign of the true light which enlighteneth every man that cometh into this world; and he honors and esteems it for God's sake. And secondly, he knows that it has a power and use greater and higher than that of the most brilliant lamps that the hand of man can make; that, though it be but a material thing, it has a spiritual value, like holy-water and other things which the church has blessed and sanctified; and specially that it is a defence against our spiritual enemies, Satan and the other fallen angels, and all the more so because these proud spirits cannot bear to be put to flight, as they are, by such a common and simple thing as a candle or a few drops of water.

You know these things, my friends; the spirit of faith teaches them to you. But you do not bear them so constantly in mind as you should. How often does the priest go to a house on a sick-call, and find that there is no candle to be had! The law of the church requires it when the sacraments are to be administered; but one would think it would not need a law to make any one who had the faith see that at least this honor should be given to them. Strange to say, however, the people of the house never thought of the matter at all. They keep our Lord waiting while they run out to borrow, if possible, a candle from some pious neighbor. Perhaps they buy one at the grocery-store; I do not know what blessing they think that has received. When they get the candle, such as it may be, there is probably nothing to put it in; it is likely enough that a bottle is all that can be found.

It would look much better, in some houses which we have to visit, if there were fewer bottles and more blessed candles. It would look as if the people who lived there thought at least as much of their souls as of their bodies. It is very unpleasant for all parties —and our Lord is one of them—to have such things happen as I have described.

Get rid of the bottle and have a candlestick in its place. I know that candlesticks, as well as candles, are rather out of fashion; but the supply will always follow the demand. For the honor and for the fear of God, do not remain any longer without a blessed candle in your house, and something worthy of it to hold it. There will be no harm in burning it, even though no one be sick and the priest not there, if it be at a proper place and time.

And, if it be possible, offer a candle to be burned in the place and at the time most pleasing to God of all—that is, on his holy altar while Mass is being offered, or his blessing being given to you in the Sacrament of his love. Honor and glorify him everywhere, but specially in the place where his glory dwelleth, and where he is daily offered up for you.

Fifth Sunday after Epiphany.

Epistle. *Coloss. iii.* 12–17. Brethren : Put ye on therefore, as the elect of God, holy, and beloved, the bowels of mercy, benignity, humility, modesty, patience, bearing with one another, and forgiving one another, if any have a complaint against another : even as the Lord hath forgiven you, so do you also. But above all these things have charity, which is the bond of perfection : and let the peace of Christ rejoice in your hearts, wherein also you are called in one body ; and be ye thankful. Let the word of Christ dwell in you abundantly, in all wisdom : teaching and admonishing one another in psalms, hymns, and spiritual canticles, singing in grace in your hearts to God. All whatsoever you do in word or in work, do all in the name of the Lord Jesus Christ, giving thanks to God and the Father by Jesus Christ our Lord.

Gospel. *St. Matt. xiii.* 24–30. At that time : Jesus spoke this parable to the multitude, saying : The kingdom of heaven is likened to a man that sowed good seed in his field. But while men were asleep, his enemy came and oversowed cockle among the wheat, and went his way. And when the blade was sprung up, and brought forth fruit, then appeared also the cockle. Then the servants of the master of the house came and said to him : Master, didst thou not sow good seed in thy field ? whence then hath it cockle ? And he said to them : An enemy hath done this. And the servants said to him : Wilt thou that we go and gather it up ? And he said : No, lest while you gather up the cockle, you root up the wheat also together with it. Let both to grow until the harvest, and in the time of the harvest I will say to the reapers: Gather up first the cockle, and bind it into bundles to burn; but gather the wheat into my barn.

SERMON XXVIII.

Gather up first the cockle, and bind it into bundles to burn; but gather the wheat into my barn.—ST. MATT. xiii. 30.

THE parable which is the subject of the Gospel of to-day is explained by our Lord himself a little further on. The disciples asked him to expound it to them; and he told them that the good seed were the children of the kingdom—that is, all good and faithful Christians; and that the cockle were the children of the wicked one—that is, all those who refuse to believe in the faith which God has revealed, or who will not obey his law. These two kinds of people, said he, live together in this world, but at the end of the world they shall all be for ever separated, the wicked to be cast into the furnace of fire, and the just to shine as the sun in the kingdom of their Father.

Our Lord calls the sinful the children of the wicked one—that is, of the devil. But he does not mean that the devil created them, for he can create no one; no, God created us all, and has, furthermore, redeemed us all with his precious Blood. There is something about them, though, which the devil may be said to have created, and that it is which makes them his children. It is sin, which he first brought into God's creation, to which he tempted our first parents, and to which he is all the while tempting us now. Sin is the devil's work; and sinners are his children, because they do his work.

But few people, at least few Christians, are all the time sinners and children of the devil. Sometimes they repent and become, at least for a time, children of God. Good and evil are mixed up in them, as they are in the world. So our Lord's parable is true of each one of them as it is of the world at large. Each of our hearts is a little field in which God is sowing the good seed of his holy inspirations, and the devil the bad seed of his wicked temptations; and sometimes consent is given to one, sometimes to the other.

Perhaps we may have asked ourselves the question (for it is a very natural one to ask): "Why has God allowed the devil to sow his bad seed in the world and in the hearts of men? And why, if he lets it be sown, does he not root out this bad seed, and not let it grow and choke what is good?" I should not wonder at your asking this question, and you should not wonder if we cannot give all of God's reasons for it, for it is one of the mysteries of his providence. But he has himself given one reason for it in his explanation of this parable. The servants, you will remember, wanted to go and root out the cockle; but the master said: "No, lest while ye gather up the cockle, you root up the wheat also together with it." Would it not be so with us, too, if God should take away all the bad seed of temptation out of our hearts? A great deal of our virtue would be rooted up, too, and what was left would not be very strong and solid. You can see that often. A person seems very good, but what is the reason? It is because he is not much tempted. Let a strong temptation come, and perhaps such a person will sin more easily than one who has seemed much worse, but has really been acquiring solid virtue by faithfully combating with difficulties the other has not had. And not only would our virtue not be solid, but our merits would not be very abundant, without temptation; for most of our merit is gained by resisting sin.

Our Lord, then, does not mean to pull up the cockle out of the way of the wheat, but wants the wheat to live and outgrow the cockle. It is for us to see that it does so; for if there is any cockle left when we come to die there will be something to do before the wheat goes to the barn—that is, to cast the cockle into the furnace of fire; and that furnace of fire, for those who die in the grace of God, is the fire of purgatory. We shall have to wait there till the cockle of sin is all burned before we can go to heaven with our wheat of virtue and of merit.

Let us not think, then, in this month of November, only of praying for those who are in those purging flames, but also of avoiding them ourselves. Our Lord does not want us to go to purgatory. He would infinitely rather take us to heaven from our death-bed than let us remain in that state of suffering. What he wants is to have the wheat grow over the whole field and choke the cockle instead of being choked by it—in a word, he wants us to be saints. That is what St. Paul says: "This is the will of God, your sanctification." Let this, then, be our devotion in the month of November and all the year round: to imitate those (and there are many of them) who have died and gone before their Lord with plenty of wheat and no cockle on their hands.

SERMON XXIX.

Bearing with one another, and forgiving one another, if any have a complaint against another: even as the Lord hath forgiven you, so do you also.—COL. iii. 13.

THESE words, my dear brethren, are taken from the Epistle of to-day. They certainly contain a most important lesson for us, and one which we are too apt never even to begin to learn. You will find plenty of people who are near the end of a long life—who have, as the saying is, one foot in the grave—who do not seem to know how to overlook and to pardon injuries any better than when they first began to be exposed to them.

There are two very good reasons, my brethren, why you should learn this lesson. The first is that, unless you do, you can never be happy in this life; the second, that, unless you have learned it, there is great reason to fear for your happiness in the life which is to come.

You can never be happy, I say, in this life, unless you know how to pardon and overlook the injuries you receive from others. And the reason of this is very plain. It is, in the first place, because it is very uncomfortable to be brooding over injuries received—that is plain enough; and, in the second place, you will always be exposed to them. There is a way to avoid them, it is true: it is to go out into the desert and live there in some cave or hut all alone. But I think there are very few nowadays who have any vocation to that; and if you should undertake to live the life of a hermit without any vocation for it, the chances are that you would be ten times as miserable as you would be with the very worst neighbors in the world.

This is the only way to avoid them; for, however good the people are among whom you live, they will always be somewhat selfish; they will want to have their own way sometimes, at least, and it will often happen that they cannot have their way and at the same time let you have yours. And they will always be somewhat thoughtless. They will not be so very careful not to offend you; and you cannot expect it of them, for you are not so careful yourself. You would be surprised if you should know how often you have given offence to others.

The fact is, there is not room enough in this world for us all to get along without sometimes treading on each other's toes. There are a great many of us sailing together down the stream of life, and it will take the most careful steering to prevent our now and then running foul of each other. And such careful steering cannot be expected of every one, or of any except one or two here and there. If you really should try it yourselves you would find how difficult it is. The saints do try it, and that is one reason why it is a work of sanctity to be indulgent to the faults of others.

Well, I said the second reason why you should learn the lesson of forgiveness to others is that, unless you do, there is great reason to fear for your happiness in the life to come. If you can have any doubt of that, those words of our Lord in another place will settle your doubt. "If you will not forgive men," he says, "neither will your Father forgive you your offences." You may confess all your sins, and receive the sacraments over and over again, but so long as you have a hatred against your neighbor your confessions and communions will be bad; you will not be in the friendship of God; and if you go out of the world with that malice in your heart you will be shut out from his presence.

You will say to me, perhaps, "Father, I will forgive, but I cannot forget." If you say this to me I say to you: Take care. As long as you do not at least try to forget, as long as you keep in your mind that sore feeling which the injury you have received, or think you have received, has caused, it will always be an occasion of sin to you. It will always prompt you to withhold from the persons whom you blame that charity which you are bound to show to all. You will always be inclined to speak evil of them, to try to prevent others from praising them, to throw out some hint in which the venom which lies lurking in your heart comes up to the surface. And do not be too sure that you have really done all that God requires because the priest has given you absolution. He cannot read your heart, and often he is obliged to forgive uncharitable people like yourself, with great doubt in his mind whether his sentence is approved by the great Judge who cannot be deceived.

Now, that you may forgive more easily, remember what I suggested a little while ago: that is, that those who have offended you have generally done so either through selfishness or carelessness, not through malice. Believe me, real malice is quite a rare thing. If you could see the real dispositions of others you would see that on the whole they are about as good as your own; and I do not suppose you think you are malicious, and I do not believe you are. Put, then, those unworthy suspicions out of your minds, and forgive others freely and generously as you yourself wish to be forgiven.

Sixth Sunday after Epiphany.

EPISTLE. 1 *Thessalon. i.* 2–10. Brethren: We give thanks to God always for you all: making a remembrance of you in our prayers without ceasing, being mindful of the work of your faith, and labor, and charity, and of the enduring of the hope of our Lord Jesus Christ before God and our Father; knowing, brethren beloved of God, your election: for our gospel hath not been to you in word only, but in power also, and in the Holy Ghost, and in much fulness, as you know what manner of men we have been among you for your sakes. And you became followers of us, and of the Lord: receiving the word in much tribulation, with joy of the Holy Ghost: so that you were made a pattern to all who believe in Macedonia and Achaia. For from you was spread abroad the word of the Lord, not only in Macedonia and Achaia, but also in every place, your faith which is towards God, is gone forth, so that we need not to speak anything. For they themselves relate of us, what manner of entrance we had unto you; and how you were converted to God from idols, to serve the living and true God. And to wait for his Son from Heaven (whom he raised from the dead), Jesus who hath delivered us from the wrath to come.

GOSPEL. *St. Matt. xiii.* 31–35. At that time: Jesus spoke to the multitude this parable: 'The kingdom of heaven is like to a grain of mustard-seed, which a man took and sowed in his field. Which indeed is the least of all seeds; but when it is grown up it is greater than any herbs, and becometh a tree, so that the birds of the air come and dwell in the branches thereof.

Another parable he spoke to them. The kingdom of heaven is like to leaven, which a woman took and hid in three measures of meal, until the whole was leavened. All these things Jesus spoke in parables to the multitudes: and without parables he did not speak to them. That the word might be fulfilled which was spoken by the prophet, saying: "I will open my mouth in parables, I will utter things hidden from the foundation of the world."

SERMON XXX.

The kingdom of heaven is like to a grain of mustard-seed.— St. Matt. xiii. 31.

A GRAIN of mustard-seed is very little, as our Lord tells us, and also, as we know, very sharp and burning. So is God's church, which is the kingdom of Christ upon earth. First, it is little; not in numbers, but little because it is poor and lowly. The human spirit is proud above all things, disobedient, rebellious, loving to be exalted, wishing to be praised. That which lost paradise, which brought sin and death into the world, which closed heaven, which opened hell, that which robbed us, stripped us of our heavenly inheritance, was *pride*. So, then, the kingdom of God, the church, that which is to govern the heart of man, to rule its disorders, to bring us back to heaven, is poor, is lowly, in the world's eyes is little. The proud world likes to swell itself out and appear big, and makes a wide path to swagger in. Our Lord tells us, " Except ye become as little children ye shall not enter into the kingdom of heaven"; and again: "Narrow is the gate and strait the way that leadeth to life." Do not wonder, then, that our holy church, which is glorious and magnificent in the eyes of angels and saints, should be thought little, and lowly, and poor by the world, and the flesh, and the devil.

Now, it seems that this very poverty of the church ought to be a reason why we should love it. If you are poor, then remember "birds of a feather flock together." The church is poor, too. She has not (particularly in these days) much of this world's goods. Often she is much put about to build even a decent temple in which to worship God. The church sometimes can hardly "keep house" for God—can hardly buy those things which are of daily necessity for his service. Oh! then the poor ought to love the church. Are you rich? Then the poverty of the church ought to touch your heart and open your purse. "The poor you have always with you," says Jesus Christ, and the poorest of the poor is God's church. The priest is obliged to beg for church, for school, and all that is in them—for almost everything, indeed, that is needed for the service of our divine Master. So, then, it is from you who are rich that large alms ought to come, so that Jesus Christ may be able to say that we have *you* with us and him as well as the poor. Again, while I caution you against hankering after mere ease and comfort in church, and the worldly elegances to be seen in the soft-cushioned and carpeted churches of the sects, I must express my wonder that many wealthy Catholics appear to be quite content to see the churches where they go to Mass fitted up with furniture that would be too mean for use in their own houses. If our Lord finds only more straw and another manger for a cradle for his divine Majesty nowadays, it ought not to be because we furnish him no better.

Secondly, the church is like a grain of mustard-seed, because her laws are often sharp and burning to the human heart. Mustard-seed, when crushed, has, as you know, a very strong and pungent odor. If you stand over it when thus crushed it will cause tears to flow from your eyes. If applied to your flesh it will burn and smart. Yes ; and sometimes the law of God will make tears start from your eyes. There is some habit you find convenient, some little pet plan you have made, some person to whom you are attached. These things are leading you from God ; so his church says : "Change your ways." "Give it up." "It is not lawful for thee." "Cut it off." Ah! don't you feel the sharp mustard-seed getting into your eyes? Again, the flesh rebels. That drink you love so much, that sinful appetite you like to indulge, those places of evil amusement to which you want to go—what says the church about such things? "Take the pledge." "Throw away drink." "You must not gratify that sinful inclination." "You cannot go to that place of amusement." "Give up that bad company or Jesus Christ will give you up." Ah! don't you feel how the mustard-seed burns and stings? But have good courage —better be burnt here than burnt hereafter. That burning of the mustard seed will heal you, will cure you. Its warmth will bring you back to life. Lastly, one day the little seed will become a great tree, whose branches shall reach to the sky, whose boughs shall wave in heaven. Then we, like poor, homeless birds of the air, shall spread our weary wings and go and make our lodgings for ever beneath its sheltering leaves. B.

SERMON XXXI.

The kingdom of heaven is like to leaven, which a woman took and hid in three measures of meal, until the whole was leavened.—St. Matt. xiii. 33.

The kingdom of heaven, my dear friends, means, as you know, in this as well as in many other of our Lord's parables, not God's kingdom in the next world, but in this—that is, his holy Catholic Church. Understanding it in this way, it is easy to see why he compares it to a grain of mustard-seed or to leaven; for it was small in the beginning, but has grown, as the mustard-seed grows, so that it now has spread through the whole earth; and it was not noticed in the beginning, as the little leaven or yeast would not be in the dough into which it is put, but has now made its influence felt in all the world, as that of the yeast is in the bread which it makes.

This was our Lord's intention, that his church should be continually growing till every one should enter it, till every heart should be leavened by its faith. But there are some people—Catholics, too, but a very curious kind of Catholics—who seem to think that the church was only made for those nations or those families which now belong to it, and will even blame those who are converted to it for leaving the religion of their fathers. I do not know what excuse one can make for these persons, except to suppose that God has blessed them with a very small share of common sense.

I do not think that there are many people so stupid as to talk in this way; but there are a good many who act as if they thought as these people seem to think. I do not mean that there are many who give the cold shoulder to converts, for that would be an unjust reproach; but I do mean that there are many Catholics who do not seem to understand the world has got to be converted, and that they themselves have got to do their share towards it; that they are part of that leaven with which our Lord meant that the world should be leavened; that it was by means of them, according to their measure of ability and opportunity, that he meant the faith to be diffused through the world. Every Catholic ought to be a missionary in his way and place, and do something to bring others to that knowledge of the truth which he himself has received.

Not that every Catholic should go out and preach the faith on the corners of the streets, or to people who would laugh at him or do him more harm than he could do them good; but that every one should be on the lookout for those who are sincere and well disposed, and be ready to give them a helping hand, to explain any difficulties which they may have, or to persuade them to come to the priest, who can explain them more fully.

But, above all, that he should spread among those who do not believe the leaven of good example, and not scandalize them by a bad life. One can hardly be too careful to avoid scandalizing even the faithful; and much more care should be taken not to scandalize those who are seeking for the truth, and particularly about those things on which their ideas are very strict and their consciences very sensitive.

Take, for instance, the horrible vice of profane swearing, to which many of you, to your own shame you must confess, are so much addicted, and about which you are inexcusably careless. There is no doubt at all that there is many a Protestant who would not so much as think of enquiring about the faith of a person who was in the habit of blaspheming. And yet he may be really anxious to know the truth, and his soul is as dear to God as yours; and if you are the cause, by this abominable habit of yours, of his turning away in despair from the church, most assuredly you will have to give an account for it when your soul shall come to be judged. Many persons all around us are outside of the church to-day because of the prevalence of this sin of profanity among Catholics, because all the Catholics whom they know seem rather to be children of the devil than of the good God.

There are many other things, particularly drunkenness and falsehood, by which Catholics spread around them the leaven of bad example, and drive people away from the faith instead of drawing them to it; but I have not time to speak of all. It is for you, my brethren, to look to it that, when you come to die, you shall feel that you have indeed done something to diffuse through the world the leaven of faith and virtue, not of unbelief and vice and that our Lord will not require at your hands the blood of your brother, for whom he died as well as for you.

Septuagesima Sunday.

Epistle. 1 *Cor.* ix. 24; x. 5. Brethren: Know you not that they who run in the race, all run indeed, but one receiveth the prize? So run that you may obtain.

And every one that striveth for the mastery refraineth himself from all things; and they indeed that they may receive a corruptible crown; but we an incorruptible one. I therefore so run, not as at an uncertainty: I so fight, not as one beating the air: but I chastise my body, and bring it into subjection: lest perhaps, when I have preached to others, I myself should become reprobate. For I would not have you ignorant, brethren, that our fathers were all under the cloud, and all passed through the sea. And all in Moses were baptized, in the cloud and in the sea; and they did all eat the same spiritual food, and all drank the same spiritual drink (and they drank of the spiritual rock that followed them, and the rock was Christ). But with the most of them God was not well pleased.

Gospel. *St. Matt.* xx. 1–16. At that time: Jesus said to his disciples this parable: The kingdom of heaven is like to a master of a family, who went early in the morning to hire laborers into his vineyard. And when he had agreed with the laborers for a penny a day, he sent them into his vineyard. And he went out about the third hour and saw others standing in the market-place idle. And he said to them: Go you also into my vineyard, and I will give you what shall be just. And they went their way. And again he went out about the sixth and the ninth hour, and did in like manner. But about the eleventh hour he went out and found others standing, and he saith to them : Why stand you here all the day idle ? They say to him : Because no man hath hired us. He saith to them : Go you also into my vineyard. And when evening was come, the lord of the vineyard saith to his steward : Call the laborers and pay them their hire, beginning from the last even to the first. When, therefore, they came, who had come about the eleventh hour, they received every man a penny. But when the first also came, they thought that they should have received more, and they also received every man a penny. And when they received it, they murmured against the master of the house, saying : These last have worked but one hour, and thou hast made them equal to us, that have borne the burden of the day and the heats. But he answering one of them, said : Friend, I do thee no wrong; didst thou not agree with me for a penny ? Take what is thine and go thy way : I will also give to this last even as to thee. Or, is it not lawful for me to do what I will ? is thy eye evil because I am good ? So shall the last be first, and the first last. For many are called, but few chosen.

SERMON XXXII.

Why stand ye here all the day idle ?—St. Matt. xx. 6.

This life, my dear friends, is often spoken of in Scripture as a day, both on account of its shortness and because the night of death follows. Now, there are certainly many persons who do stand all their lives idle ; that is to say, they do not try to "*work out their own salvation*"; they do not try to do anything in the Lord's vineyard, the church, by helping forward good works either by their means or by their active service. There are a great number of men and women who never think of caring for the great business of their salvation. Day after day goes by, week after week, and they have done no good works, corrected no faults, made absolutely no advancement or improvement. It is too much trouble for them to examine their consciences, too tiresome to stir themselves to go to Mass and the sacraments. They have sunk into a state of spiritual drowsiness by the world's fireside; in a word, they are all the day idle. Oh! if there are any such here, let them take warning. For the night will surely come, and then it will be too late. Perhaps this is the eleventh hour for you. God has called you often before; now, by the voice of his priest, he speaks once more and says: "Why stand ye here all the day idle?" To-day you see again the purple vestments and hangings; they tell you that Lent is fast approaching, that a time of grace is coming round once more. Oh! then, you that have yet a few hours of the day of life left, go into the vineyard of your own souls, root up the weeds, till the soil, plant good seed, that the Father of all may be able in the end to give you the wages of everlasting life.

Again, such among you as have means, or who are able to help your pastor by active service in the charge of the sick and the poor, who can teach the uninstructed, help along in sewing-schools and in forming sodalities and pious organizations of various kinds—to you also the cry comes, "Why stand ye all the day idle?" Why, when called upon to bear a little part of the priest's burden, are so many people like an old gun that hangs fire? Why is it often so difficult for the priest to get the active co-operation of the lay people? Why does he so often get the "cold shoulder," as people say, when he asks a little help? Is it not because people won't go into the vineyard, won't work, won't take trouble? Because they would rather not be bothered? How often they say: "I have no time"; "What are the priests for, anyhow?" "Let *them* look after these things." Thus they stand all the day idle, and the hard work falls on the priests and just a few self-sacrificing helpers. When you are called on, then, by your pastors to help in the parish, "don't be backward in coming forward"; make up your minds that you will not stand idle, but that it shall be "a long pull and a strong pull, and a pull all together."

Why should we be so afraid of idleness in spiritual things and in works of charity? Because, my dear friends, the time is short. Life is passing swiftly. The night of death is at hand. Soon the cry will be heard: "Behold, the Bridegroom cometh; go ye forth to meet him." Soon the Master of the vineyard will come and look at our work. Woe to us if he finds that we either never went into the vineyard at all, or, at best, the work there was so ill done that our part of the land is choked with docks and darnels and every kind of weed! You know, doubtless, that people sometimes give to each of their children a little garden to plant; ah! how these children try to make "my garden" the best one. How careful they are of it, how grieved if the frost or some noxious insect should destroy the flowers or fruits! We are all children; God has given us each a little garden, a little piece of his great vineyard, to care and tend. Let us, then, like the little ones, try to make our garden the finest, that when our Father, God, and our dear Mother, Mary, come to look at it they may find it full of beauty and fragrance, and say concerning us: "This one, at least, did not stand all the day idle."

B.

SERMON XXXIII.

They murmured against the master of the house.—St. Matt. xx. 11.

We can hardly fail, my dear brethren, to understand the meaning of this parable of our Lord, though he himself has given no explanation of it. He is the master of the house; we are the laborers whom he has hired to work in his vineyard, and hired, too, at a very great price; for the penny which the laborers all received represents the reward of eternal life which he has promised to all who die in his service, even though they come to that service at the eleventh hour—that is, at the end of their lives.

Now, I do not know that we are inclined to find fault with our Lord for forgiving one who has sinned during his whole life and sincerely repents, though it be on his death-bed. We are generous enough to be glad when one is really converted and saves his soul; and perhaps all the more if it be at the last moment. We do not find fault with God for his mercy, but rather we thank him for it.

But we are inclined to murmur against him for what seems to us to be an unjust and partial distribution of his mercies, as the laborers murmured against their master. They did not complain that the last received a penny, but that they themselves did not receive more. They thought that the master ought to have proportioned the wages to the service rendered; but we can see plainly enough that he was not so bound. All he was bound to was to give the penny to all those to whom he had promised it; as for the rest, he might have given any one of them his whole property, if he had taken a special fancy to him. You would not say that a man acted unjustly if he should single out any one of his servants and make him a special present over and above his regular wages. You would say, as the master of the house said, that he could do what he liked with what remained after his debts were paid.

Now, let us apply this, which is nothing but common sense, to our Lord's relations to us. He has a debt to pay to us to which he has bound himself. It is a real debt to us, because it rests on a real promise which he has made. And that debt is to forgive us when we really turn to him and repent of our sins, and to give us, through his own merits and the shedding of his own Blood, the eternal happiness which that precious Blood has purchased for us. But he is not bound to give us graces which will force us to repent; nor is he bound to give to each one of us the same graces inclining us to repent. He has promised forgiveness to those who repent, but not repentance to those who sin. Still less is he bound to give to all the same impulses to perfection, the same interior consolations, the same extraordinary supernatural gifts of any kind. He is no more bound to this than he is bound to give us all the same amount of natural strength, whether of mind or body, or the same amount of worldly goods. He has his reasons for the distribution of his gifts, it is true, and they are wise and holy ones, we may be sure; for he does not act from caprice, as we might do. But they are not reasons of justice to us, but mercy. If we were treated according to strict justice I do not know who among us would be saved.

Remember this, then, my brethren, when you are inclined to find fault with our Lord for his treatment of you or others. Remember that you have already received many times more than in strict justice was your due. Remember the countless favors, both temporal and spiritual, which you have already received at his hands, and be ashamed of complaining that others have received even more. Beware of envying them those things which God, in his great mercy, has freely bestowed on them; take care not to covet your neighbor's goods, for that is exactly what you are in danger of doing. And remember, specially, the great gift which he has given you all, and which many others who certainly seem, even in your own eyes, as good as yourselves have not received; that is, the light of the one true faith. Remember that you have not had to struggle in darkness and uncertainty; that you have always been able to know what to believe and what to do. Others, it is true, might have this, too, if they would do their own part; but that part God has done for you. Thank him, then, for this unspeakable mercy, and do not complain of other things which he has given or withheld.

SERMON XXXIV.

So run that you may obtain.—1 COR. ix. 24.

THERE is a great rage just now, my brethren, as you are aware, for walking, running, or footing it in any way. He or she is the best man or woman who can go the greatest number of miles in a week, or the greatest number of quarter-miles in the same number of quarter-hours. The interesting question of the present day is who can plod along with the greatest number of big blisters on each foot, or best endure being stirred up every fifteen minutes from a few winks of much-needed sleep, and go to sleep again the soonest after accomplishing the required number of laps on a tan-bark track.

This is all very well in its way. Walking is not a bad thing for the health at any time ; and just now it is a decidedly good thing for the pocket, if one is strong enough to excel in it. But for most people there are better ways of getting over the ground. Even the professional pedestrian will not refuse, now and then, to make use of the elevated railway.

There is one journey, however, which we all have to make on foot. That is the journey to heaven, where we all want to go. There is no elevated railway to take us there. If we are to get there it must be by our own exertions. We may, it is true, save part of the labor by availing ourselves of the very uncomfortable and slow transit provided in purgatory ; but that is a thing which we must surely wish to avoid as far as possible.

Yes, my brethren, every sensible person will try to escape that means of conveyance, and make this journey on foot over the road prepared in this world. Furthermore, as he has this long walk to take—for heaven is not very near to most of us—he will try to fit himself for it ; to go into training, and to keep in training, so that he may not break down on the way, or find himself with a short record when the end of his time arrives. He will bear in mind the warning of St. Paul in to-day's Epistle: "So ru that you may obtain."

How does the pedestrian manage to run so as to obtain his fame, his thousand dollars, and his gate-money? In the first place he works hard and sticks to his work. He does not waste his time by sitting down on the benches and watching the other man. He keeps on the track as long as he is able. When he cannot keep on any longer he takes the rest and food that he needs—not a bit more—and goes at it again. Sometimes he feels ready to drop; but he keeps on, and the fatigue passes away.

Secondly, he not only keeps to his work, but he avoids everything else that can interfere with it. He does not live on plum-cake and mince pie, or fill up with bad whiskey and drugged beer. He adopts a good, plain, wholesome diet—something that will stick to his bones and go to muscle, not to fat.

Thirdly, he does not stagger round the ring with a Saratoga trunk on his back. Far from it. He lays aside every weight that he can. He even makes his clothes as light as possible. He does not care to carry anything more than himself over the five hundred miles that he has to go.

Lastly, he has a director. He does not call him by that name—he calls him a trainer; but it comes to the same thing. He does not trust his own judgment, but has some one else to feed him, to tend him, to check him, or to urge him on.

Now, in all things, my friends, the pedestrian sets us a good example: in the earnestness which inspires him, and the means he takes to ensure success.

Imitate him in them in the great journey before

you, in which so much more than fame and gate-money is involved. In the first place, keep to your work; let every waking moment be a step toward heaven. Be not weary in well-doing. Secondly, do not indulge sensuality; use what the world has to give so that it may help you on your course, and not for its own sake. Eat and drink so that your body may be strong enough to serve your soul, but not strong enough to rule it. Thirdly, do not put a great load of riches on your back, unless you have got some good use to make of it. You will have to drop it at the end of your race, and it will only keep you back and prevent your winning. Lastly, do not trust yourself too much. Have some one to help you—a director who will guide you and tell you when you make mistakes, when you are going too fast or too slow.

This is nothing but common prudence; use it, and your transit to the kingdom of heaven shall be both rapid and sure.

Sexagesima Sunday.

EPISTLE. *2 Cor. xi. 19–xii. 9.* Brethren You gladly suffer the foolish : whereas you yourselves are wise. For you suffer if a man bring you into bondage, if a man devour you, if a man take from you, if a man be extolled, if a man strike you on the face. I speak according to dishonor, as if we had been weak in this part. Wherein if any man is bold (I speak foolishly) I am bold also. They are Hebrews; so am I. They are Israelites; so am I. They are the seed of Abraham; so am I. They are the ministers of Christ (I speak as one less wise), I am more ; in many more labors, in prisons more frequently, in stripes above measure, in deaths often. Of the Jews five times did I receive forty stripes, save one. Thrice was I beaten with rods, once I was stoned, thrice I suffered shipwreck ; a night and a day I was in the depth of the sea ; in journeys often, in perils of rivers, in perils of robbers, in perils from my own nation, in perils from the Gentiles, in perils in the city, in perils in the wilderness, in perils in the sea, in perils from false brethren : in labor and painfulness, in watchings often, in hunger and thirst, in many fastings, in cold and nakedness. Besides those things which are without : my daily instance, the solicitude for all the churches. Who is weak, and I am not weak? Who is scandalized, and I do not burn? If I must needs glory, I will glory of the things that concern my infirmity. The God and Father of our Lord Jesus Christ, who is blessed for ever, knoweth that I lie not. At Damascus the governor of the nation under Aretas the king, guarded the city of the Damascenes to apprehend me.

And through a window in a basket was I let down by the wall, and so escaped his hands. If I must glory (for it is not expedient indeed); but I will come to visions and revelations of the Lord. I know a man in Christ above fourteen years ago (whether in the body I know not, or out of the body I know not: God knoweth), such an one caught up to the third heaven. And I know such a man, whether in the body or out of the body, I know not: God knoweth; that he was caught up into paradise; and heard secret words which it is not granted to man to utter. Of such an one I will glory: but for myself I will glory nothing, but in my infirmities. For even if I would glory, I shall not be foolish: for I will say the truth. But I forbear, lest any man should think of me above that which he seeth in me, or anything he heareth from me. And lest the greatness of the revelations should puff me up, there was given me a sting of my flesh and angel of Satan, to buffet me. For which thing I thrice besought the Lord, that it might depart from me; and he said to me: My grace is sufficient for thee; for power is made perfect in infirmity. Gladly therefore will I glory in my infirmities, that the power of Christ may dwell in me.

GOSPEL. *St. Luke viii.* 4–15. At that time: When a very great multitude was gathered together and hastened out of the cities to him, he spoke by a similitude. A sower went out to sow his seed. And as he sowed some fell by the wayside, and it was trodden down, and the fowls of the air devoured it. And some fell upon a rock; and as soon as it was sprung up, it withered away, because it had no moisture. And some fell among thorns, and the thorns growing up with it, choked it. And some fell upon good ground; and sprung up, and yielded fruit a hundredfold. Saying these things, he cried out: He that hath ears to hear, let him hear. And his disciples asked him what this parable might be. To whom he said: To you it is given to know the mystery of the kingdom of God; but to the rest in parables, that seeing they may not see, and hearing they may not understand. Now the parable is this: The seed is the word of God. And they by the wayside are they that hear: then the devil cometh, and taketh the word out of their heart, lest believing they should be saved. Now they upon the rock, are they who when they hear, receive the word with joy: and these have no roots; who believe for a while, and in time of temptation fall away. And that which fell among thorns, are they who have heard, and going their way, are choked with the cares, and riches, and pleasures of this life, and yield no fruit. But that on the good ground, are they who in a good and perfect heart, hearing the word, keep it, and bring forth fruit in patience.

SERMON XXXV.

And some seed fell upon a rock.—St. Luke viii. 6.

THE sentence which forms the text is sometimes translated "and some fell upon stony ground"—that is to say, the good seed scattered by the sower fell in a place that was hard and rocky. The sower in the parable is Jesus Christ, the seed is the word of God. The great Chief Sower, dear friends, has gone away, but the good seed, the word of God, the doctrines of holy church, her precepts, her laws, the rules of morality, the standard by which we can tell good deeds from sin—all this good seed is still sown by God's priests, by the divinely appointed and ordained ministers of the word of God. Chiefly this sowing is done in the confessional and in the pulpit. In the confessional the sower scatters the good seed into each heart individually; in the pulpit the seed is scattered over the multitude gathered together. It seems a hard thing to say, but alas! in these days the word of God, the good seed, falls for the most part upon stony ground. The priest exhorts, entreats, persuades, threatens, tells of God's justice, speaks of his mercy, holds up the joys of heaven as a reward, points to the abyss of hell as a punishment; and it all falls upon stony ground. It falls upon the high crags of inaccessible rocks, upon the heart of the hardened sinner, upon the stony, adamantine hearts of those who have given up even the thought of repentance. It falls upon you, wretched man, who come to Mass for the sake of appearances every Sunday; upon you who drag a dead, corpse-like, blackened, devil-marked soul here before the altar of God every Sunday morning, without ever thinking of taking that soul to one of those confessionals which *stare* you in the face. Yes, the good seed falls upon you, and it falls upon a rock waiting to be calcined by the fires of hell.

The word of God falls upon the pavement, hard and stony as it is. It falls upon the hearts of frivolous, giddy, conceited girls. It falls upon the hearts of blaspheming, drinking, impure young men. It falls upon the hearts of men of business whose only aim is wealth, and of the women who are votaries of fashion; for what are the hearts of all such but a pavement, a thoroughfare, along which pass every evil beast, every low, degrading passion, and every unholy desire? O you girls and young men of this city and this day! you men and women of the world! you who come and hear the sermon, and afterwards go away with a simper on your powdered faces and a sneer upon your lips! you young ladies and young gentlemen "of the period"—to you I say, your hearts are stony ground. The good seed **can** never grow upon it. Nothing can flourish there but thorns and briers, whose end is to be burnt. O dear brethren, young and old, rich and poor! tear up the paving-stones, shiver to atoms your pride, your love of the world and its vanities; and when you hear the word of God, when the good seed is scattered, let your hearts be not stony, but soft and moist to receive it.

There are others whose hearts are like the pebbly beach. The seed falls there, and then the sea of their pride comes and washes it all away. They know what is said from the pulpit is true, they know the advice in the confessional is good, but they are too proud to change their lives, too proud to own that the priest knows better than they do. They say: Why should the church interfere between my wife and me, or between my children and myself? Why should the head of the family be ruled by the clergy? and the like. On such as these the word falls, but it falls on stony ground. To all of you, then, the Gospel says this morning, "He that hath ears to hear, let him hear." Open your ears and soften your hearts. Sermons are not for you to criticise; they are for you to profit by, for you to form your lives upon. The words of the priest are the words of God. The seed that he sows is the good seed. Woe to you if your hearts are stony ground! There is a rank growth which is called stone-crop, which clings to walls and stones; there is a weed-like, yellow grass that sprouts upon neglected house-tops. What do men do with such plants? They cast them forth into the smouldering weed-fire. And so will God cast into the fire that is never quenched those who receive the word of God on stony ground. B.

SERMON XXXVI.

A sower went out to sow his seed.—St. Luke viii. 5.

You all know, my brethren, what this seed is, and who it is that sows it; for our Lord himself explains the parable, and you have just heard the explanation.

The seed, he says, is the word of God; and it is God that sows it. And what is the word of God? Protestants tell us that it is the Bible; and their idea of sowing it is to leave a copy of it with everybody, whether they can read and understand it or not. That is not the way, however, that the Divine Wisdom has followed. He has put his word, of which the Bible is no doubt a great part, in the hands and the heart of his church, and told her to preach it to all nations—not to leave copies of it with them.

The word of God is, then, the religious instruction which you are all the time receiving, mainly from the priests of the parish to which you belong. It is God that gives it to you through them. It ought to bring forth fruit a hundred-fold, like the seed falling on good ground. You ought not only to hear it but to keep it. Do you?

What was the sermon about last Sunday? Don't all speak at once. Well, I am not going to tell you, though I am pretty sure that many of you will never know unless I do. And if you don't remember the last one there is not much chance that you remember the one before that. In fact, I have no doubt that there are plenty of people in the church at this moment who do not remember any sermon at all. All that they ever listened to—or did not listen to—in the many years they have been going to church, went in, as the saying is, at one ear and out at the other.

And yet you talk enough about what you hear, some of you at least. You make yourselves a standing committee to decide on the merits of the various preachers that you sit under. You say to each other: "What a fine discourse that was!" or, perhaps: "That was the worst sermon I ever heard." But what either of them was about it would puzzle you to tell. Your ears were tickled, or they were not, and that was all.

Perhaps you think I am rather hard on you. You will say: "Father, surely you cannot expect our memories to be so good. And then we hear so much that one thing puts out another." Well, there is some truth in that. Even if you try to remember I know you will forget a good deal; but the trouble is that you do not try.

You do not hear sermons in the right way. You think whether they are good or not, but you don't think whether or not there is anything in them that is good for you; and if so, what it is. If, perchance, you do hear anything that comes home to you, you fail to make a note of it. You don't get any fruit from the word of God, though you often think your neighbors ought to. You say: "I hope Mr. or Mrs. Smith, Brown, or Jones heard that"; but you do not hear it yourself. You do not apply it to your own case. You do not try to find out whether anything has been said that it would be well for you to know, or to think of if you do know it.

Try, then, to amend in this respect. Listen, when you hear a sermon or instruction, to the word of God in it speaking to you. Do not think who says it, but what is said, and what use you are going to make of it. One day you will be called to account before God's judgment-seat for all these words of his that you have heard ; look to it that they bear fruit in your heart. It is better than remembering them, to have them change your lives ; but if they do that you will remember them. And they will do that, unworthy as his servants are through whom they come to you, if you listen to them in the right way. Remember, now, what this sermon is about, and don't forget it before next Sunday.

SERMON XXXVII.

A sower went out to sow his seed.—St. Luke viii. 5.

Our Divine Saviour, in his explanation of this parable, points out four kinds of soil upon which the seed fell, three of which gave no harvest. The barren soils represent those souls which either do not keep the word of God—and they are the wayside ; or, keeping it, do not bring forth fruit—and they are the stony and the thorny ground. Wayside souls are hardened by the constant tramp of sin and dried by the scorching wind of passion. On such ground the seed remains on the surface ; it cannot penetrate. "So it is trodden down, and the birds of the air—that is, the devil, swift and noiseless in his flight—come and take the word of God out of such hearts, lest believing they might be saved." Stony soil looks fair enough, but it is shallow ; the rock underneath hinders moisture, and the seed, though it sprouts, has but weak roots, which soon wither. There are souls " who hear and even receive the word with joy ; and these have no roots," because their Christianity is shallow; right under the fair appearances of religion is the hard rock of worldliness and self-love. Now, the soil in "which we should be rooted," says St. Paul (Eph. ii. 7), "is charity." Again, there are "those who believe for a while, and in time of temptation fall away." The word of God has entered into your souls; it has converted you. But have not evil habits to which you cling, and cherished sins repeated at the first onset of temptation, taken all firmness out of your purpose of amendment and nipped in the bud your good resolution? I hope the mission will have more lasting fruit among you.

Thorny soil is full of the germs and roots of useless and hurtful plants. In such ground, says our Saviour, the good and bad seed started up and for a time grew together. Soon the thorns shot ahead, sucked up for themselves all the juices of the earth, shut out the warmth of the sun from the wheat, closed in upon it, and finally choked it. In our fallen nature are the germs of evil, the hot-bed of concupiscence. They are part of ourselves; we cannot get entirely rid of them, as no ground, however well worked, can be freed from bad seeds. There they are with the good, and will sprout up with it; the mischief is in letting them grow until they kill the grace of God and absorb our souls; then, indeed, we are in a state of spiritual suffocation; the divine seed is choked in us. Now, the thorns, says our Saviour, " are the cares, the riches, and the pleasures of life." As long as we are in the world we shall have to bear with its cares. Yet the great care, you know, is your salvation. All other concerns become choking thorns when they take precedence of this. Riches are not the best claim to heaven. Yet it is only the unjust getting, the absorbing love, and the sinful use of them that choke off the life of the soul. And in riches there is danger for the poor, strange as it may seem. As the shadow of St. Peter cured, so the shadow of wealth diseases by causing envy, want of resignation. The poor should beware of the "evil eye" of riches; it is poverty *in spirit* which is a passport to heaven. The pleasures of life, as you know from your own experience, unless checked by mortification, are fatal to the growth of God's word within us. The sunshine of the world is peculiarly favorable to the tropical vegetation of noxious or useless weeds.

Remember that your soul is a field in which Satan has put germs of evil as well as God, of good. Both are watching the growth and looking out for the final result. On you it depends which crop your soul will produce, wheat or thorns. The wheat will be gathered in God's granary, the thorns are only fit to burn. Be ye, therefore, good ground—*i.e.*, "hearing the word, keep it, and bring forth fruit in patience."

Quinquagesima Sunday.

Epistle. 1 *Cor. xiii.* 1–13. Brethren: If I speak with the tongues of men and of angels, and have not charity, I am become as sounding brass or a tinkling cymbal. And if I should have prophecy, and should know all mysteries, and all knowledge, and if I should have all faith, so that I could remove mountains, and have not charity, I am nothing. And if I should distribute all my goods to feed the poor, and if I should deliver my body to be burned, and have not charity, it profiteth me nothing. Charity is patient, is kind: charity envieth not, dealeth not perversely, is not puffed up, is not ambitious, seeketh not her own, is not provoked to anger, thinketh no evil, rejoiceth not in iniquity, but rejoiceth with the truth: beareth all things, believeth all things, hopeth all things, endureth all things. Charity never faileth: whether prophecies shall be made void, or tongues shall cease, or knowledge shall be destroyed. For we know in part, and we prophesy in part. But when that which is perfect shall come, that which is in part shall be done away. When I was a child, I spoke as a child, I understood as a child, I thought as a child. But when I became a man, I put away the things of a child. We see now through a glass in an obscure manner: but then face to face. Now I know in part: but then I shall know even as I am known. And now there remain faith, hope, and charity, these three: but the greatest of these is charity.

Gospel. *St. Luke xviii.* 31–43. At that time: Jesus took unto him the twelve, and said to them: Behold we go up to Jerusalem, and all things shall be accomplished which were written by the prophets concerning the Son of Man. For he shall be delivered to the Gentiles, and shall be mocked, and scourged, and spit upon: and after they have scourged him, they will put him to death, and the third day he shall rise again. And they understood none of these things, and this word was hid from them, and they understood not the things that were said. Now it came to pass that when he drew nigh to Jericho, a certain blind man sat by the wayside, begging. And when he heard the multitude passing by, he asked what this meant. And they told him that Jesus of Nazareth was passing by. And he cried out, saying: Jesus, son of David, have mercy on me. And they that went before, rebuked him, that he should hold his peace. But he cried out much more: Son of David, have mercy on me. And Jesus stood and commanded him to be brought to him. And when he was come near, he asked him, saying: What wilt thou that I do to thee? But he said: Lord, that I may see. And Jesus said to him: Receive thy sight: thy faith hath made thee whole. And immediately he saw, and followed him, glorifying God. And all the people, when they saw it, gave praise to God.

SERMON XXXVIII.

Jesus, son of David, have mercy on me.—St. Luke xviii. 38.

THERE are two points, dear brethren, in the conduct of the blind man of whom we have just read, that seem to be particularly noticeable. First, although he could not *see* Jesus, he nevertheless knew that he was passing by, and cried out: "Jesus, son of David, have mercy on me." Secondly, when "the crowd rebuked him, that he should hold his peace, he cried out *much more*: Son of David, have mercy on me." Now, that blind man is an image of the souls who are grievously tempted, and also of those who have fallen into the darkness of sin. Now, there are, as we all know, some who are dreadfully tempted. There are good, pious souls who are afflicted with the lowest and most degrading temptations. Crowds of evil imaginations fill their minds; the basest suggestions are made to them by the evil one; the foulest mind-pictures are produced in them; they are urged to be proud, to be vain, unloving, uncharitable, and the like. Such people are for the moment blind. They cannot *see* Jesus. He is hidden behind these gathering clouds. It seems to them as if the light of God's grace had gone out in their hearts, and they sit down by the wayside, weary and blind. Suddenly they hear sounds in the distance; it is the Mass-bell, the voice of the priest in the confessional, a word from the pulpit, the choir chanting out at High Mass or Vespers. These sounds mingle; they sound like the tread of a multitude, and in the midst of the clamor a still, small voice says: "'Tis Jesus of Nazareth who passes by." Oh! then, poor tempted souls, and you too, unfortunate ones, upon whom has settled the stone-blindness of mortal sin, never mind if you cannot *see* Jesus; never mind if your darkened orbs cannot gaze upon his sweet face nor meet the look of compassion that he casts upon you; stretch out your hands towards him, all covered with the roadside dust as they are, lift up your choked and faltering voice, and cry aloud to your Saviour: "Jesus, son of David, have mercy on me!" He will hear you; he will have mercy; he will touch your poor closed eyes and you shall receive your sight. But now another word of advice, both to those who are trying to get rid of besetting temptations and to those who are striving to shake off the chains of grievous sin. When you have given the first heartfelt cry, when you have made the first move in the right direction, when you have roused yourselves to make the first real effort either to shake off your temptations or to get free from the slavery of sin, then it will very likely happen to you as it did to the blind man: "The crowd will rebuke you that you should hold your peace." There are a good many well-known characters in that crowd. Their names are Timid Conscience, Old Habit, Fear, Despair, Human Respect, Cowardice, Weak Resolution, Want of Firm Purpose, False Shame, No Hope, and a host of others. Now, all these will rebuke the poor, blind, tempted ones and the stone-blind sinners. What, then, must they do? They must take example from the blind beggar in the Gospel. When the crowd rebuked him he cried out *much more:* "Son of David, have mercy on me!" He knew that he must cry out louder to make his voice drown the buzzing murmurs of the crowd. Jesus did not seem to hear him, so he shouted louder. O you that are blind from temptation, you that are blind in sin, you that have given the first cry, and whose voices seem about to be drowned by the voice of the crowd of old habits and want of trust, cry louder, cry much more: "Son of David, have mercy on me!" Then, no matter if your blindness be never so dark, Jesus will stand still; he will command you to be brought to him; he will say to you: "What wilt thou that I do to you?" And then will be the time for you to pray: "Lord, that I may *see.*" O my God! grant that all the tempted and all the sinners may have the grace to make that petition. May God "enlighten all our eyes, that we sleep not in death," and bring us all "to *see* the God of Gods in Sion"!

B.

SERMON XXXIX.

And they understood none of these things, and this word was hid from them, and they understood not the things that were said.—St. Luke xviii. 34.

If you have listened attentively to this Gospel, my dear brethren, it seems to me that you must have been astonished at this part of it. For our Lord certainly could not have told his apostles more clearly about what was going to happen to him than he had told them in the words which immediately preceded these. "The Son of Man," he says, "shall be delivered to the Gentiles, and shall be mocked and scourged and spit upon; and after they have scourged him they will put him to death, and the third day he shall rise again." What more clear account could he have given them of his approaching passion, death, and resurrection? And yet it made no impression on them at all. When the time of his Passion actually came they were quite unprepared for it, as much so as if he had said nothing about it beforehand.

How can we account for this? What reason can we give for this blindness to what was put so plainly before their eyes? It was as complete a blindness as that of the poor man whose cure is told in the latter part of the Gospel.

There is only one way to account for it. You know there is a proverb that "none are so blind as those who do not want to see." That was the trouble with them, and that was the reason why their blindness was not cured, as was that of the poor man of whom I have just spoken, and who did most earnestly wish and beg to receive his sight. They had a fixed idea before their minds, and they did not want to look at anything else. That idea was that their Master was going to have a great triumph, overcome all his enemies, and set up his kingdom in this world as a great prince; and they were going to have high places in that kingdom, to be rich, powerful, and be respected by everybody. What he said did not fit in with that idea, so they paid no attention to it. They thought he could not be talking about himself, that he must mean somebody else, when he spoke about the "Son of Man."

Perhaps you think this was very foolish on their part, and would lay it to some special stupidity or prejudice on the part of these poor, ignorant men. But I think, if you look into your own hearts, you will find them pretty much the same.

Most Christians, I am afraid, have got an idea very much like this in their minds. They know, indeed, that Christ did not come into the world to be a great king, as the world understands the word; that he did not acquire great wealth for himself or his friends; that he did not enjoy what we call prosperity and happiness. But they think that is what they themselves have a right to expect. They know, of course, all about the Passion of Christ, but they think it is all over now.

And yet there are words for us just as plain as those which the apostles heard and did not understand. We do not see their meaning, and for the same reason ; that is, because we do not want to see it. They are not only once repeated, but so many times that I could preach you a long sermon made up of them alone. Their meaning is that the Passion of Christ is not over ; that each one of us has our share in it ; that the life which he means for us is the same kind of one that he himself led. St. Paul understood it well when he said : " I fill up those things that are wanting of the sufferings of Christ."

Try, then, my brethren, to get the idea out of your minds that you have come into the world to enjoy yourselves and have a good time. It is an idea unworthy of Christians. Not those who prosper, but those who suffer, are the ones to excite our envy, for they are most like our Divine Lord. And, moreover, those who suffer are really the happiest, if they remember this, for their suffering is a pledge of eternal happiness. It is a sign that he has a place waiting for them in his kingdom very near to him.

And let us, like the blind man of the Gospel, ask him to take away our blindness, that we may really see this and believe it ; that our eyes may be opened to the light coming from the next world. That will make pain and adversity beautiful and glorious ; and we will even hardly wish to hasten the day when, if we are faithful, God himself shall wipe away all tears from our eyes.

SERMON XL.

SOME very important notices have just been read to you, my brethren. Do you know what they are ?

You ought to by this time, for you have heard them many times before; and yet I am sure that some of you to whom they have been read ten or twenty times already know no more about them now than before you ever heard them at all. Why is this? It is because, as I said last Sunday, you do not listen, and do not try to remember, nor care to understand.

What were these notices, then? They were the notices about this great season on which we are entering: the holy season of Lent, the most important one of the whole year.

What is the first one of these notices which you have or have not just heard? You don't know. Well, it is this: *All the week-days of Lent, from Ash Wednesday till Easter Sunday, are fast-days of precept, on one meal, with the allowance of a moderate collation in the evening.* Fast-days—do you know what that means? I venture to say that many of you do not; or, if you do, you do not act as if you did. Some people that you would think had more sense seem to think that a fast-day is about the same thing as a Friday through the year, except that it is not so much harm to eat meat on a fast-day as on a Friday. It is hard to understand how any one can be so stupid.

What is a fast-day, then? It is a day, as you hear in the notices, on one meal. That does not mean two other full meals besides, and plenty of lunches in between. It means what it says—one full meal, and only one. The church has, it is true, allowed, as the notices say, a moderate collation in the evening. What does that mean? As much as you want to take? No. How much, then? Eight ounces is the amount commonly assigned. That is to say, you have your dinner, and a supper of eight ounces in weight. Is that all? No, not quite. Custom has also made it lawful to take a cup of tea or coffee and a small piece of bread, without butter, in the morning. This is an important point; for if this will prevent a headache and enable you to get through with your duties as usual, you are bound to take it, and not get off from the fast on the ground that you cannot keep a strict fast on nothing at all till noon.

This, then, is what is meant by a fast-day. It may be a day of abstinence from flesh-meat, or it may not be. Monday, Tuesday, and Thursday you can have meat, but at dinner only; and no fish, oysters, etc., when you have meat—the tea or coffee and the eight ounces the same those days as on the others. But on Wednesday, Friday, and Saturday no meat at any time. And remember, nothing can be eaten on a fast-day but just as I have described—no lunches, large or small, between meals.

But you say: "I will get very hungry and lose a good many pounds on such a scant diet as that." Yes, that is quite likely; and that is just what Lent was made for, that you might get hungry and lose as many pounds as you can spare. That never seems to occur to some people. It wouldn't do some of you any harm to lose a few pounds; you will recover from it, I am sure. The papers say that one of the pedestrians (a woman, too, by the way) lost over thirty in a long walk she has just finished. Is it not as easy to suffer a little for the honor of God as a great deal for one's own?

But is there no excuse? Oh! yes. There are plenty. They are given in the last paragraph of the notices. If you are weak or infirm—really, that is;

not with a weakness beginning on Ash Wednesday and ending on Easter Sunday—if you are too old or too young; or if from any reason, like hard work, you really need abundant food. In case of doubt consult a priest.

But these excuses do not allow one to eat meat. They excuse, as you hear in the rules, from fasting, but *not from abstinence.* And yet you will hear people saying: "They told me I was not bound to fast," and forthwith eating meat as often as they can get it, just the same as if it was not Lent at all. Understand, then, it takes a much greater reason to excuse from abstinence than from fasting. Never eat meat at forbidden times in Lent without getting proper permission. Ordinary work is no excuse.

I would like to say much more about these matters, that you might fully understand them, were there time to do so. But remember that the rules of Lent are binding, like the other laws of the church, in conscience; and if you break them in any notable way you commit a mortal sin. Suffer a little now, that you may not suffer for ever, banished from the kingdom of God.

First Sunday of Lent.

EPISTLE. *2 Cor. vi.* 1–10. Brethren: We do exhort you, that you receive not the grace of God in vain. For he saith: "In an accepted time have I heard thee; and in the day of salvation have I helped thee." Behold, now is the acceptable time: behold, now is the day of salvation. Giving no offence to any man, that our ministry be not blamed: but in all things let us exhibit ourselves as the ministers of God, in much patience, in tribulation, in necessities, in distresses, in stripes, in prisons, in seditions, in labors, in watchings, in fastings, in chastity, in knowledge, in long suffering, in sweetness, in the Holy Ghost, in charity unfeigned, in the word of truth, in the power of God; by the armor of justice on the right hand and on the left: through honor and dishonor: through infamy and good name: as seducers, and yet speaking truth: as unknown, and yet known: as dying, and behold we live: as chastised, and not killed: as sorrowful, yet always rejoicing: as needy, yet enriching many: as having nothing, and possessing all things.

GOSPEL. *St. Matt. iv.* 1–11. At that time: Jesus was led by the spirit into the desert, to be tempted by the devil. And when he had fasted forty days and forty nights, he was afterwards hungry. And the tempter coming, said to him: If thou be the Son of God, command that these stones be made bread. But he answered and said: It is written, "Man liveth not by bread alone, but by every word that proceedeth from the mouth of God." Then the devil took him up into the holy city, and set him upon the pinnacle of the temple, and said to him: If thou be the Son of God, cast thyself down, for it is written: "That he hath given his Angels charge over thee, and in their hands shall they bear thee up, lest perhaps thou hurt thy foot against a stone." Jesus said to him: It is written again: "Thou shalt not tempt the Lord thy God." Again the devil took him up into a very high mountain, and showed him all the kingdoms of the world, and the glory of them. And said unto him: All these will I give thee, if falling down thou wilt adore me. Then Jesus saith to him: Begone, Satan, for it is written: "The Lord thy God shalt thou adore, and him only shalt thou serve." Then the devil left him: and behold, Angels came and ministered to him.

SERMON XLI.

Thou shalt not tempt the Lord thy God.—St. Matt. iv. 7.

WHAT is it to tempt God? The words sound very strange; for we know that God is infinitely good, and that he cannot be tempted, like us, to commit sin. So that cannot be what is meant by tempting him.

We shall see easily enough what is meant by it if we consider what it was that the devil suggested to our Lord. He said to him: "Throw yourself down from this pinnacle of the temple; no harm will happen to you, for your life is too precious to God for him to allow it to be lost. His angels will carry you down safely; a miracle will be worked in your behalf."

That which Satan wished our Lord to do is what is meant by tempting God. It is to try and see if he will not do some extraordinary thing for us which there is no need for him to do; to presume on his mercy and providence. That is what the Latin word means from which our word "tempt" comes. It means to try, to make an experiment. That, in fact, is the real meaning of our word "to tempt." When the devil tempts us he is trying us, to see how far our love of God will go; he is making an experiment to find out the strength of our souls. God does not let him try all the experiments he would like to.

He has no right to try us in this way; but God lets him do it for our own good. But God does not allow us to be trying any experiments on his mercy and goodness. He does not allow us to depend upon it, except when we know that we have a right to do so.

And yet that is what people, and even Christians, are doing all the time. Perhaps you do not know how; but you ought to know, and I will tell you.

A man tempts God when he puts himself, without necessity, into an occasion of sin. He knows, or ought to know, that he cannot depend on God's grace to keep him from sin in such a case. He knows that God may indeed help him through, so that he will not sin, and perhaps that he has done so before; but he knows, or ought to know, that God has not promised him such a grace, and that it will be nothing surprising if he does not give it to him.

Such is the case of the drunkard who has some sort of a desire to reform his life, and who goes into a liquor-store. He ought to know that he must have God's grace if he is to avoid getting drunk; and so he tries God, to see if he will give him that grace. But there is no need for him to make the experiment, for he could avoid it by simply keeping outside; and that is what God will certainly give him the grace to do, if he prays and is in earnest. Let such a man remember, before he goes near the place, those words: "Thou shalt not tempt the Lord thy God."

Such is the case, too, of young men or women who trust themselves in company of one with whom they have often acted immodestly before. They may pretend to have great sorrow for these past sins, but it is false; they may deceive themselves or their confessors, but not Almighty God, who reads their hearts. No one is truly sorry for his sins when he continues in the great sin of tempting God.

I will tell you of some other people who tempt God. They are those who remain quietly in mortal sin, day after day, week after week, month after month. They say to themselves: "God is good; he will give me time to repent." God may well say to such a one: "Thou fool, who has told thee that? This very night I will require thy soul of thee." He has a right to do it; and you have no right to expect another day of him. When you do so you are trying his patience; you are making an experiment on his mercy. This present moment is all you have a right to depend on. And yet you will sleep night after night in sin, forgetting that, if God should treat you justly, the morning would find you dead; forgetting that your whole life is nothing but a long temptation of God.

SERMON XLII.

Man liveth not by bread alone, but by every word that proceedeth out of the mouth of God.—ST. MATT. iv. 4.

ONE of the greatest, if not *the* greatest, of the defects of the present time is an inordinate care for temporal and material things. How shall we live? what shall we eat? wherewithal shall we be clothed?—these are the questions which men are all too much exercised about at the present day. We see persons who rise, and cause their children to rise, at a very early hour, and from that time till late at night they are working and toiling. We see men of the world who really injure their health, and perhaps shorten their days, by their close and unflagging attention to business. Why do people act thus? All for the sake of the bread that perisheth, all in order to heap up a few dollars which at best they can keep but for a few years. So great has this thirst for money-making become that we see it even in our young boys. They don't want to stay at school; they don't want to store up learning; by the time they are fourteen or a little older (having nothing in their heads but reading, writing, and a little confused arithmetic) they want to be off to the store, the workshop, or the factory. Why? Because they want to join as soon as possible in the wild-goose chase after the goods of the world. Now, all these classes of persons have to learn "that man liveth not by bread alone." My dear friends, besides that poor body which you work so hard to feed, to clothe, and to please, you have an immortal soul. Body and soul united form what we call man. So, then, you must not act as if you were all body. You cannot do so without peril to your soul. Suppose you were to try an experiment of this kind. You say to yourself: "I will eat nothing; I will have prayers for breakfast, confession for lunch, prayers and devotions for dinner, and meditation on death for supper." Then you try it for a week. What an elegant skeleton you would make for a museum at the end of that time! Yet people treat their souls just in that way. Instead of refreshing it with prayers and devotions, etc., they give it clothes, meat and drink, calculations of stock, calculations of profits, cares of this world, etc., and thus the soul is starved just as the body would be by improper food. So then, dear brethren, don't try "to live by bread alone." You can't do it. Try also to live "by every word that proceedeth out of the mouth of God"—that is to say, by doing those things which, either by his church or by the interior inspirations of his grace, he wishes you to do. Are you in business, or at work? Very well; take care of your affairs prudently, work faithfully, but remember this is not all. You must also find time to pray, find time for confession and the hearing of holy Mass. Don't leave piety to priests, religious women, and children, but let the men also be seen in the church and at the altar-rail. It is a custom in some places that the men should sit on one side of the church and the women on the other. Don't you think if we tried that plan that the numbers on the men's side would often be rather slim? Why? Because they are out in the world trying to live by "bread alone." O my dear friends! why care so much for the goods of this world? Why lay up so much treasure where rust and moth destroy, and where thieves break through and steal? We cannot take a cent with us when we go, and our poor body, even *that* which we have pampered so much, must decay and return to dust. Let us, then, this morning make a good resolution, that when the devil comes and tempts us to give ourselves up too much to thoughts about our food, our raiment, and our temporal affairs, we will repulse him with these words: "It is written, 'Man liveth not by bread alone, but by every word that proceedeth out of the mouth of God.'" B.

SERMON XLIII.

Jesus was led by the Spirit into the desert, to be tempted by the devil.—St. Matt. iv. 1.

Do you know what the word "tempt" means, my brethren? I have no doubt that you know what it is to be tempted. You know that, as St. James says, "every man is tempted, being drawn away, by his own concupiscence, and allured." You yourselves have often been tempted; your concupiscence—that is, your sinful passions of one kind or another—have often tempted you, allured you, enticed you away from the law of God.

But the word "to tempt" does not mean "to allure" or "to entice." It means "to try." To tempt any one is to try him to see what sort of stuff he is made of; that's the real meaning of the word—just as a gun, for instance, is tried by putting in an overcharge to see if it will burst, though I would not advise any of you to tempt a gun in that way. It is not a very safe experiment.

That is the kind of experiment, though, that the devil is always trying on us. He is not afraid of accidents. If an accident does happen it will not hurt him. It is just what he wants. So he tries us in various ways to find where our weak point is; for he cannot tell without trying. When he succeeds, when we break down under his temptations, he says to himself: "That's good. I hit the right spot that time. I'll try that again." For you see we are not like guns: we can be burst more than once.

Now, the Gospel tells us that our Lord himself was led into the desert to be tempted by the devil; that is, to have the devil experiment on him. This seems strange. What use was it to try him? Did not the devil know that he was God and could not sin?

No, my brethren, it is probable that he did not. If he had he would not have wasted his time in a temptation which would be of no use. But why did not our Lord let him know it? It was because, being man as well as God, he chose to be tempted or tried like the rest of us: first, that he might set us an example in resisting temptation; and, secondly, that he might merit for us a grace which should make it easy to do so. So he was led into the desert, for our sakes, by his own Spirit—by the Holy Spirit of God.

He has set us the example and merited for us the grace; and, thanks to what he has done for us, it is easy for us to resist temptation. But you do not believe it, that is the trouble.

Some of you think it is impossible to resist temptation. You say, to excuse your sin, "I could not help it." Now, that is simply a lie; or, rather, it is more: it is a blasphemy against God. It is as much as to say, "God did not give me the grace to resist temptation," and thus to make him a partaker in your sins.

You can help it. When our Lord drove away the devil, as the Gospel to-day tells us, he made it easy for us to do the same. And it is a great shame not to do it. What a disgrace to God, and what a laughing-stock to the devil, is a man or a woman who breaks down every time he or she is tried! Yet I am afraid there are plenty of such.

God does not tempt you. St. James tells us that. He has no need to, for he knows what you are made of. But he lets the devil do it, that you may merit by resisting; and he does not let you have any more temptation than you can bear. Remember that, then, the next time you are tempted. Say to yourself: " I have got strength enough to resist this with the help of God. I'll turn the laugh on the devil, instead of his having it on me. I'll show him he was a fool to try to tempt me. I'll let him see that he hit the wrong spot instead of the right one; in fact, that there isn't any right spot to hit. Here's a chance for me to get some merit, and to show that I am good for something; that I am of some use after all the labor that my Maker has spent on me."

Say this in the name of God and in the strength which he gives you, and you will be surprised to see how the devil will run away. No doubt he will try you again, but if you persevere he will give it up as a bad job at last, and you will enter heaven with the reward the Lord wishes to give you—that is, a great stock of merit instead of sin from the temptations which you have had.

Second Sunday of Lent.

Epistle. 1 *Thess. iv.* 1–7. Brethren : We pray and beseech you in the Lord Jesus, that as you have received from us, how you ought to walk, and to please God, so also you would walk, that you may abound the more. For you know what commandments I have given to you by the Lord Jesus. For this is the will of God, your sanctification: that you should abstain from fornication. That every one of you should know how to possess his vessel in sanctification and honor, not in the passion of lust, like the Gentiles who know not God: and that no man overreach, nor deceive his brother in business: because the Lord is the avenger of all such things, as we have told you before, and have testified. For God hath not called us unto uncleanness, but unto sanctification in Christ Jesus our Lord.

Gospel. *St. Matt. xvii.* 1–9. At that time: Jesus taketh unto him Peter and James, and John his brother, and bringeth them up into a high mountain apart. And he was transfigured before them. And his face did shine as the sun: and his garments became white as snow. And behold, there appeared to them Moses and Elias talking with him. And Peter answering, said to Jesus : Lord, it is good for us to be here : if thou wilt, let us make here three tabernacles, one for thee, and one for Moses, and one for Elias. And as he was yet speaking, behold a bright cloud overshadowed them. And behold, a voice out of the cloud, saying : This is my beloved Son, in whom I am well pleased: hear ye him. And the disciples hearing, fell upon their face, and were very much afraid. And Jesus came and touched them, and said to them: Arise, and be not afraid. And when they lifted up their eyes they saw no man, but only Jesus. And as they came down from the mountain, Jesus charged them, saying: Tell the vision to no man, till the Son of Man be risen from the dead.

SERMON XLIV.

And he was transfigured before them. And his face did shine as the sun: and his garments became white as snow. . . . Behold a bright cloud overshadowed them. And behold! a voice out of the cloud, saying: This is my beloved Son, in whom I am well pleased.—ST. MATT. xvii. 2, 5.

I THINK, brethren, one can hardly read the above account of the Transfiguration of our dear Lord without having suggested to our minds one of the most beautiful of the many services of the Catholic Church. I mean the rite of Benediction of the Blessed Sacrament. We ourselves are the three disciples. The mountain up into which our Lord brings us is the holy altar. His face, shining as the sun, is represented to us by the bright lights that cluster round his throne, and by the refulgence of the rays of the monstrance which contains him. Then his garments are indeed as white as snow; for he veils his divinity under the form of the purest wheaten bread, and hides himself beneath its appearances as though he should wrap his sacred Body in pure white raiment. Then the bright cloud is the floating incense, and the voice out of the cloud the tinkling bell, which seems to say to us as Jesus is held aloft and as we bend low in adoration: "This is

God's beloved Son, in whom he is well pleased." So then, the Gospel for to-day naturally suggests to our minds a few reflections on this great devotion of the church—Benediction of the Blessed Sacrament. Now, a great many persons seem to think that Benediction is only "tacked on," as it were, to the office of Vespers. This idea is all wrong. To be sure, Benediction is often given directly after Vespers, but it is an entirely separate and distinct service. Vespers end with the Antiphon of the Blessed Virgin; Benediction begins when the Holy Sacrament is taken from the tabernacle and placed in the costly metal frame called the monstrance, or ostensorium. So, then, Benediction is not part of Vespers, or of any function which may precede it; and I want to make this very clear, because I think the false notion that it is merely something supplementary is a reason why so many people neglect it. What, then, is Benediction? It is the solemn exposition of the same Jesus whose face shone so bright on Thabor. He stays there upon the altar for a little while, that we may kneel before him, adore him, praise him. Then he is lifted up in the hands of his priest, and he gives us his blessing. Remember, it is not the priest who blesses you at Benediction; it is Jesus himself who does so. Now, it is very true, dear friends, that people are not *bound* to come to Benediction; yet surely, if each one realized what a blessed thing Benediction is, no one who could come would stay away. Jesus is there on the altar. He is waiting to hear your prayers, waiting to receive your acts of love and adoration, waiting to bless you. Oh! then come often to Benediction. Do not say, "There is nothing but Vespers this afternoon"; remember there is something **more**

—Benediction of the Blessed Sacrament. There is a day fast approaching on which the Holy Sacrament will be carried in procession, and then placed in the most solemn manner in the repository. I mean Maundy Thursday. Now, that is also an exposition of the Blessed Sacrament, and, although Jesus is not held aloft by the priest as at ordinary Benedictions, who can doubt but that Jesus blesses us as he passes by? I pray you, then, when that day arrives to remember who it is who comes to you. Let us see the church full, not of gazers at the lights and flowers, but of faithful worshippers of their King and God. If you go from church to church on that day don't go to peer, don't go to see, but go to pray. So when the devotion of the Forty Hours is announced in your church—that devotion which is the most solemn of all the expositions and benedictions through the year —be devout; spend at least an hour in the day before the Lamb of God. Remember that the Holy Sacrament is Jesus Christ—the very same who was born in Bethlehem and died on Calvary. Lastly, come to Benediction always with a living faith and a burning love. Never let your place be vacant, if you can help it, when you know it is to be given. Set a great store by it. In the words of a living preacher: "Night by night the Son of God comes forth to you in his white raiment, wearing his golden crown; night by night his sweet voice is heard, and he looks for you with a wistful gaze; do not turn away from such blessedness as this; do not refuse to listen to his pleading words; do not let your places be empty before the altar when Jesus comes." B.

SERMON XLV.

And that no man over-reach, nor deceive his brother in business; because the Lord is the avenger of all such things.— 1 Thess. iv. 3.

These words are from the Epistle of to-day, my dear brethren, and are certainly suggestive, or at least should be so, at this season which the church has assigned as a time for examination of conscience and repentance for sin.

The sin which St. Paul warns us against goes, when it is practised in other ways, by worse names than the one which he gives it here. A man meets you on a lonely road and takes your money forcibly from you; what do you call it? You call it robbery. A man enters your house at dead of night and carries off your property; what do you call it? You call it burglary. A man picks your pocket on the street; what do you call it? You call it theft. Well, it is all one and the same thing. All these are various ways of breaking the Seventh Commandment; and what is that? *Thou shalt not steal.*

And what is it to deceive or over-reach some one else in business? It is just the same thing as these; it is the breaking of this same commandment; it is stealing, just as much as robbery, burglary, and theft are, only it does not go by so bad a name, and is not so likely to be punished by the laws of the land. And what do I mean by this over-reaching or deceiving? I mean selling goods under false pretences for more than they are really worth; using false weights or measures; evading in one way and another the payment of one's just debts; taking advantage of one's neighbor's difficulties to make an undue profit for one's self; in short, all the many ways in which men turn a dishonest penny or dollar; in which they get rich by trickery and injustice. All these are stealing, just as bad and a great deal more dishonorable than robbery, burglary, or theft, because not attended with so much risk to the person who is guilty of them.

Now, it seems to me that this sin of cheating—for that is the bad name such sharp practices ought to go by, though they often do not—is a most strange and unaccountable one; much more so than those other kinds of stealing. The man who breaks into your house or who picks your pocket is generally one who is pretty badly off, and who needs what he takes more than the people do from whom he takes it. You do not expect to find rich men setting up as burglars or pickpockets. It is true, sometimes you do find people who have a passion for stealing things when they have plenty of money to buy them; but that is commonly considered to be a special kind of insanity, and they have a name made on purpose for it; they call it "kleptomania." The people who do this are supposed to be crazy on this particular point; but is it not really just the same thing for a man who has enough and to spare to be trying to cheat his neighbor? Such a man, it would seem, must be crazy too.

And there is another way in which cheating is a strange thing, and especially in a Catholic. For every Catholic at least must know that if he tries to cheat he himself gets cheated worse than the people he is trying to impose on. For he gets himself into a very bad position. He has got to do one of two things. One is to restore, as far as possible,

what he has cheated other people out of; and that is
a very hard thing to do sometimes—much harder
than it would have been to have left cheating alone.
But hard as this is, the other is much harder. For
the other thing is to go to hell; to be banished from
God for ever; to pay for all eternity the debt which
he would not pay here.

Do not, then, my brethren, get yourselves into this
position. But if you are in it do the first of these
two things. Restore your ill-gotten goods. Do it
now; not put it off till you come to die. It will
cost you a struggle then as well as now; and even
if you try to do it then, it is doubtful if those who
come after you will carry out your wishes. A purpose to restore which is put off till a time when you
cannot be sure of carrying it out is rather a weak
bridge on which to pass to eternal life. Remember
now what you will wish at the hour of death to have
remembered; remember those words of our Lord:
"What doth it profit a man, if he gain the whole
world and suffer the loss of his own soul?"

SERMON XLVI.

THOSE of you, my brethren, who are keeping Lent
as it should be kept are beginning by this time, if I
am not mistaken, to think that it is a pretty long
and tedious season. Fasting and abstinence, giving
up many worldly amusements, getting up early in
the morning and going to Mass as so many of you
do, and other such things, get to be rather tiresome
to the natural man after a few days; and I have no
doubt you are quite glad that Lent does not last the

whole year, and are looking forward to the time when it will be over. I have always noticed that there were not many at Mass in Easter week, and there are very few, I imagine, who fast or abstain much then.

And perhaps you are even inclined to say : "What ever did the church get up Lent for at all ? Certainly we could be good Christians without it, or save our souls, at any rate." But when you come to think of it you know well enough why Lent was instituted. You know that we cannot save our souls without abstaining from sin, and that we shall not be likely to abstain from sin unless we abstain sometimes also from what is not sinful. You know also that we cannot get to heaven without doing penance for our sins, and that it is better to do penance here than in purgatory. And you know, too, that most people will not abstain much or do much penance beyond what the church commands ; so you know why the church got up Lent.

She did it that we might get to heaven sooner and more surely. That ought to be our encouragement, then, in it, that every good Lent brings us a good deal nearer to heaven ; that heaven is the reward of penance and mortification. And it is partly to keep this before our minds that the church tells us in to-day's Gospel the story of our Lord's transfiguration : how he took Peter and James and John up with him on Mount Thabor, and there appeared to them in his glory ; and filled their hearts with renewed courage and confidence in him, and with a firm belief that it was worth their while to follow him, even if they had to sleep out at night, and not get much to eat, and suffer in many ways—that it was worth while for the sake of the good time coming, of which his glory was a promise, though they did not know just when or what it would be.

They thought, perhaps, it would be in this world; that their Master would come out in the power and majesty that they could see that he had, put down all his enemies, and reign as a great king on the earth. We know better; we know, or ought to know, that it will not be in this world. But we know that the good time coming will be something a great deal better than anything that can be in this world.

So we ought to be a great deal more encouraged than they were, especially when we think how little, after all, we have to suffer compared with what was asked of our Lord's chosen apostles. We do not have to sleep on the ground, or live on grains of wheat picked off the stalk in the fields, as they sometimes had to do. We have not got to look forward, as they did after his death, to long and painful labors and journeyings, to being driven from one city to another, to being scourged and buffeted, and put at last to a cruel death. No; on the whole, we have got a pretty easy time. We probably will not starve; nobody will persecute us; we will most likely always have a house to live in, and die in our beds.

It is not much, then, is it, to eat fish instead of meat, to fast enough to have a good appetite, to lose a little sleep and get a little tired? Perhaps if we would think more of the reward for such little things, and think a little more of the good time coming in heaven, we might even wish that Lent was more than forty days long.

Third Sunday of Lent.

Epistle. *Eph.* v. 1-9. Brethren: Be ye followers of God, as most dear children. And walk in love as Christ also hath loved us, and hath delivered himself for us an oblation and a sacrifice to God for an odor of sweetness. But fornication and all uncleanness, or covetousness, let it not so much as be named among you, as becometh saints: nor obscenity, nor foolish talking, nor scurrility, which is to no purpose: but rather giving of thanks. For know ye this, and understand that no fornicator, nor unclean, nor covetous person which is a serving of idols hath any inheritance in the kingdom of Christ and of God. Let no man deceive you with vain words. For because of these things cometh the anger of God upon the children of unbelief. Be ye not therefore partakers with them. For you were heretofore darkness, but now light in the Lord. Walk ye as children of the light: for the fruit of the light is in all goodness, and justice, and truth.

Gospel. *St. Luke* xi. 14-28. At that time: Jesus was casting out a devil, and the same was dumb; and when he had cast out the devil, the dumb spoke; and the multitude admired: but some of them said: He casteth out devils in Beelzebub, the prince of the devils. And others tempting, asked of him a sign from heaven. But he, seeing their thoughts, said to them: Every kingdom divided against itself shall be brought to desolation, and a house upon a house shall fall. And if Satan also be divided against himself, how shall his kingdom stand? because you say, that in Beelzebub I cast out devils. Now if I cast out devils in Beelzebub, in whom do your children cast them out? Therefore they shall be your judges. But if I, in the finger of God, cast out devils, doubtless the kingdom of God is come upon you. When a strong man armed keepeth his court, those things which he possesseth are in peace. But if a stronger than he come upon him and overcome him, he will take away all his armor wherein he trusted, and will distribute his spoils. He that is not with me, is against me: and he that gathereth not with me, scattereth. When the unclean spirit is gone out of a man, he walketh through places without water, seeking rest: and not finding, he saith: I will return into my house whence I came out. And when he is come, he findeth it swept and garnished. Then he goeth and taketh with him seven other spirits more wicked than himself, and entering in they dwell there. And the last state of that man becometh worse than the first. And it came to pass, as he spoke these things, a certain woman from the crowd lifting up her voice, said to him: Blessed is the womb that bore thee, and the paps that gave thee suck. But he said: Yea, rather, blessed are they who hear the word of God and keep it.

SERMON XLVII.

Every kingdom divided against itself shall be brought to desolation.—St. Luke xi. 17.

WE can see at once how true the sentence just read is; for if the head of a kingdom were to rise against the members, the king against his ministers, the people against both king and government, and the army and navy against their proper commanders—if all this should take place, then I say that kingdom would certainly be brought to desolation, and any enemy could easily come along and take possession of it. Now, dear brethren, the Christian family is a little kingdom. The father and mother are the king and queen, the older and more experienced members of the family are the counsellors, the children the subjects of that kingdom. The Christian family ought to be most closely united, and this for many reasons. Each member has been baptized with the same baptism, been sanctified by the same Holy Spirit. They have all been pardoned for their sins through the same Precious Blood, do all eat of the same spiritual food, the Body and Blood of Christ. Then, to come to natural reasons, they are bound together by the tie of blood, by the tie of parental and filial affection; they live together, pray together, rejoice together, suffer together. So there is every reason why the Christian family should be united; and if it is to fulfil its mission properly it *must* be united, or it will be brought to desolation. O my dear friends! how many of these little kingdoms which should go to make up the grand empire of Jesus Christ upon earth fall away from their allegiance to him, and all because they are divided against themselves. We see a father, for instance, given over to habits of drunkenness; he comes home either in a dull, heavy stupor or else in a perfect fury of rage; he worries his wife, scares his children, disgraces himself; all his family shrink from him. There you see at once the head divided against the members. Or there is in the family a cross, ill-tempered, scolding wife, and, as the Scripture says, "there is no anger above the anger of a woman: it will be more agreeable to abide with a lion and a dragon than to dwell with a wicked woman. As the climbing of a sandy way is to the feet of the aged, so is a wife full of tongue to a quiet man." Such a woman would divide any family; she destroys the unity thereof just as much as the drunken husband. What, also, must be thought of interfering relations, cousins, aunts, uncles, and last, but not least, mothers-in-law? How often do they make mischief and destroy the kingdom of the Christian family! So, too, rebellious children, quarrelsome brothers and sisters—they all destroy peace, they all help to divide the kingdom, they all help to bring it to desolation; and in the end, instead of a fair kingdom, strong and united, nothing remains but a wretched scene of strife and contention, and in comes the devil and takes possession of everything. Now, my dear friends, when by your drunkenness, your crossness, your mischief-making and party-spirit, by your rebellion against parental authority, you divide the kingdom of your family, not only you yourselves will suffer, not only will you and your family have to endure spiritual injury and perhaps loss of salvation, but the great kingdom of Christ, now militant here on earth, and one day to be triumphant in heaven, suffers also. Who make up the church on earth? Individuals, families. Who are to fill the ranks of the heavenly kingdom? The same. Oh! then, if you are divided against yourselves, if you are brought to desolation, you are part of the devil's kingdom on earth, and will form part of his empire of sin and death in hell. For God's sake, brethren, *stop this evil war*. Stop these things which make the family miserable. Have peace in your homes. Let men see that the peace of Christ and the union of Christ dwell there. Correct your faults; curb your tongues and your tempers; be obedient. Remember, the first words the priest says when he comes to your homes on a sick-call are these: "Peace be to this house and all that dwell therein." Try to profit by that benediction. Try always to have the peace of God, which passeth all knowledge, and then shall your kingdom stand.

B.

SERMON XLVIII.

"Are you going to make your Easter duty?" This is an important question just now, my dear brethren. You should put it to yourselves, and your answer should be: "Yes, certainly." The church commands it; and you know very well that he who will not hear the church is to be held as a heathen and a publican; that he who despises the church despises our Lord, and he who despises the Lord despises his Father who is in heaven. Surely you will not make yourselves guilty of this frightful sin of contempt; surely you do not wish to be held as a heathen. But knowing, as you do, the precept of the church binding at this time, how can you expect, if you do not fulfil it, to escape from the consequences of your disobedience, as expressed in the words of our Lord which I have just recited?

To go against the church in one of her commands is to spurn her authority altogether. It is strange that people should make, of their own wits or fancy, distinctions between the precepts of the church, when the church makes and acknowledges no such distinctions. The authority in all cases is the same, and, therefore, the commands are all equally binding. Yet how many Catholics who would scruple to eat meat on Friday or miss Mass on Sunday think nothing at all of breaking, without reason, the fast and abstinence of Lent, and give no heed whatever to the obligation of going to confession and communion in Easter-time! It really looks, to judge from their conduct, as if this Easter duty was not on an equal footing with the other commands of the church; as if the church did not mean what she prescribes. Now, the truth of it is, to this precept is attached a more severe sanction than to any other. The church makes any Catholic who violates it liable to excommunication, and deprivation of burial in consecrated ground. So you see the obligation is very strict and the church is terribly in earnest about it, if you are not.

To take matters in your own hands, as so many Catholics do on this point, and call little what she calls great, and slight an order that she is so anxious about, is to be a heathen, or, at any rate, a Protestant; it is to set your private judgment above her authority; it is to despise God, who commands through her. If you would only take this view of it—and this is the true view to take—you would think more than once before you would say: "O pshaw! any other time will do. Once a year? All right; I find it more convenient to go at Christmas." No, any other time will not do; once a year will not do, unless it be just now at this time. Christmas is a glorious feast, and Christmas-tide a joyful season, but it is not the season prescribed by the church for your annual communion; and, heathen that you are, your convenience is not the main point to be considered. The question is: Has the church power from God to command me, and what does the church command?

Oh! then, my brethren, let not the penances, the **prayers, the instructions, the special graces of this** holy season go to naught and be of no avail; but rather let them lead you up to the end for which they are intended—that is, to bring you to repentance for past sins, amendment for the future, to restore you to the friendship of your God, and strengthen you, for further battling in life, with the bread of heaven, his most precious Body and Blood.

SERMON XLIX.

He saith: I will return into my house whence I came out.—
St. Luke xi. 24.

THE warning which our Lord gives us in this Gospel is certainly a most terrible one, my brethren, but it may not seem plain to whom it is addressed; who they are who, now and at all times, are in danger of having the devil come back to them in this way of which he speaks. For nowadays, thank God! it is not very often that we find people who are really possessed by the devil, in the proper sense of the word.

But, in a more general sense of it, there are plenty of people who are possessed by the devil. They are those who are in a state of mortal sin. In them Satan has regained the possession from which he was driven out in holy baptism—that is, the soul which was his at least by original, if not by actual, sin. And he is in them as a dumb devil, like the one which the Gospel tells us that our Lord cast out; that is, he makes the people dumb whom he possesses, by keeping them from telling their sins and getting rid of them by confession.

But the dumb devil is often cast out, particularly at times of special grace and help from God, like this holy season of Lent through which we are now passing, or at the time of a mission or of a jubilee. At such times you will always find people, who have been away from the sacraments for years, coming back to them and making an effort to amend their lives and save their souls.

Now, this is very unpleasant to the devil, who has counted on these people as his own. He has a special liking for the souls which have been his so long. So when he is driven out of them he does not simply go off on other business, as we might expect; but he always has an eye on his old home. He says to himself, when he finds that he does not get along so well elsewhere: "I will return into my house whence I came out. I will see if I cannot get in again."

So he comes back to his old house, to the soul which has been his, and too often he finds it pretty easy to get in again. He finds it, in fact, "swept and garnished," as our Lord says, and all ready for his reception. So, of course, he goes in and takes his old place. The soul, which has escaped from sin by a good confession, relapses into it again.

What a pity this is! And yet how common it is! How many, how very many, there are who a month or so after a mission, or some other occasion when you would think they would really be converted in good earnest, are back again in their old sins just the same as if they had never confessed them at all!

It seems strange, perhaps. And yet it is not so strange when you come to think of it. The reason is not very hard to find. It is just the one that our Lord gives: it is that the house of the soul, from which the devil has been driven, is empty, "swept and garnished." Nothing has been put there in the place of the vices and bad habits that were there before. There is no habit of prayer; there is no remembrance of the good resolutions that were made at confession; there is no attempt to avoid the occasion of sin; and, above all, there is no grace coming from the sacraments. That is the great mistake these converted sinners have made. They have promised at confession to go every month for the future; but they have not kept that promise. Now, it is perfect folly and madness for one who has been in the habits of sin to hope to persevere by saying a few short prayers and going to confession once a year. Such a way of going on leaves the soul empty of grace, and without anything to prevent its enemy from coming in.

If you want to persevere after a good confession, go every month to the sacraments. This is not a practice of piety; it is only common prudence. This is the means which God has appointed in his church to fill the soul with grace, and leave no room for the devil in his old home from which he has once been driven away.

Fourth Sunday of Lent.

EPISTLE. *Gal. iv.* 22–31. Brethren: It is written that Abraham had two sons: the one by a bondwoman, and the other by a free-woman: but he that was by the bond-woman was born according to the flesh: but he by the free-woman was by the promise. Which things are said by an allegory: for these are the two testaments: the one indeed on Mount Sina which bringeth forth unto bondage, which is Agar: for Sina is a mountain in Arabia, which hath an affinity to that which now is Jerusalem, and is in bondage with her children. But that Jerusalem which is above, is free: which is our mother. For it is written: "Rejoice, thou barren, that bearest not: break forth and cry out, thou that travailest not; for many are the children of the desolate, more than of her that hath a husband"; now we, brethren, as Isaac was, are the children of promise. But as then he, that was born according to the flesh, persecuted him that was according to the spirit: so also now. But what saith the Scripture? "Cast out the bond-woman and her son: for the son of the bond-woman shall not be heir with the son of the free-woman." Therefore, brethren, we are not the children of the bond-woman, but of the free: by the freedom wherewith Christ has made us free.

GOSPEL. *St. John vi.* 1–15. At that time: Jesus went over the sea of Galilee, which is that of Tiberias: and a great multitude followed him, because they saw the miracles which he did on them that were infirm. And Jesus went up into a mountain, and there he sat with his disciples. Now the Pasch, the festival day of the Jews, was near at hand,

When Jesus therefore had lifted up his eyes, and seen that a very great multitude cometh to him, he said to Philip: Whence shall we buy bread that these may eat? And this he said to try him, for he himself knew what he would do. Philip answered him: Two hundred pennyworth of bread is not sufficient for them, that every one may take a little. One of his disciples, Andrew, the brother of Simon Peter, saith to him: There is a boy here that hath five barley loaves, and two fishes; but what are these among so many? Then Jesus said: Make the men sit down. Now there was much grass in the place. So the men sat down, in number about five thousand. And Jesus took the loaves: and when he had given thanks he distributed to them that were sat down. In like manner also of the fishes as much as they would. And when they were filled, he said to his disciples: Gather up the fragments that remain, lest they be lost. So they gathered up, and filled twelve baskets with the fragments of the five barley loaves, which remained over and above to them that had eaten. Then those men, when they had seen what a miracle Jesus had done, said: This is the prophet indeed that is to come into the world. When Jesus therefore perceived that they would come and take him by force and make him king, he fled again into the mountain himself alone.

SERMON L.

When, therefore, Jesus had lifted up his eyes and seen that a very great multitude cometh to him, he said to Philip: " Whence shall we buy bread that these may eat ?"—St. John vi. 5.

To-day is mid-Lent Sunday, dear brethren. Half of the holy season has passed away, and the Pasch is near at hand. All through Lent the church has been praying, fasting, and preaching, making extra efforts to bring in the sinners who have so long stayed without the fold. Like the Divine Master, she looks down upon the crowd and she has pity on them. She wants to heal the sick; they will not be healed. She wants to feed the hungry; they will not be fed. The church looks round upon the vast crowd of her children and wants them to make their Easter duty; alas! how many neglect it. Why should you make the Easter duty? First, because it is a strict law of the church. If you fail to make it by your own fault you commit a grievous mortal sin and put yourself in a position to be excommunicated from God's church. Secondly, for your own spiritual good. What kind of a Christian can he be who does not go to confession or communion at least once in a year? How shall you make it? First go to confession, and then, when you have received absolution, go to communion. That is all simple and plain enough. Why, then, do some people stay away from their Easter duty? Let us tell the truth. Confession must come first, and confession is the difficulty. A man has been engaged for years in an unlawful business, or he has stolen a sum of money, or he has been the receiver of stolen goods, or in some way or other cheated in trade. Such a man is a thief. He knows it, and he is also aware that if he goes to confession the priest will say: "Give up the ill-gotten money, sell your fine house and your gilded furniture, and make restitution; you must restore or you will damn your soul." They won't do that, won't give up the dishonest gains, and so they won't make the Easter duty. Or there are some who have committed sins of impurity; they have been unfaithful husbands, dissolute wives. They won't give up their bad habits or won't tell their shameful sins, and so they won't make the Easter duty. There are others on whom the fiend of drunkenness has settled; they are always on a spree, always pouring the liquor which stupefies them down their throats; they won't repent and they won't make the Easter duty. Ah! then, if there be any such sinners here—if there be any thieves, if there be any who are living upon dishonest gains, if there be any who are wallowing in impurity and drunkenness—tell me, how long is this going to last? How many more years will you slink away from your Easter duty like cowards and cravens? Will you go on so to the end of your lives? Oh! then you will go down to hell, and your blood be upon your own heads. No one stays away from Easter duty except for disgraceful reasons. There is always something bad behind that fear of the confessional, and such a man deserves to be pointed at by every honorable Catholic. Suppose you *have* stolen, or been an adulterer, or a fornicator, or a drunkard, or what not. Now is the time to repent, and amend, and make reparation. Don't you see the church looking down with eyes of mercy upon you? Why, then, stay? There can be only one reason, and that reason is because you want to go on being thieves, adulterers, and drunkards. O brethren! do not, I pray you, so wickedly. The church is kind. The blood of Christ is still flowing. The confessionals are still open. Go in there with your heavy sins and your black secrets. Go in there with your long story of sin. Go in, even if your hands are red with blood—go in, I say, and if you are truly penitent you will be cleansed and consoled. Let there not be a single man or woman in this church who can have it said of them this year: "**You missed** your Easter duty." And you that have been away for years and years, don't add another sin to your already long list of crimes. You are sick, you are fainting with hunger, you are a poor wandering sheep; but never mind, remember Jesus looks with pity upon you, and he will heal your sickness in the sacrament of penance, and feed you with his own Body and Blood. B.

SERMON LI.

Gather up the fragments that remain, lest they be lost.—St. John vi. 12.

It seems rather odd, does it not, my brethren, that our Divine Lord should have been so particular about saving all the broken bits of those loaves and fishes? He had just worked a wonderful miracle, and he could have repeated it the next day without any difficulty. When he or his apostles or the crowd who came to hear him were hungry, he had nothing to do but to say the word, and they could all have as much to eat as they wanted. Why, then, be so particular about hunting up all the crusts of bread and bits of fish that were lying round in the grass?

Perhaps you will say: "It was to show what a great miracle he had worked; to show that, in spite of their all having dined heartily, there were twelve basketfuls of scraps left over—much more than they had to start with."

I do not think that was it. The greatness of the miracle in feeding five thousand men on five loaves and two fishes was plain enough. At any rate, that was not the reason that he himself gave.

He said: "Gather them up, *lest they be lost.*" "Well, then," a prudent housekeeper would say, "the reason is plain enough. It was to teach us economy—not to let anything go to waste; to save the scraps, and make them up into bread-puddings and fish-balls."

I know you do not think that was it. Most people who are not forced to this kind of economy are apt to turn up their noses at it, and connect it in their minds with a stingy disposition, which they very rightly think is not pleasing to God.

But, after all, I don't see what it could very well have been but economy that our Lord meant to teach. I don't see what other meaning you can get out of his command to gather up the fragments, that they might not be lost. If that does not mean economy, what does it mean?

No, my brethren, economy, or a saving spirit, is not such a contemptible thing when rightly understood. There may be stinginess with it, but stinginess is not a part of it. Economy, rightly understood, is setting a proper value on the gifts of God.

Yes; what comes from him—and everything does—is too valuable to be thrown away. To despise his gifts is very much like despising him.

And besides, there is not, in fact, an unlimited supply of them, though there might be. He might have fed his followers in that miraculous way every day; but he only did so twice in his life.

Our Lord, then, did mean, I think, to set us an example of economy. Practise it as he did, my brethren. Prize God's gifts, whatever they may be; do not waste them. But especially his spiritual gifts; for they are infinitely more precious than the material ones. Don't count on having a future extraordinary supply of them.

You have got enough to save your souls now, and to sanctify them, if you will only make use of it. You have got the faith, the sacraments, and the word of God. You don't need to have any one rise from the dead to convert you. Our Lord tells us that a certain rich man who was in hell wanted to go back to earth and appear to his brothers, that they might take warning by his example. He was told that it was not necessary; that they had Moses and the prophets. Well, you have got a great deal more. You know just as well what you must do to save your souls, and even to become saints, as if you had been beyond the grave yourselves. Don't expect more yet.

Save up your spiritual gifts, my brethren; you have got plenty now, but you do not know how much more you will get. When God gives you any grace make the most of it; perhaps it will be the last you will have. Bring back to your minds what you have heard, and the good thoughts and purposes which the Holy Ghost has given you; serve up the spiritual feasts you have had, not only a second time, but over and over again. Make what you have got go as far as possible, and your souls will grow stout and strong. Wait for unusual graces like a mission or a jubilee, and they will be thin and weak all the time. Be economical, especially in spiritual things; that is a very important lesson of the Gospel of to-day.

Passion Sunday.

EPISTLE. *Heb. ix.* 11–15. Brethren: Christ being come a high-priest of the good things to come, by a greater and more perfect tabernacle not made with hands, that is, not of this creation : neither by the blood of goats, nor of calves, but by his own blood, entered once into the Holies, having obtained eternal redemption. For if the blood of goats and of oxen, and the ashes of a heifer being sprinkled, sanctify such as are defiled, to the cleansing of the flesh : how much more shall the blood of Christ, who by the Holy Ghost offered himself unspotted unto God, cleanse our conscience from dead works, to serve the living God ? And therefore he is the mediator of the new testament : that by means of his death, for the redemption of those transgressions, which were under the former testament, they that are called may receive the promise of eternal inheritance in Christ Jesus our Lord.

GOSPEL. *St. John viii.* 46–59. At that time : Jesus said to the multitude of the Jews : Which of you shall convince me of sin ? If I say the truth to you, why do you not believe me ? He that is of God, heareth the words of God. Therefore you hear them not, because you are not of God. The Jews, therefore, answered and said to him : Do not we say well that thou art a Samaritan, and hast a devil ? Jesus answered : I have not a devil ; but I honor my Father, and you have dishonored me. But I seek not my own glory : there is one that secketh and judgeth. Amen, amen, I say to you : if any man keep my word, he shall not see death for ever. The Jews therefore said : Now we know that thou hast a devil. Abraham is dead, and the prophets; and thou sayest: If any man keep my word, he shall not taste death for ever. Art thou greater than our father Abraham, who is dead? And the prophets are dead. Whom dost thou make thyself? Jesus answered: If I glorify myself, my glory is nothing. It is my Father that glorifieth me, of whom you say that he is your God. And you have not known him, but I know him. And if I shall say that I know him not, I shall be like to you, a liar. But I do know him, and do keep his word. Abraham your father rejoiced that he might see my day: he saw it, and was glad. The Jews therefore said to him: Thou art not yet fifty years old, and hast thou seen Abraham? Jesus said to them: Amen, amen, I say to you, before Abraham was made, I am. They took up stones therefore to cast at him. But Jesus hid himself, and went out of the temple.

SERMON LII.

But Jesus hid himself.—St. John viii. 59.

THICK and fast, dear brethren, the shadows of the Great Week begin to fall upon us. Only a few more days and it will be Palm Sunday, the first day of Holy Week. To-day we are left, as it were, alone. The crucifix, with its figure of the dead, white Christ, is veiled; the dear, familiar faces of the Blessed Virgin and St. Joseph are veiled also; and even the saints before whom we were wont to kneel are all hidden behind the purple veil of Passion-tide. Not till Good Friday will Jesus look upon us again, not till Holy Saturday will the Blessed Virgin, St. Joseph, and the saints once more come forth to our view. We are, then, alone by ourselves. God wants us to stand up before him just as we are. Jesus has hidden his face for a while. The crucifix has bidden you good-by. In what state were you last night when devout hands veiled the figure of Christ? Will you ever look upon the old, familiar crucifix again? It may be, before the purple veil is lifted from this cross, you will have looked upon the face of Christ in judgment. O brethren! to-day the face of Jesus is hidden. May be the last time you looked upon it you were in mortal sin, and are so still. When and how shall you look upon it again? If you live till Good Friday you will see it then held aloft by the priest, and afterwards kissed by all the faithful. If you die before then, and die, as you may, without warning or preparation, then you will look upon the face of Christ upon the judgment seat, then you will hear the awful words: "Depart from me, ye cursed, into everlasting fire." Or perhaps—and may God grant it!—you will next see the face of Jesus in the person of his priest in the confessional, and there it will be turned upon you in mercy and forgiveness. There are some of you, I know, who are as *dead men*. There are some of you who, even up to this late hour, are holding out against grace. Still in mortal sin! I point you to the veiled Christ. I ask you, here in the sacred presence of God, I ask you in the most solemn manner, when and how will you look upon his face again? He has bidden you good-by to-day, he has said farewell, and as he said it he saw that you were a blasphemer, a drunkard, an adulterer, a slanderer, a creature full of pride, full of sloth, full of all kinds of sin. Oh! say, shall he still find you so when he returns? Say, when he is uncovered on Good Friday can you, dare you add to his grief by still being what you are now? And to us all, even the most devout, this lesson of the veiled crucifix ought not to pass unheeded. Christ has gone from us to-day! How will he come back to us? All torn and bloody, all thorn-scarred, all spear-pierced, nailed to the cross, and all for love of us! We, too, brethren, who are trying to walk strictly in the narrow path—we, too, may ask ourselves, When and how shall we see him again? Perhaps before Good Friday, ay, perhaps even before our hands can grasp the green palm-branch of next Sunday, we may see the unveiled face of our Beloved. Are we afraid of that? Oh! no. We have loved the face of suffering too well to dread the face of glory. We only expect to hear from his lips words of love and welcome. Brethren, there is a day coming when all veils shall be lifted. There is a time nearing us when all must look upon the face that died on Calvary's Mount. On that day and at that time will take place the great unveiling of the face of Christ: I mean the day of general judgment. O solemn, O awful thought for us to-day before the veiled image of our Lord! May be the judgment day will come before that light veil is lifted from the well-known crucifix. Great God! our next Good Friday may be spent either in heaven or in hell. Go home, brethren, with these thoughts fixed deeply in your hearts. Come here often to pray. If you have sins come here and confess them; and often and often as we turn to the veiled Christ, let us most devoutly cry: "Jesus, when and how shall we look upon thy face again?" B.

SERMON LIII.

UNDER the false accusations of the Jews how calm and self-possessed our Lord remains! He does not return passion for passion, anger for anger, accusations for accusations, violence for violence; but he meets calumny with the assertion of truth, and confounds his enemies by humility and meekness. They accuse him of sin; with the sublime simplicity of a pure conscience he dares them to convince him of sin. They call him names: "Thou art a Samaritan"; to so evident a falsehood he deigns no reply. Blinded by anger, they accuse him of being possessed: "Thou hast a devil"; a simple denial, "I have not a devil," the leaving of his own glory to his Father, the assertion of his divine mission, is the answer to the blasphemous calumny. "Now we know thou hast a devil," repeat they, waxing more passionate; but, unimpassioned, Jesus rises above their rage to the calm heights of the Godhead, and affirms his eternal generation. Finally, losing all control of themselves, they take up stones to cast at him; but he quietly goes out of the temple and hides himself, for his hour—the hour when he would bear in silence the accusations and indignities of man, and allow himself to be led to slaughter—had not yet come.

In this our Saviour teaches us how we should behave when the passions of others fall upon us and we are made the butt of accusations, just or unjust. In such circumstances what is generally your conduct? By no means Christian, I am afraid, but very worldly; for the world counts it true valor and justice to give tit for tat, to take tooth for tooth and eye for eye. Do you not give back as good—and often worse—than you get? Prudence, let alone Christianity, should dictate to you quite another conduct. Your counter-accusations do but strengthen and confirm the calumny; they allow it to stand. "You're another" and "you're no better" are poor arguments to clear yourselves. It's a flank movement that does not cover your position, a feint that does not save you from attack. The answering of a question by asking another question is a smart trick, but no answer. A calm denial, if you could make it, or dignified silence would do the work more surely and thoroughly. And so the fight of words goes on in true Billingsgate style; to and fro they fly thick and hot, hotter and hotter as passion rises on both sides. "One word brings on another," until white heat is reached and all control of temper lost. Then, as the Jews ended with stones, so you perhaps come to more serious passion than mere words. The result is quarrels, deadly feuds, bodily injuries, and worse, may be—bloodshed and the jail. A cow kicked a lantern in a stable, and Chicago was on fire for days. Some frivolous accusation that you pick up, while you should let it fall, starts within you a fire of anger that makes a ruin of your whole spiritual life and throws disorder all around you; families are divided; wife and husband sulk, quarrel, live a "cat and dog" life; friends are separated, connections broken. Peace flies from your homes, your social surroundings, your own hearts; the very horrors of hell are around you. Christian charity has been wounded to death, and the slightest of blows, the lightest of shafts has done it. All for the want of a little patience and self-possession! How often we hear it said: "Oh! I have such a bad temper; I'm easily riz, God forgive me! I've a bad passion entirely." Well, my dear brethren, learn from this Gospel how you should control yourselves, how you should possess your souls in patience. One-half the sins of the world would be done away with, if only the lesson of this Gospel were laid to heart and put into practice. What is the lesson?

Firstly, never seek self-praise in self-justification. Jesus turns aside the calumny of the Jews, but leaves the glorifying of himself in the hands of his Father, "who seeketh and judgeth." Secondly, pay no attention to accusations that are absurd, evidently untrue, and frivolous. When Jesus is called names and is made out to be what every one knows he was not—"a Samaritan"—he makes no answer. Thirdly, if serious calumny, calculated to injure your usefulness in your duties and state of life, assail you, it then becomes your right, and sometimes your duty, to repel the calumny, as Jesus did when he was accused of "having a devil." But in this case your self-justification, like that of our Saviour, should ever be calm, dignified, and Christian. It should be a defence, never an attack. The true Christian parries, he does not give the thrust; he shields himself from the arrows of malice, he does not shoot them back. Superior to revenge, he pities enemies for the evil they do; he forgives them and prays for them, as our Lord has commanded. This is Christian charity, and Christian humility as well. But as it avails little to know what we should do, if we have not God's grace to enable us to do it, let us often say, especially in temptations to impatience: "O Jesus, meek and humble of heart! make me like unto thee."

SERMON LIV.

Why is to-day called Passion Sunday, my brethren? There does not seem to be any special commemoration of our Lord's sacred Passion in the Mass, as there is next Sunday, when the long account of it from St. Matthew's Gospel is read; and most people, I think, hardly realize that to-day is anything more than any other Sunday in Lent.

But if you look into the matter a little more you will notice a great change which comes upon the spirit of the church to-day, and remains during the two following weeks. The Preface of the Mass is not that of Lent, but that of the Cross; the hymns sung at Vespers and at other times are about the cross and our Lord's death upon it; and all the way through the Divine Office you will see evident signs that the church is thinking about this mystery of the cross, the commemoration of which is consummated on Good Friday.

And if you look about the church this morning you will see the pictures all veiled, to tell us that during these two weeks we should think principally of our Lord's suffering and humiliation; that we should, as it were, for a while forget his saints and everything else connected with his glory. And even the cross itself is concealed, for it is after all a sign of triumph and victory to our eyes; it is waiting to be revealed till Good Friday, when the sacrifice shall be accomplished and the victory won.

To-day, then, is called Passion Sunday because it is the opening of this short period, from now till Easter, which the church calls Passion-time.

What practical meaning has this Passion-time for

us, my brethren? It means, or should mean, for us sorrow, humiliation, sharing in the Passion of our Lord. Lent, all the way through, is a time of penance; but more especially so is this short season which brings it to a close. Now, surely, is the time, if ever, when we are going to be sorry for our sins, when we cannot help thinking of what they have made our Divine Saviour suffer. Now is the time to think of the malice and ingratitude of sin; to see it as it really is, as the one thing which has turned this earth from a paradise into a place of suffering and sorrow; to see our own sins as they truly are, as the only real evils which have ever happened to us, and to resolve to be rid of them for our own sake and for God's sake; for he has suffered for them as well as we.

Now is the time to go to confession, and to make a better confession than we have ever made before, or ever can make, probably, till Passion-time comes round again. For now is it easier for us to be sorry for our sins, not only because we have everything to show us how hateful they are, but also because God's grace is more liberally given. He has sanctified this time and blessed it for our repentance and conversion. He calls us and helps us always to penance, but never so much as now.

Hear his voice, then, my brethren, and, in the words with which the church begins her office to-day: "To-day if you shall hear his voice, harden not your hearts." Do not obstinately remain in sin, and put off your repentance and confession to a more favorable time. There is no time nearly as good as this; this is the time which God himself has appointed. You must make your Easter duty, if you would not add another terrible sin to the many which you have already made our Lord bear for you; make it now before Easter comes. Take your share now in the Passion, that you may have your share of the Easter joy.

And there is another reason why you should come now to confession; for there is another unusual grace which God now offers you—the grace of the Jubilee, which you heard announced last Sunday. Now, a Jubilee is not a mere devotion for those who frequent the sacraments; it is a call and an opportunity for those who have neglected them. I beg you not to let it be said that you have allowed this opportunity to go by. Come and give us some work to do in the confessional; the more the better. We will not complain, but will thank you from the bottom of our hearts. The best offering you can make to your priests, as well as to the God whose servants they are, is a crowded confessional and a full altar-rail at this holy Passion-time.

Palm Sunday.

EPISTLE. *Phil. ii.* 5–11. Brethren: Let this mind be in you, which was also in Christ Jesus: who being in the form of God, thought it not robbery himself to be equal with God: but debased himself, taking the form of a servant, being made to the likeness of men, and in shape found as a man. He humbled himself, becoming obedient unto death, even the death of the cross. Wherefore God also hath exalted him, and hath given him a name which is above every name: that in the name of Jesus every knee should bow, of those that are in heaven, on earth, and in hell. And that every tongue should confess that the Lord Jesus Christ is in the glory of God the Father.

GOSPEL. *St. Matt. xxvii.* 62–66. And the next day, which followed the day of preparation, the chief priests and the Pharisees came together to Pilate, saying: Sir, we have remembered that that seducer said, while he was yet alive: After three days I will rise again. Command therefore the sepulchre to be guarded until the third day: lest his disciples come and steal him away, and say to the people, He is risen from the dead: so the last error shall be worse than the first. Pilate said to them: You have a guard; go, guard it as you know. And they departing, made the sepulchre sure with guards, sealing the stone.

SERMON LV.

Behold thy King cometh to thee meek.—St. Matt. xxi. 5.

Through humility and suffering to exaltation and glory—that is the way our Lord went to heaven, dear brethren, and that is the way we must go if we wish to follow him. To-day is Palm Sunday, the day on which our Lord rode in triumph to begin his Passion. Yes, in triumph; but what an humble one! He rode upon a lowly beast; there were no rich carpets spread along the way, only the poor and well-worn garments of the apostles and of the multitude thrown together with the boughs and branches torn from the wayside trees. All was humble, and doubly so if we think that he was riding to his death. Yes, brethren, those palm-branches were scarce withered, the dust had hardly been shaken from those garments, when the cross was laid upon his shoulders and the thorny crown pressed upon his brow. Dear brethren, let us ask ourselves this morning if we want to go to heaven. Do we want to be where Jesus is now, and where he will be for all eternity? If we do we must follow him through suffering and humility to exaltation and glory. We must be content with little and short happiness in this world; for, as I have said, the triumph of Palm Sunday was short-lived indeed. What followed? Jesus was brought before Pilate. He was condemned to death, forsaken, set at naught, buffeted, mocked, spit upon. He, the innocent Lamb of God, was scourged, stripped of his garments, crowned with thorns. Then upon his poor, torn shoulders was laid a heavy cross, which he carried till he could no longer bear it. And, lastly, outside the city gates they nailed him to that same cross, and he died. But after that came the glory and the triumph—the glory of the resurrection; the triumph over sin, and death, and hell.

Brethren, we needs *must* think of heaven to-day; the waving palms, the chanted hosannas, all speak to us of that delightful place. We cannot help thinking of that great multitude, clad in white robes and with palms in their hands, of whom St. John speaks, and of those others who cast down their golden crowns before the glassy sea. We want to reach that blessed place; we want to hear the sound of the harpers harping upon their harps; we want to hear the angels' songs and see the flashing of their golden wings; we want to gaze upon Jesus and Mary and all the heavenly host. But, brethren, not yet, not yet. See the long path strewn with stones and briers; see that steep mount with its cross of crucifixion at the top. That way must be trodden, that mountain scaled, that cross be nailed to us and we to it, or ever we may hear the golden harps or the angels' song. Through humility and suffering to exaltation and glory. Oh! let us learn the lesson well this Holy Week. Let us learn it to-day as we follow Jesus to prison and to death; let us learn it on Holy Thursday when we see him humble himself to the form of bread and wine; let us learn it on Good Friday when we kiss his sacred feet pierced with the nails. Yes, let us learn the lesson and never forget it. Heaven has been bought for you. Heaven lies open to you: but there is only one way there, and that way is the way of suffering. So, then, brethren, when your trials come thick and fast; when your temptations seem more than you can endure; when you are pinched by poverty, slighted by your neighbors, forsaken—

as it seems to you—even by God himself, then remember the way of the cross. Remember the agony in the garden; remember the mount of Calvary. Grasp the palm firmly in your hand to-day; let it be in fancy the wood of the cross. Cry aloud as you journey on: "Through humility and suffering to exaltation and glory." Keep close to Jesus. Onward to prison! Onward to crucifixion! Onward to death! Onward to what comes afterwards! Resurrection! Reward! Peace! B.

SERMON LVI.

He humbled himself, becoming obedient unto death, even the death of the cross.—Phil. ii. 8.

WE are entering to-day, my dear brethren, on the great week, the Holy Week, as it is called, of the Christian year—the week in which we commemorate the Passion and death of our Lord; and at this time our minds cannot, when we assist at the offices of the church, be occupied with any other thoughts than those which are suggested by his sufferings for our redemption.

And surely there is enough to occupy them not only for one short week, but for all our lives. The Passion of Christ is a mystery which we can never exhaust, in this world or in the world to come. It is the book of the saints, and there is no lesson of perfection which we cannot learn from it. So we must needs look at it to-day only in part, and learn one of its many lessons; and let that be one suggested to us by the words of the text, taken from the Epistle read at the Mass: "He humbled himself, becoming obedient unto death, even the death of the cross."

What is this lesson? It is that of humility, which is the foundation of all supernatural virtues, and yet the last one which most Christians try to acquire.

In fact, it would seem that many people, who are very good in their way, are rather annoyed than edified by the examples of humility that they find in the lives of the saints. It seems to them like hypocrisy when they read that the saints considered themselves the greatest sinners in the world. But it was not hypocrisy; they said what they really felt. They were not in the habit, as most people are, of noticing their neighbors' faults and making the most of them, and of excusing their own. So, though it was not really true that they were such great sinners when compared with others, it seemed to them that it was.

And, moreover, they were willing that others should think them so. In that they differed very much from some whom you would think were saints. The real saints are willing to bear contempt; they are willing to be considered sinners, even in their best actions, as long as God's glory is not in question; and, what is really harder, though it ought not to be, they are willing to be considered fools. Almost any one would rather be thought a knave than a fool. There are very few good people who like to be told of their faults; there are fewer still who like to be told of their blunders.

Now, it is with regard to this matter that we need specially to think of our Saviour's example. He, who could not be deceived, could not believe himself to be a knave or a fool; but he consented that others should consider him so, to set us an example of humility. He was reckoned among sinners in his life as well as in his death; and he hid the treasures of his divine wisdom and knowledge under the appearance of a poor, simple man of the lower classes. But it was in his sacred Passion that his humility is seen most plainly; he became obedient unto death, even the death of the cross; he, our Lord and our God, suffered the most disgraceful punishment that has ever been devised for common criminals.

There is the example, then, my brethren, for us poor sinners to follow. And the humility which we need most is nothing but the pure and simple truth. It is nothing but getting rid of the absurd notion that we are wiser and better than other people whom anybody else can see are our equals or superiors; for, strangely enough, it is always hardest to be humble when it is most clear that we ought to be. And depend on it, it is high time to set about acquiring this virtue; for, simple as it seems, to get even as much as this of it will take, for most of us, all our lives.

SERMON LVII.

I WILL say a few words to you this morning, my brethren, on the Jubilee just proclaimed by our Holy Father.

What is a Jubilee? It is the proclamation of a great spiritual favor which may be obtained by any Catholic in the world during a specified time. This spiritual favor is a special plenary indulgence which, if gained in a way that perfectly fulfils all the conditions and completely satisfies the intentions of the church, will surely wipe out not only all the actual sins one has committed in all his life before, but take away also all the temporal punishment one would have to undergo in this life or in purgatory on account of those sins, be they great or small.

No wonder that all the children of the Catholic Church rejoice to hear such a favor proclaimed by their Holy Father, and that everybody is so anxious to partake of its benefits.

What is to be done? Just what the Pope says, and in a way specially directed for his diocesans by each bishop. There are visits to be made to certain churches, and prayers to be said there. There is a fast to be observed on one day. There are alms to be given. There is confession to be made and Holy Communion to be received. And all to be done by or before next Pentecost Sunday.

First. The visits. For this city there are three churches named by His Eminence the Cardinal—viz., St. Patrick's Cathedral, St. Stephen's, and the Church of the Epiphany. Each one of these three churches must be visited twice All the visits may be made in one day or on different days, and one may, if he pleases, pay the two visits to the same church at once before going to another.

Second. Prayers are to be said in the churches; and they ought, of course, to be devout ones, and offered for all the intentions laid down by the Holy Father. No particular prayers are prescribed. One can hear Mass, or say the beads, or say five times the Our Father and Hail Mary, or one of the Litanies; or any of these prayers will do.

Third. The fast. This may be in Lent or after,

on any day that meat is allowed. But on the day you choose for the fast you must also abstain from meat.

Fourth. The alms. The amount or kind is not prescribed, but is left to your own generosity. It may be in money, in food, or in clothing, and it may be given to an orphan asylum or other such charitable institution, or to build a church. It may be given when making the visits; and special alms-boxes will be found in those churches to be visited, into which the offering can be put.

Fifth. Confession and Communion; and both ought to be prepared for and made the very best one can. Moreover, as one gains the more merit by doing actions in a state of grace, one will likely make the Jubilee better if he begins by making a good confession. Now is the time for great sinners to return to God and obtain his merciful forgiveness; for the Pope has given special privileges to confessors, in order that they may absolve the hardest kind of cases. Let no one, therefore, despair, nor think himself too hard a case. That is what the Jubilee is for—to bring down the mercy and forgiveness of God upon this sinful generation. To ensure this the father of the faithful sets the whole Catholic world together praying, and fasting, and giving alms, and confessing their sins, and making holy, devout communion, so as to take heaven by storm, as our Lord said we might. "For the kingdom of heaven suffereth violence, and the violent bear it away." What a sublime spectacle, which only the Catholic Church can show—two hundred and fifty millions of people all turning to God at once! No wonder the Catholic Church saves the world. Look out that you are not found, in eternity, to be one of those whom she failed to turn to God, and lost for ever because you would not hear her instruction and counsel, nor be guided by her into the way of eternal life.

Easter Sunday.

EPISTLE. I *Cor. v.* 7, 8. Brethren: Purge out the old leaven, that you may be a new mass, as you are unleavened. For Christ, our pasch, is sacrificed. Therefore let us feast, not with the old leaven, nor with the leaven of malice and wickedness, but with the unleavened bread of sincerity and truth.

GOSPEL. *St. Mark xvi.* 1-7. At that time: Mary Magdalen, and Mary the mother of James and Salome, bought sweet spices, that coming they might anoint Jesus. And very early in the morning, the first day of the week, they come to the sepulchre, the sun being now risen. And they said one to another: Who shall roll us back the stone from the door of the sepulchre? And looking, they saw the stone rolled back, for it was very great. And entering into the sepulchre, they saw a young man sitting on the right side, clothed with a white robe: and they were astonished. And he said to them: Be not affrighted; ye seek Jesus of Nazareth, who was crucified: he is risen, he is not here; behold the place where they laid him. But go, tell his disciples and Peter that he goeth before you into Galilee; there you shall see him as he told you.

SERMON LVIII.

Mary Magdalen.—ST. MARK xvi. 1.

DEAR brethren, you have all felt the great contrast that there is between the awful rites of Good Friday and the joy of to-day. Still fresh in your minds is the memory of the darkened church, the uplifted crucifix, the wailing of the reproaches. You remember, too, "the silence that might be felt" that reigned in God's temple on Holy Saturday. You can recall how still the church seemed yesterday at early morning, just as if some awful deed had been done there the day before; you may remember how unspeakably solemn seemed the silent procession to the porch to bless the new fire ; how quiet and subdued all that followed. But suddenly a voice rang out into the darkness—the voice of the sacrificing priest at the altar; an "exceeding great cry" pierced the stillness, and instantly every veil fell ; the sunlight streamed in through every window; chiming bells, pealing organ, and choral voices burst upon your senses ; everything seemed to say, "He is risen ! he is risen !" And we felt it was almost too much, almost more than the feeble human heart could bear and not break for very joy. If, then, this contrast is so marked and this joy so great after a lapse of eighteen hundred years and more, oh ! what must have been the joy of the first Easter day. The first crucifix bore no ivory or metal figure; it had nailed to it the flesh of the Son of God. The first Good Friday was no commemoration of an event ; it was the event itself. Oh ! then how great, how great beyond mind to imagine or tongue to tell, must have been the joy of the first Easter. Jesus had died, left all his beloved. He had been buried, and there he rested in the quiet garden. Very early in the morning come Mary Magdalen and the other women to the tomb. The sun was just rising ; the flowers of that blessed garden were just awaking ; the dewdrops sparkled like rubies in the red sunrise ; the vines and the creepers, fresh with their morning sweetness, hung clustering round the sacred tomb. To that spot the women hasten; the sun rises; she, Mary Magdalen, stoops down; her Lord is not there, but lo! the great stone is rolled away; a bright angel sits thereon; other angelic spirits are in the tomb. The angel speaks: "He is risen; he is not here. Behold, he goes before you to Galilee. Alleluia! alleluia!" The Lord is risen indeed. And now, brethren, wishing you every joy that this holy feast can bring, I will ask the question, Where or of whom shall we learn our Easter lesson? We will learn it from her whose name, whose lovely, sainly name, forms the text of this discourse. In pointing you to Mary Magdalen, the great saint of the Resurrection, I do but follow the mind of the church; for in to day's sequence the whole universal church calls upon her, "*Dic nobis, Maria, quid vidistis in via?*"—Declare to us, O Mary! what sawest thou in the way? She saw the sepulchre of Christ, in which were buried her many sins. In the way, the sorrowful way of the cross, she saw the Passion of Christ; in the way, the glorious way of the triumph of Christ, she saw the glory of the Risen One and the angel witnesses. Oh! is not our lesson plain? Like Magdalen, let us see the sepulchre, and let us cast our sins in there. Let us see the way of the cross and walk therein; let us see the glory of the Risen One and the angel witnesses in the heavenly kingdom. O poor, repentant sinners! you who during Lent have kissed the feet of Jesus and stood beneath his cross in the confessional, what a day of joy, what a lesson of consolation comes to you! Who was it **upon whom fell the first ray of Resurrection glory?**

Who is it upon whom the great voice of the church liturgy, in the Holy Sacrifice, calls to-day? Ah! it was and is upon the "sometime sinner, Mary." Joy! joy! for the forgiven sinner to-day. Alleluia! alleluia! to you, blood-washed children of Jesus Christ; for she who saw the Master first was once a sinner—a sinner like unto you. Alleluia, and joy and peace, unto you all in Jesus' name, and in the name of the redeemed and pardoned Mary! Alleluia, and joy and peace! whether you be sinner as she was, or saint as she became. Alleluia, and joy and peace! for "Christ our hope hath risen, and he shall go before us into Galilee." Alleluia, and joy and peace! for we know that Christ hath risen from the dead. Lord, we know that we are feeble and sinful, but lead, "Conquering King," lead on; go thou before to the heavenly Galilee. Time was when we feared to follow; but she, "more than martyr and more than virgin"—she, Mary Magdalen, is in thy train, and, penitent like her, we follow thee. Alleluia, and joy and peace, to young and old! Alleluia, and joy and peace, to saint and pardoned sinner! for Christ hath risen from the dead.

B.

SERMON LIX.

He is risen.—ST. MARK xvi. 6.

THIS is Easter Sunday, and the heart of every Christian is full of joy; for on this day the voice of God is heard assuring us that the dead can and will rise again to enter upon a new and never-dying life. To die is to suffer the most poignant grief, the greatest loss, the most grievous pain that man is called upon to endure.

However long or sweet may be the pleasure of the draught of life, and health, and prosperity that one may drink, all must find this *one* bitter drop at the bottom of the cup. It is death; and if God himself did not tell us, how could we know but that it is the end of all? "But now Christ is risen from the dead and become the first fruits of them that sleep." Who says Christ is risen again? God. How do we hear his voice of truth, which cannot deceive nor be deceived? We hear him when we hear the voice of his divine church, which he has made "the pillar and the ground of the truth." This is, then, her joyful and triumphant news to-day. All who die shall rise again from the dead, because our Saviour, Jesus Christ, first of all rose from the dead, and promised that the change of a similar resurrection should come upon all mankind. And I say again that we know that to be true because the Catholic Church, the only divine voice there is in the world, assures us that it is true. Bitter as death may be, the hope of the resurrection is its complete antidote. Now I understand why the words, "a happy death," is so common a speech among Catholics. It implies an act of faith in the resurrection, and a confidence that he who dies has not only prepared himself to die but also to rise again. This is an important reflection to make on Easter Sunday, for there is a resurrection unto eternal life and a resurrection unto damnation, which, compared to eternal life, is eternal death. A philosopher said: "Happy is that man who, when he comes to die, has nothing left but to die." But the Christian says: "Happy is that man who, when he comes to die, leaves the world and all he has to do or might do in it, sure of a happy and glorious resurrection."

All Catholics believe that they will rise again from the dead, but I am free to say that many of them do not prove their faith by their works. They seem to think so much of this world, and give so much of their thoughts and words and actions to it, that certainly no heathen would imagine for a moment that they thought even death possible, or that there was any future state to get ready for. I wonder how any one of us would act or what we would be thinking about, if we were absolutely sure that in less than an hour's notice we would some day be called to be made a bishop or a pope, or a king or queen ; or would be carried off to a desert island, and left there to starve and die without help.

We do not believe either fortune likely to happen to any of us, therefore we do not prepare for it. Alas ! so many Catholics do not prepare for the sudden call to rise to a glory and dignity far higher than that of any prelate or prince, or to sink to a miserable state infinitely worse than to starve and die on a desert island ; and why not ? I say the heathen would answer, because they do not believe that either fortune will be likely to happen to them. If they did their lives would prove their faith.

Now, I know I have set some of you thinking, and that has just been my purpose. Have I a right to participate in the Easter joy of to day, or am I only making an outside show of it, while my conscience tells me I am a hypocrite ? Have I kept the commandments of God and of the church ? Have I **made my Easter duty, or resolved to make it?** What kind of a life would I rise to on the day of resurrection, if I died to-night? What would Jesus Christ, my Judge and Saviour, find in me that looked like him, and therefore ought to give me the same glorious resurrection as he had? Dear brethren, that is what he wants to find in us all. That is what he died to give us. That is what the Holy Spirit is striving hard to help every one of us to obtain. Come, a little more courage. and let us rise *now* from all that is deathly, or dead, or corrupt, or rotten in this life we are leading, and Jesus will be sure to find in us what will fashion us unto the likeness of his own resplendent and divine resurrection to eternal life.

SERMON LX.

Christ, our pasch, is sacrificed. Therefore let us feast, not with the old leaven, nor with the leaven of malice and wickedness, but with the unleavened bread of sincerity and truth.— 1 COR. v. 7, 8.

THERE are none of us, my dear brethren, I am sure, who can fail on this Easter morning to have something of the spirit of joy which fills the church at this time, and which runs through all her offices at this season. "This is the day that the Lord hath made," she is continually saying to us; "let us rejoice and be glad in it."

Yes, we are all glad now; we all have something of the Easter spirit, in spite of the troubles and sorrows which are perhaps weighing on us, and from which we shall never be quite free till we celebrate Easter in heaven—in that blessed country where death shall be no more, nor mourning, nor crying, nor sorrow shall be any more; where God shall dwell with us, and he himself with us shall be our God.

But what is the cause of our joy? Is it merely that the season of penance through which we have just passed is over, that the church no longer commands us to fast and mortify ourselves? That may, indeed, be one reason, for there are certainly not a great many people who enjoy fasting and abstinence; but there should be another and a much better one. It should be that Lent has not left us just where it found us; that we can say to-day not only that Christ has risen, but that we also have risen with him.

Yes, my brethren, that is the joy that you ought to be feeling at this time. What is Easter, or Christmas, or any other feast of the church worth without the grace of God? It is no more than any secular holiday; merely a time for amusement, for sensual indulgence, and too often an occasion of sin. If you are happy to-day with any happiness that is really worth having, it is then because you have the grace of God in your souls, either by constant habits of virtue, or by a good confession and communion which you have made to-day or lately. It is now, as at the last day, only to those who are really and truly the friends of Christ that he can say: "Well done, good and faithful servant: . . . enter thou into the joy of thy Lord." For this is the day, the great day of his joy; and it is only by being united with him that you can share in it.

This, then, is the desire which I have when I wish you to-day a happy Easter, as I do with my whole heart: that if you have not made your Easter duty, you will make it soon; and that if you have made it, you will persevere—that, having risen from the dead, you will die no more. It is the wish compared with which all others are as nothing; for the happiness of the world is but for a few short years, but the joy of the soul is meant to last for ever.

And if you would have it, there is one thing above all which you must do—which you must have done, if you have made a really good communion. Holy church reminds us of it in a prayer which is said to-day at Mass, and which is repeated frequently through the Easter season. This is to put away all that old leaven of malice and wickedness, that spirit of hatred and uncharitableness for your neighbor, which is so apt to rankle in your hearts. If you would be friends with God you must be friends with all his children. Let there be no one whom you will not speak to, whom you would avoid or pass by. When there has been a quarrel one of the two must make the first advances to reconciliation; try to have the merit of being that one, even though you think, probably wrongly, that you were not at all in fault. This day, when we meet to receive the blessing of our risen Saviour, is the day above all others for making friends. Unite, then, with your whole hearts in this prayer of the church which I am now about to read at the altar, first translating it for you: "Pour forth on us, O Lord! the spirit of thy charity, that by thy mercy thou mayest make those to agree together whom thou hast fed with thy paschal mysteries; through Christ our Lord. Amen."

Low Sunday.

EPISTLE. 1 *St. John v.* 4–10. Dearly beloved: Whatsoever is born of God overcometh the world; and this is the victory which overcometh the world, our faith. Who is he that overcometh the world, but he that believeth that Jesus is the Son of God? This is he that came by water and blood, Jesus Christ; not in water only, but in water and blood. And it is the spirit that testifieth, that Christ is the truth. For there are three that give testimony in heaven, the Father the Word, and the Holy Ghost. And these three are one. And there are three that give testimony on earth: the spirit, the water, and the blood, and these three are one. If we receive the testimony of men, the testimony of God is greater. For this is the testimony of God, which is greater, because he hath testified of his Son. He that believeth in the Son of God, hath the testimony of God in himself.

GOSPEL. *St. John xx.* 19–31. At that time: When it was late that same day, being the first day of the week, and the doors were shut, where the disciples were gathered together for fear of the Jews, Jesus came and stood in the midst, and said to them: Peace be to you. And when he had said this, he showed them his hands, and his side. The disciples therefore were glad when they saw the Lord. And he said to them again: Peace be to you. As the Father hath sent me, I also send you. When he had said this he breathed on them; and he said to them: Receive ye the Holy Ghost. Whose sins you shall forgive, they are forgiven them; and whose you shall retain, they are retained. Now Thomas, one of the twelve, who is called Didymus, was not with them when Jesus came. The other disciples therefore said to him: We have seen the Lord. But he said to them: Unless I shall see in his hands the print of the nails, and put my finger into the place of the nails, and put my hand into his side, I will not believe. And after eight days his disciples were again within, and Thomas with them. Jesus cometh, the doors being shut, and stood in the midst, and said: Peace be to you. Then he saith to Thomas: Put in thy finger hither, and see my hands; and bring hither thy hand, and put it into my side; and be not incredulous, but faithful. Thomas answered, and said to him: My Lord. and my God. Jesus saith to him: Because thou hast seen me, Thomas, thou hast believed; blessed are they that have not seen, and have believed. Many other signs also did Jesus in the sight of his disciples, which are not written in this book. But these are written that you may believe that Jesus is the Christ, the Son of God: and that believing you may have life in his name.

SERMON LXI.

Unless I shall see in his hands the print of the nails, and put my finger into the place of the nails, and put my hand into his side, I will not believe.—ST. JOHN xx. 25.

"IT is no vain question," says Father Matthias Faber, of the Society of Jesus, from whose writings this sermon is adapted—"it is no vain question whether we do not owe more to St. Thomas, who was slow in believing the fact of Christ's resurrection, than to the other apostles, who credited it instantly." Then he goes on to quote St. Gregory, who says that "the doubt of St. Thomas really removed *all* doubt, and placed the fact that our Lord had really risen with his human body beyond all dispute." So to-day, following the good Jesuit father, I am going to be St. Thomas. I shall hear from many of you something of this kind : "O father! I am so delighted : my wife or my husband, my son, my brother, my friend, has risen from the dead. He or she has been to confession, given up his bad habits, come again into our midst ; has been to Communion, has said, Peace be to you, has altogether reformed and become good." Ah! indeed. Is that so ? Of course it is quite possible; but towards those whose resurrection you announce to me I am St. Thomas this morning, and say to them : "Unless I shall see in their hands the print of the nails, and put my finger into the place of the nails, and put my hand into their side, I will not believe." In a word, I will not believe that any of you have risen from the dead, I will not believe that you have come out of the grave of mortal sin, unless I see in you the signs of a former crucifixion. First, I want to see the print of the nails. I want to see in your hands and feet—that is, in your inclinations and passions—the print of the nails that the priest drove in, in the confessional. I want to see that these hands strike no more, handle no more bad books, pass no more bad money, write no more evil letters, sign no more fraudulent documents, are stretched forth no more unto evil things, raised no more to curse. I want to see these hands lifted in prayer, stretched out to give alms, extended in mercy, busy in toiling for God and his church. I want to see these hands smoothing the pillows of the sick, giving drink to the thirsty, food to the hungry, and raiment to the naked. I want to see the print of the nails, or I will not believe. These feet, too—I must see them bearing you to the confessional regularly, taking you to Mass, carrying you to Benediction, bent under you in prayer. In a word, I must see in you the signs of a true conversion, or I will not believe that you have really risen from the death of sin. Then, like St. Thomas, I must "put my finger into the place of the nails." That is, when you are taken down from the cross, when, as it were, you have persevered for quite a while in God's service, I want at any time to be able to assure myself that the wound is really there. I want to be sure that those old charlatans, the world and the flesh, haven't been round and healed those wounds with their salve of roses, their pleasures of life, and their elixir of youth. I want to know for certain that you have, by God's grace, raised your body from the grave, having first nailed it to the cross, and to be sure that it is the same body. I want to put my finger into the scars of crucifixion. Lastly, I want to put my hand into your side to see if the heart is wounded. I want to see if there is true contrition there. I want to find out if the old designs, the old loves, the old plans are driven out; I want to find out if that heart has really upon it the scar of the spear of God. O brethren! to say, "I have risen with Christ," is an easy thing; for others to tell the priest that you are truly converted presents no difficulty; but I am St. Thomas, and I want to *see* the wounds. Then what a consolation for the priest if he can perceive plainly the print of the nails, put his hand into the place of the nails, and put his hand into the side! Then, like St. Thomas, he can cry: ' My Lord and my God." For in the truly crucified and converted sinner he can see clearly the work of the Almighty. Ah! then, brethren, strive to crucify your flesh every day; strive to know nothing but Jesus, and him crucified. Try to bear about in your bodies the "stigmata of the Lord Jesus," for they will be your best credentials on earth and your brightest glory in heaven. B.

SERMON LXII.

For this is the charity of God, that we keep his commandments.—1 St. John v. 3.

We have in these words the infallible test of a true Christian life. He alone truly loves God who keeps his commandments. I once heard of a man who used to get down on his knees every morning and recite the Ten Commandments as a part of his morning prayers. I believe that that man's religion was practical. He certainly had in his mind the right idea of what religion meant. We are apt to keep the commandments too much in the background. True, we have them and know them well enough, but they don't shine out in our lives as they should. Here is a man that prays, but don't pay his honest debts. Here is another that always goes to Mass, but has the habit of cursing. Another is honest and just with his neighbors, but, as everybody knows, gets drunk.

People sometimes talk about the difficulties of having faith; but this is not where the trouble lies. The real struggle and conflict of religion is to correct the morals of men. True religion insists upon the keeping of the commandments, and that is why it is so repugnant to men. Faith is easy to the virtuous; if men wished to be moral there would be no difficulties about faith. We sometimes hear people say: "Your religion is a perfect tyranny." Yes, if you choose to call the Ten Commandments tyranny. This is the only tyranny that I have ever found. I think, also, that every Catholic will testify that these Ten Commandments are what really make religion hard, and that if these could only be set aside men would never complain of its being hard. I never heard of a Catholic who was willing to keep the Ten Commandments who thought that anything else connected with his religion was hard. Here we have, then, in a nutshell, the whole secret of the opposition of men to the true religion; but, inconsistent as it may seem and really is, men, while they hate, have yet to admire what they hate. An apostate monk may set himself up as a reformer and talk about "justification by faith alone," but the world laughs at such nonsense. It trembles, though, when it hears our Lord say: "Every tree, therefore, that bringeth not forth good fruit shall be cut down and cast into the fire." "If any man loves me he will keep my commandments." This pretended reformer, Doctor Martin Luther, who called that wonderful Epistle of St. James, in which we are taught that "faith without good works is dead," "an epistle of straw," proved, however, to the world by his own life that it was this straw of being obliged to keep the commandments which broke his back, as it has broken the backs of so many others. But people do not have to leave the church to be thus broken, for we have in the bosom of the church, also, those who try to have piety without morality; but they are the hypocrites, the sham followers of Christ. They will some day, unless they speedily change their lives, hear our Lord saying to them: "I never knew you; depart from me, ye that work iniquity." Ah! may we not some of us have good reason to fear that we shall one day be judged as hypocrites? The bankrupt merchant is afraid to look at his books, and trembles at the thought of attempting to calculate his liabilities; so those false Christians dare not look at the law of God to examine their lives by it. But, to their shame and grief, the day of reckoning will come. The devil may whisper to such, "Soul, take thy ease," but, thank God! there is the voice of God's church, which will not allow us to delude ourselves.

If we Catholics go to hell it will be with our eyes wide open. The waves of passion can never drown that voice. It will always tell us of our sins, and will never let us be content in being hearers of the law, unless we are also doers. This is the way which is certainly pointed out to us; "and it shall be called the holy way."

SERMON LXIII.

Jesus came, and stood in the midst, and said to them, Peace be to you.—St. John xx. 26.

In spite of there being so much fighting in the world, I think, my brethren, that there are not many of us who really like it for its own sake, or who would not rather have peace. Of course we are not willing to sacrifice everything for it; we do not want peace at any price. We do not want the peace of slavery—that which comes from being beaten. We want an honorable one—that which comes from having had the best of our adversary in a just war.

There is another kind of peace besides these two. It is that which comes from being let alone. But **that is something which is not intended for us in this** world. Somebody will always be interfering with us; if nobody else does, the devil, at any rate, will be sure to do so. No, arrange it as we may, our life will always be full of annoyances and conflicts, both from without and from within.

And this kind of peace was not what our Lord wished and gave to his apostles on that glorious day when he arose from the dead. He knew very well that they, of all men in the world, were not going to be let alone. They were going to be put in the very front of the battle. Not only their neighbors but the whole world was going to rise up against them; and Satan, with his infernal host, was going to single them out as the special objects of his hatred and vengeance.

No, the peace which our Lord gave to his apostles was not this, but that which comes from victory. And that is the peace which he wishes us also to have.

Over whom, then, are we going to be victorious? In the first place, over the devil and all his temptations.

Many Christians, I am sorry to say, make the opposite kind of peace with the devil—that is, the peace of slavery; one which they would be ashamed to make with anybody else. Should they be tempted by him to impurity, drunkenness, hatred, or blasphemy, they give in and strike their colors at once. Being tempted and sinning are all the same thing to them. Well, they have peace in a certain way by this; that is, the devil, when he finds what miserable and cowardly soldiers of Christ they are, does not trouble himself much about them. He feels pretty sure of them; they are his prisoners of war, and it is for his interest to treat them well as long as they are in this world.

Yes, if you want to make peace with the devil you can surrender to him at once. But shame, I say, on such a peace as this! It is a base, contemptible, and cowardly one, and it will not last long. Satan only waits for this life to be over to satisfy all his malice and hatred on those he now seems to love.

But you may have, if you will, the peace and satisfaction of victory over him. Make up your mind to have it—to have it every time he tempts you. It is not so hard as you think; it is easy by the merits of our Lord's sacred Passion, which are at your command. He showed this to his apostles on that first Easter day, when he said to them: "Peace be to you." He showed them his hands and his side, bearing those glorious wounds, the marks and the pledge of victory.

And you can also have the peace of victory over all others who trouble you in this world, however unjust and strong they may be. How? Why, in the same way as our Lord and his apostles had it. Not by fighting with them, and giving back as good as you get—no, but by giving much better than you get; by doing them all the good you can. Evil is not to be conquered by evil, but by good. "Love your enemies; do good to them that hate you"; that is what the Eternal Wisdom has said; that is the way to have victory and peace, not only in the next world but also in this; and the sooner you believe it and act on it the happier will you be.

Second Sunday after Easter.

EPISTLE. 1 *St. Peter ii.* 21-25. Dearly beloved: Christ has suffered for us, leaving you an example that you should follow his steps. "Who did no sin, neither was guile found in his mouth." Who, when he was reviled, did not revile: when he suffered, he threatened not: but delivered himself to him that judged him unjustly. Who his own self bore our sins in his body upon the tree: that we, being dead to sins, should live to justice: by whose stripes you were healed. For you were as sheep going astray: but you are now converted to the pastor and bishop of your souls.

GOSPEL. *St John x.* 11-16. At that time: Jesus said to the Pharisees: I am the good shepherd. The good shepherd giveth his life for his sheep. But the hireling, and he that is not the shepherd, whose own sheep they are not, seeth the wolf coming and leaveth the sheep, and flieth; and the wolf snatcheth and scattereth the sheep: and the hireling flieth, because he is a hireling: and he hath no care for the sheep. I am the good shepherd: and I know mine, and mine know me. As the Father knoweth me, and I know the Father; and I lay down my life for my sheep. And other sheep I have, that are not of this fold: them also I must bring, and they shall hear my voice, and there shall be one fold and one shepherd.

SERMON LXIV.

I am the Good Shepherd.—St. John x. 11.

It is not requisite for me to prove to you, dear brethren, that our Lord was and is, in every sense, the "Good Shepherd," nor is it my intention to speak of him this morning in that character. I want to bring this fact before your minds—namely, that although the "great Shepherd and Bishop of our souls" has gone from us, yet he has left other authorized pastors to take charge of his flock. The Pope is a shepherd, the bishops are shepherds, and, to bring it down close to you, the priests of God's church are shepherds. You and your children are the sheep and the lambs of Christ's flock; we are your shepherds appointed by Jesus Christ to feed you, to watch over you, to keep you in the fold, to check you when you want to go astray. Now, then, every priest can say, "I am the good shepherd." And what does a good shepherd do? First, he tends his flock with care; and, secondly, he derives from it his means of support. Now, brethren, the priest's duty is to watch over and care for you; and that he does so you will not deny. He must hear your confessions, give you Holy Communion, come to you when you are ill, administer the sacraments to you, advise you, preach to you, instruct you, shield you from the wolves and seek you when you are lost, and often serve you at the risk of his own life. Now, the priest does all these things, not because he is paid, not because the people hire him and pay him a salary, but *simply* and *solely* because he is the good shepherd; because it is his mission, his office to do so; because he is placed over you by authority. Now, it follows from this that it is your duty to be fed, to be kept in the fold, to be checked when you are going wrong, to hear his voice and obey him. I am afraid some don't understand this. How is it we hear of milk-and-water Catholics going to be married before magistrates, or, what is worse, before ministers of a false religion? How is it that we find Catholics denying their faith and going to a Protestant place of worship for the sake of a little food and clothing? The priest has God's own authority; you are the sheep. The priest has you in charge. God does not come and ask you if you would like a shepherd; he places one over you, and that he may guide you, and not that you may guide him. I say this for the benefit of those who are always talking about their priests, always picking holes in the conduct of their pastors. Such people forget their position, forget their obligations, and make themselves appear very ignorant, much wanting in faith, and very impertinent. Again, the shepherd lives by his flock; so the priest must be supported by the people. A priest has a body as well as you have, and he can't live on air or on shavings. Then he wants to build and keep in repair God's temples. He wants money to build schools and support them; he wants money to feed and clothe the poor. He wants money because it is your *duty* to give it; for one of the laws of the church is, "To pay tithes to your pastors." Often, too, it is a great kindness for us to accept some of your worldly riches, which otherwise would, perhaps, prevent your entry into heaven. We can do with the riches what the shepherd does with his wool: make clothes for the naked and destitute, exchange what we get for building and decorating God's church, and a hundred other things of which you, the sheep, and your children, the lambs of Christ's flock, will get the heavenly merit and the everlasting profit. Oh! then, brethren, have faith, try always to cling to the priest as the good shepherd, so that at the last day we may call you all by name, and find that of the little flock of sheep and lambs not one is missing. B.

SERMON LXV.

Christ suffered for us, leaving you an example that you should follow his steps.—1 St. Peter ii. 21.

THE holy church is not going to let us forget the cross, my brethren, even in this joyous Easter season. There is a prayer, or Commemoration of the Cross, which she orders to be said in the divine Office even more frequently now than during the rest of the year; and here in the Epistle of to-day she warns us that we all must take up our cross as our Lord took his, if we would have a share in the triumph which we now celebrate.

"Christ," says St. Peter, "left us an example that we should follow in his steps." St. Peter had not forgotten those words which his Master after his resurrection spoke to him on the shore of the Sea of Galilee: "Do thou follow me." He tried to do it; and he did follow his Lord in a life of toil and suffering, ended by a painful death on the cross like to that which his Saviour had borne. He followed the example which had been set him; he believed what he says in this Epistle of his, and acted on it. How is it with us?

Many Christians seem to imagine that our Lord, by his resurrection, took away, or ought to have taken away, all trouble from the earth. They cannot understand how it is that in this redeemed world, whose sins his Blood has expiated, the cross still keeps coming down on them at every turn. They honor the cross, and are grateful for the redemption which it has brought them; but even when they kiss it on Good Friday they do not understand that they have got to take it, embrace it, and bear it themselves.

And yet that is the fact. The cross is to free us from eternal suffering, but not from that which passes away. Our Lord did not suffer in order that we might have no suffering at all, but that we might be able to bear our sufferings better, and to bear greater ones than we could otherwise have borne. He might have redeemed us without suffering as he did; but one of the reasons why he did not choose to was that we, the guilty, to whom the cross belongs, may bear it cheerfully when we see Him who was innocent taking it on his shoulders.

But why did not our Lord suffer enough to free us from suffering at all? I think there are not many who are ungenerous enough to ask such a question plainly, though it seems to be in a great many people's minds. Well, I will tell you why he left us a share of his cup. It was for the same reason that he took his own share: it was because he loved us, and chose what was for our best good. And he knew it was better for us to be saved through our own sufferings as far as possible. They could not be enough of themselves; so he did what was enough, and then enough more to bring down our own share to just what we could make the best use of with his grace and by his example.

That is the reason, then, why the cross is left in the world. Try to see it and acknowledge it yourselves; that is better than to have the cross meeting you as a strange and unaccountable thing. For it will meet you at Easter as well as at other times of the year; even when you are happiest there will always be some cloud in your sky. There will never be any real and true Easter for you till you shall, like your Redeemer, have exchanged this temporal life for that which is eternal. But do not be too much in a hurry for that time. He knows best how much suffering is good for you. Count it a joy and an honor that he has thought you worthy to follow in his steps, and thank him for the example which he has given you to help him to do so, as well as for his merits which he has also given you that your following might not be in vain.

SERMON LXVI.

And other sheep I have that are not of this fold; them also I must bring, and they shall hear my voice, and there shall be one fold and one shepherd.—St. John x. 16.

IF we only knew how much our Lord loves those "other sheep" who are not in the one true fold, we should think and act differently from what we do towards them. As we look upon the sacred image of our Divine Lord upon the cross, we behold his arms and hands stretched to their utmost extent to embrace the whole world.

He is the second Adam, who came to undo the work of the first Adam; and as the terrible consequences of the first transgression have extended to *all* men without exception, so, also, to repair this evil which has come upon all men it was necessary that the grace of salvation should be offered to *all* without exception. And from this we may infer that God does not simply will that men should be saved, but that he actually gives to every man that is born sufficient grace to accomplish this great work. But are those who stay outside of the one fold in the way to use this sufficient grace? Certainly they are not, or our Lord never would have said: "Them also I must bring, and they shall hear my voice, and there shall be one fold and one shepherd." No one, therefore, can be said to be in the way of salvation who stays outside of the one true fold of the Catholic Church. We cannot, of course, know what extraordinary means of grace God may use for those who are ignorant of the church, yet we do know with perfect certainty that the Catholic Church, with its doctrine, sacraments, and other means of grace, is the only divinely-established means of salvation for all men.

Knowing, then, that our Divine Lord, inasmuch as he died for all men, wills to bring all men into the one true fold, where they may be under one shepherd, we must feel it to be our duty, if we have the love of Christ in our hearts, by our prayers, words, and good example to bring the "other sheep" of whom our Lord speaks so lovingly to the knowledge of this one fold. It is only a coldness of faith and charity which can make us look upon those who are outside of the church as if they were already where they ought to be, and where God wishes them to be, or make us think that it is a hopeless task to try to bring them into the true church. Our Lord has promised that they shall hear his voice. We know, then, that he will co-operate by his all-powerful grace with what we do for their salvation.

Our first duty is that of prayer for these "other sheep." Every prayer that we offer up for the conversion of infidels and heretics will be heard, and will bring down upon them additional grace. Prayer opened the hearts of the Irish people, when they were in the darkness of paganism, to receive the true faith from St. Patrick. In our own day, also, prayer has brought thousands of Protestants and infidels into the true church. Father Ignatius Spencer, of the Order of Passionists, was raised up by God to spread among the Catholics of Ireland and England the devotion of prayers for England, and we behold the results of these prayers in the great "Oxford movement," which brought so many into the church and has opened the way for so many more conversions. Can we ever by our words bring others into the church? Yes. An explanation of some point of Catholic doctrine, an invitation to come and hear a sermon, the lending of a Catholic book, may be the means which God has chosen for the conversion of our Protestant neighbor. "Who knows," said St. Alphonsus Liguori, "what God requires of me? Perhaps the predestination of certain souls may be attached to some of my prayers, penances, and good works."

But, above all, by our good example we should lead others into the "one fold." "Actions speak louder than words," but woe to us if our actions belie the truth of our faith! What shall we answer if accused before the tribunal of God by souls who would have known and have been saved by the truth but for our bad example? We must never forget, dear brethren, our duty towards those "other sheep" for whom our Lord died just as much as he did for us.

Third Sunday after Easter.

FEAST OF THE PATRONAGE OF ST. JOSEPH.

EPISTLE. 1 *St. Peter ii.* 11-19. Dearly beloved, I beseech you as strangers and pilgrims to refrain yourselves from carnal desires, which war against the soul; having your conversation good among the Gentiles; that whereas they speak against you as evildoers, considering you by your good works they may glorify God in the day of visitation. Be ye subject therefore to every human creature for God's sake; whether it be to the king as excelling, or to governors as sent by him for the punishment of evildoers and for the praise of the good; for so is the will of God, that by doing well you may silence the ignorance of foolish men: as free, and not as making liberty a cloak of malice, but as the servants of God. Honor all men; love the brotherhood; fear God; honor the king. Servants, be subject to your masters with all fear, not only to the good and gentle, but also to the froward. For this is thankworthy, in Christ Jesus our Lord.

EPISTLE OF THE FEAST. *Gen. xlix.* 22-26. Joseph is a growing son, a growing son and comely to behold; the daughters run to and fro upon the wall. But they that held darts provoked him, and quarrelled with him, and envied him. His bow rested upon the strong, and the bands of his arms and his hands were loosed by the hands of the mighty one of Jacob: thence he came forth a pastor, the stone of Israel. The God of thy Father shall be thy helper, and the

Almighty shall bless thee with the blessings of Heaven above, with the blessings of the deep that lieth beneath, with the blessings of the breasts and of the womb. The blessings of thy father are strengthened with the blessings of his fathers: until the desire of the everlasting hills should come; may they be upon the head of Joseph, and upon the crown of the Nazarite among his brethren.

GOSPEL. *St. John xvi.* 16–22. At that time: Jesus said to his disciples: A little while, and now you shall not see me: and again a little while, and you shall see me: because I go to the Father. Then some of his disciples said one to another: What is this that he saith to us: A little while, and you shall not see me: and again a little while, and you shall see me, and because I go to the Father? They said therefore: What is this that he saith, a little while? we know not what he speaketh. And Jesus knew that they were desirous to ask him; and he said to them: Of this do you inquire among yourselves, because I said: A little while, and you shall not see me: and again a little while, and you shall see me? Amen, amen I say to you, that you shall lament and weep, but the world shall rejoice: and you shall be sorrowful, but your sorrow shall be turned into joy. A woman, when she is in labor, hath sorrow, because her hour is come: but when she hath brought forth the child, she remembereth no more the anguish, for joy that a man is born into the world. So also you now indeed have sorrow, but I will see you again, and your heart shall rejoice; and your joy no man shall take from you.

GOSPEL OF THE FEAST. *St. Luke iii.* 21–23. At that time it came to pass, when all the people were baptized, that Jesus also being baptized and praying, heaven was opened: and the Holy Ghost descended in a bodily shape as a dove upon him: and a voice came from heaven: Thou art my beloved Son, in thee I am well pleased. And Jesus himself was beginning about the age of thirty years: being (as it was supposed) the son of Joseph.

SERMON LXVII.

Our Holy Father, Pope Pius IX., as you know, dear brethren, has made his reign glorious by defining the dogma of the Immaculate Conception; thus placing in our dear Lady's diadem the brightest gem that adorns it. He has further rendered his pontificate glorious by declaring the chaste spouse of Mary Immaculate, St. Joseph, to be the patron of the universal church. When we celebrated the feast of St. Joseph, on the 19th of last month, his statue was veiled by the hangings of Passion-tide; but to-day his image is exposed to our gaze, and I have thought that this discourse cannot be better occupied than by considering how fitting it is that good St. Joseph should be the patron of the universal church, and how great a devotion we should have towards him.

St. Joseph is a fitting patron for the rich and for those whom God has placed in the high positions and stations of this world; for let us never forget that St. Joseph, although poor, was, by lineal descent, of the royal house of David. He was of high birth, of noble blood, and yet how humble, how willing to work for his living when it became necessary!

So, then, here is a lesson for those who hold their heads high in the world. Some day, dear friends, you may come down, you may be brought low. You may lose your money, lose position, lose your place in society. Take example, then, from St. Joseph. Do not say like the unjust steward: "To dig I am unable, and to beg I am ashamed"; but remember that the fairest hands that ever were, and the noblest blood that ever flowed, are never disgraced by honest labor or necessary toil.

St. Joseph is a fitting patron also for the poor. He had to work hard. He had, for the safety of the Divine Child and his Immaculate Spouse, to take long and weary journeys. He had the pain of seeing Jesus and Mary turned from the doors of Bethlehem, while those who had money were safely and comfortably lodged. Yet he never complained, never murmured. He worked, and bore all the inconveniences of poverty without a word. Is it so with you who are poor? Don't you sometimes envy the rich, get discontented with your position, feel rebellious against the will of God? If so, I point you to St. Joseph. He is your model. He is your example; strive to imitate him in all things. Are you humiliated? Bear it for Christ's sake. Are you punished by cold and hunger? Bear it for Christ's sake. Are you weary after your day's labor? Bear it, bear it all for Christ's sake, as good St. Joseph did.

St. Joseph, too, is a model for the married. He cared tenderly for the Virgin Mother and her Divine Child. He loved them, he guarded them. He is a model for the unmarried in his purity of life. He is a model for the priest, a model for the people, a model for the young, an example for the old. Oh! then how wisely our Holy Father acted in making him patron of the universal church. But not only is St. Joseph patron of the living, but also of the dying and the dead—of the dying, because *he* died in the arms of Jesus and Mary. Beautiful death! The Son of God at his side, the Mother of God to support his dying form! O brethren! we who are here to-day *living* will one day be *dying*. Let us, then, pray St. Joseph that he will obtain for us the grace of a happy death—the grace to die, as he died, in the arms of Jesus and Mary. Then, no matter if flames devour us, or waters overwhelm us, or disease slays us, we shall be safe—safe, for the Son of God will hold us by the hand; safe, for the Mother of God will throw around an all-protecting mantle of defence.

And, lastly, St. Joseph is the patron of those who are dead and in purgatory. He waited long in limbo before he entered into the joy of heaven. Separated from all he loved on earth, and seeing the pearly gates of heaven, not yet opened by the bloodshed of Calvary, shut against him, oh! how great must his longing have been. Ah! then I am sure St. Joseph feels for and loves the holy souls in purgatory, who, like himself, have lost earth and not yet gained heaven.

Let us all, then, hasten to St. Joseph to-day. Let us pray for ourselves and others. Let us pray for the living and pray for the dead. Let us say: "O great patron of the whole church! look down from the loftiness of thy mountain to the lowliness of our valley; obtain for us to live like thee, to die like thee, and to reign *with* thee in everlasting bliss." B.

SERMON LXVIII.

On this Sunday, my dear brethren, the church celebrates every year the feast of the Patronage of St. Joseph. You have often heard it read out from the altar, you heard it just now; and yet I am afraid most of you might as well not have heard it, for all the impression it made on you. If you thought anything about the notice you probably thought that it was only something to interest the pious people, to let them know when to say their prayers and go to Communion.

If you did you made a great mistake. St. Joseph is not a saint for pious people only, but for every Christian. That is true of all the saints, but specially so of St. Joseph. All the saints take an interest in all of us, however weak and imperfect, or even sinful, we may be; they all love us and care for us far more than our friends in this world. Still, they have perhaps a particular care for some, as we have, or should have, a particular devotion to some of them as our patrons.

But St. Joseph is everybody's patron. That is what holy church means by inviting us all to celebrate this feast of his Patronage, and by giving him the title, as she did only a few years ago, of patron of the universal church. He is the patron of the church in general and of each member of it in particular.

What is a patron? The word has rather gone out of common use. Well, it is a friend at court. A patron is one who has got influence and power to use for our advantage. If we want anything he is the one to get it for us. He is the man that you go to if you want to get an office or employment of any kind from the powers that be; and generally you will find it pretty hard to get a place, if you have not such a friend to go to.

Well, St. Joseph is such a friend for all of us in the court of heaven, and that is the one where we all want to have an interest ; for there is where all matters are really arranged, whether regarding heaven or earth. If you want anything whatever St. Joseph is the one to go to, whether it be the most important thing of all—that is, the grace of final perseverance and salvation—or merely to pay your debts or save you from want. He will get you either one, though I do not know that he will get you the dollar, if you do not want the grace also.

But you will say, perhaps : "I do not need St. Joseph's help so much, for I have Our Blessed Lady to go to ; is not she more powerful even than he is ?" Well, I do not deny that, of course, nor that she is the best of all patrons. Neither does the church ; for she celebrates, as you know, the feast of Our Lady's Patronage also. But I would not give much for your devotion to her, neither would she herself, unless you include St. Joseph in it. You might as well try to separate her from her Divine Son as St. Joseph from her.

Besides, you know the saints have what I may call their specialties. It is not, for instance, a superstition to ask the help of St. Anthony of Padua to find for us what we have lost. St. Joseph has several specialties ; and one of them, and one which I know you will think quite important, is the help which he will give to us in temporal necessities when we are hard pressed for money, or things seem in any way to be going very much against us. Let me, then, suggest to you a very practical form of devotion to him. When anything goes wrong, instead of worrying about it and making it keep you from prayer, or even, perhaps, from Holy Mass, go to St. Joseph about it ; ask him to get you what you want or to relieve your from your trouble. He will do it for you, unless it be bad for your soul.

Perhaps you think this is all fancy. Well, all I say is, just try, and you will see whether it is or not. You will find plenty of people who will tell you that what I say is true. But ask St. Joseph to help your soul, too, for he does not want to have you neglect that. See if you cannot make the patronage of St. Joseph, both temporally and spiritually, more of a reality to yourselves before another year has gone by.

SERMON LXIX.

Be ye subject therefore to every human creature for God's sake.—1 St. Peter ii. 13.

IF we stop to consider these words of the Epistle, my dear brethren, they must certainly have a strange sound to us in this age of the world, and especially in this country, which makes liberty its great boast. Many of us, I am afraid, in spite of their reverence for St. Peter, who gives this instruction, would be tempted to say that this doctrine of his is a very curious one. "Be subject to every human creature." indeed! Why, on the contrary, in this free and enlightend republic, we do not acknowledge subjection to any one; we hold that every man is equal; we are all sovereigns and make laws ourselves—not subjects, obedient to laws made by others. We observe the laws of the land, it is true, but that is because they are arrangements made by the majority for the good of the nation, state, or city, and because we must have some sort of law if we are to have any kind of order.

Well, this creed, which some of you, perhaps, have adopted, may sound well enough in itself, but unfortunately it does not seem to agree very well with St. Peter's inspired and infallible teaching. We must, if we are Catholics, acknowledge that instead of claiming that no one has a right to control us, we ought, as he says, to "be subject to every human creature." The only thing, then, is to find out just what he means by this.

Does St. Peter mean, then, that we must be willing to obey every human creature, every man, woman, or child that undertakes to command us? Yes, there is no doubt that such is his doctrine. We must be *willing* to obey every one; we must have a spirit of subjection and humility, not of superiority and pride. We must not think that we are too good or too wise to be commanded by any one, however bad or however foolish he may seem to be. We must have a desire to obey, not to command.

But does St. Peter mean that we actually must always obey every one, man, woman, or child, who chooses to command us? No, of course he does not mean that. We shall see what he does mean by bringing in the rest of the text.

"Be ye subject," he says, "to every human creature *for God's sake.*" That is, be subject, as a matter of counsel, to every human creature, whenever we can suppose that creature to be speaking in the name of God; and as a matter of precept whenever we are sure that such is the case.

The first is a counsel, as I said, to be followed by those who would be perfect; to mortify our own will and submit to the direction of others when it is not evidently wrong or foolish. But the second is a strict duty to be practised if we would be saved: to submit to the commands of those who certainly do speak in God's name, when their commands are not plainly wrong. And who are those who speak in God's name? First, they are those whom he has appointed to rule his church—your Holy Father the Pope, the bishops, and your pastors. Remember, when they speak to you they speak in the name of God; do not murmur against them, but obey cheerfully for his sake, whether their commands come to you directly or through others whom they appoint to duties connected with the church.

Secondly, they are those whom he has appointed to rule the state or nation. No state or nation can be governed except in the name of God. That is what St. Paul says distinctly: "The powers that are," he says—and he was speaking of the heathen emperors—"are ordained of God. Therefore he that resisteth the power resisteth the ordinance of God. And they that resist purchase to themselves damnation." Be submissive, then, to the authorities and officers of every degree and kind in the nation, state, or city, when you meet them in the discharge of their duty. Though you may have chosen them yourselves, when they have been chosen they speak to you in God's name.

Lastly, those who rule in the family do so in the name of God. Children should remember that when they disobey their parents it is God's commands they are disobeying, and that disobedience in any grave matter is a mortal sin. And servants—for such really are those who live out in families—should also bear in mind their duty of obedience for God's sake and as to God. "Servants," says St. Peter in this Epistle, "be subject to your masters with all fear."

Yes, we should all fear to disobey lawful authority, because God has established it, not we ourselves. And we should also understand that only in obedience for God's sake is true liberty to be found.

Fourth Sunday after Easter.

Epistle. *St. James i.* 17–21. Dearly beloved : Every best gift, and every perfect gift, is from above, coming down from the Father of lights, with whom there is no change nor shadow of vicissitude. For of his own will hath he begotten us by the word of truth, that we might be some beginning of his creatures. You know, my dearest brethren, and let every man be swift to hear, but slow to speak, and slow to anger. For the anger of man worketh not the justice of God. Wherefore casting away all uncleanness, and abundance of malice, with meekness receive the engrafted word, which is able to save your souls.

Gospel. *St. John xvi.* 5–14. At that time : Jesus said to his disciples : I go to him that sent me, and none of you asketh me : Whither goest thou ? But because I have spoken these things to you, sorrow hath filled your heart. But I tell you the truth : it is expedient to you that I go : for if I go not, the Paraclete will not come to you; but if I go, I will send him to you. And when he shall come, he will convince the world of sin, and of justice, and of judgment. Of sin indeed : because they have not believed in me. And of justice : because I go to the Father ; and you shall see me no longer. And of judgment : because the prince of this world is already judged. I have yet many things to say to you : but you cannot bear them now. But when he, the Spirit of truth, shall come, he will teach you all truth. For he shall not speak of himself : but what things soever he shall hear, he shall speak, and the things that are to come he shall show you. He shall glorify me : because he shall receive of mine, and will declare it to you.

SERMON LXX.

I tell you the truth : it is expedient for you that I go. . . . But I will see you again, and your heart shall rejoice ; and your joy no man shall take from you.—St. John xvi. 7, 22.

WE all know, dear brethren, what place our Lord was speaking about and to which he was soon to go. He was soon to leave his disciples and go to heaven. To that place we all hope to go also, that we may see him there, where, as he promises further on in the same discourse, our hearts shall rejoice, and where our joy no man shall take from us.

Now, there are three joys, it seems to me, which go to make up the happiness of heaven. First, we shall be consoled ; second, we shall be satisfied ; and, last and best of all, we shall see God.

We shall be consoled for all the evils we have suffered in this world. Oftentimes we have to fight pretty hard against the world, the flesh, and the devil, and we have received, perhaps, many a grievous wound in mind and heart. Then, again, we have endured much sickness, experienced many a bitter pang, undergone many a heavy trial. Once we are in heaven we shall be consoled for all these things there ; our wounds will be healed, our sins forgiven, our hearts comforted. There we shall see the fruits of our penance, there we shall be solaced for all we have borne. He who leads his flock like a shepherd and carries the lambs in his bosom will come to us ; he will fold us in his holy arms, and for evermore we shall be at peace.

Again, we shall be satisfied. Here we love certain places and their surroundings ; we love creatures ; we love all that is beautiful. But we are not satisfied, for all these things either leave us or we are forced to leave them. Now, in heaven exists all the beauty and loveliness of earth, only in a degree infinitely higher and fairer. There we shall have all things we can desire, and possess them without fear of change or loss. There we feel all the sweetness of prayer, all the delights of sensible devotion, all that the saints on earth felt when rapt in ecstasy, and more. Here there is always something to disappoint us, something that makes us restless and uncomfortable. There everything will exceed our highest hopes, our best desires—in a word, in heaven, and in heaven alone, we shall be perfectly satisfied.

Then, lastly, O joy of joys! we shall see God. We shall see him face to face. We shall see the beauty of God. We shall behold his wisdom and his everlasting glory. Yes, brethren, these poor eyes, that have shed so many tears, they shall see God. The poor eyes so weary from watch and vigil, so tired of looking up into heaven after Jesus and Mary, so sick of looking around on earth, so terrified from looking down into hell—these eyes shall see God. We shall gaze on all the blessed. We shall see Jesus, and Mary, and Joseph. Our eyes will look upon the golden pavement of the celestial streets, the gates of pearl, and the walls of amethyst. We shall see all the brightness and glory of heaven, for we shall see God.

Brethren, these joys are waiting for you. Every baptized member of Christ's mystical body has a right to a home in that land of peace! Ah! then be careful, I pray you, not to lose the way. See where the Standard-bearer leads! See the cross that he bears. Oh! you all want to go to heaven, I am sure you do. There is only one thing that can keep you out, and that is mortal sin. Stain your soul with mortal sin by grievous violation of any one of the commandments, and that is enough, should you die impenitent, to keep you for ever from being consoled, from enjoying eternal happiness, from seeing God. Ah! then, brethren, walk in the narrow road. Be faithful and loving children of the church, and then one day you will leave this poor, weary, sinful world and go to dwell for ever within the walls of the City of Peace. B.

SERMON LXXI.

Let every man be swift to hear, but slow to speak.—St. James i. 19.

I THINK that every one of you, my dear friends, will agree with me that this would be a much happier world than it is if this recommendation of St. James, in the Epistle of to-day, were carried out. For it is quite plain, I think, to every one of you that other people talk too much. If they would only say less, and listen more to what you have to say, things would go on much better. If they would only be swift to hear, but slow to speak, the world would get much more benefit from your wisdom and experience than is now the case.

But, unfortunately, this general conviction, in which, I think, we all share more or less, does not tend to produce the desired result, but rather the contrary; for it makes everybody more anxious to speak and to be listened to, and more unwilling to listen themselves. We all want everybody except ourselves to keep St. James's rule, but do not set them a good example. So our example does harm, while our conviction does no good; and things are worse than if we did not agree with St. James at all.

Now, would it not be a good idea if each one would try, if it were only for the sake of good example, to be less willing to talk and more willing to listen? And perhaps, after all, even we ourselves do sometimes say a word or two which is hardly worth saying, or perhaps a great deal better unsaid.

A story is told of a crazy man who, in some very lucid interval, asked a friend if he could tell the difference between himself and the people who were considered to be of sound mind. His friend, curious to see what he would say, said: "No; what is it?" "Well," said the crazy man, "it is that I say all that comes into my head, while you other people keep most of it to yourselves."

My friends, I am afraid the crazy man was about right, but he was too complimentary in his judgment of others. By his rule there would be a great many people in the asylum who are now at large. Really, it seems as if it never occurred to some persons who are supposed to be in their right minds whether their thoughts had better be given to the world or not. Out they must come, no matter whether wise or foolish, good or bad.

Yes, the madman, for once in his life, was pretty nearly right. One who talks without consideration, who says everything that comes into his or her head, is about as much a lunatic as those who are commonly called so; for such will have one day to give an account for all their foolish and inconsiderate words, long after they themselves have forgotten them. And to carelessly run up this account is a very crazy thing.

A little instrument has lately been invented, as you no doubt have heard, which will take down everything you say; it is called the phonograph. It makes little marks on a sheet of tinfoil, and by means of these it will repeat for you all you have said, though it may have quite passed out of your own mind. There are a great many uses to which this little instrument may be put; but I think that one of the best would be to make people more careful of what they say. They would think before they spoke, if a phonograph was around. Few people would like to have a record kept of their talk, all ready to be turned off at a moment's notice. It would sound rather silly, if no worse, when it was a day or two old.

Perhaps the phonograph will never be used in this way; but there is a record of all your words on something more durable than a sheet of tinfoil. This record is in the book from which you will be judged at the last day. Our Lord has told us that at that day we shall have not only to hear but to give an account for all the idle words spoken in our lives.

Should not, then, this thought restrain our tongues, and make us rather be swift to hear than to speak? —more especially as it is generally only by hearing that one can learn to speak well.

But what should you be swift to hear? Not the foolish or sinful talk of others no more careful than yourselves. Be willing, indeed, to listen to all with humility, believing them to be wiser or better than you are; but seek the company and conversation of those whom you know to be so. Nothing better can come out of your heads than what is put into them. **You** will be like those with whom you converse.

And therefore, above all, seek silence, that in it you may converse with Almighty God, and hear what he has to say to you. He is the one above all others whom you should be swift to hear. When you get in the way of listening to him you will be slow enough to speak. There is nothing so sure to prevent idle words as the habit of conversation with God.

SERMON LXXII.

Let every man be . . . slow to anger. For the anger of man worketh not the justice of God.—St. James i. 19, 20.

WHAT is the reason, my brethren, that people sin by anger so much? There is no temptation, it seems to me, that is more often given way to. Other ones, though frequently consented to, are also frequently resisted, even by those most subject to them; but with this it seems as if we were like gunpowder: touch the match to us, and off we go; if any one does us an injury or says an insulting word, we flare up at once and give back all we got, and more.

Afterward, perhaps, we are sorry; but that seems to do no good. Next time it is just the same. And so it goes on, till perhaps we begin to think that we really are like gunpowder; that God made us so that we cannot help going off when the match of provocation is applied.

But that is not true. It will never do to make God the cause of our sins. It is our own fault. But what is the fault? What is the matter that this temptation is not resisted like others?

I will tell you what I think the matter is. It is that the temptation to anger does not seem to be a temptation at the time. The angry word seems to you all right when you utter it. It is not so with other things—sins of impurity, for instance. You know they are wrong, and that you ought to resist them, even when they are on you; and sometimes you make up your mind to do so. But it is not so in this sin of anger.

And why does it not seem to be a temptation? Why do you think it no sin to say the angry word, to flare up when you are provoked? It is because your mind is confused at the time, so that you cannot tell what is sin and what is not.

That is the truth, if I am not mistaken. It is just the peculiar danger of this temptation that it disturbs and confuses the mind more than any other one. You cannot tell what really is right when you are under it; it is not safe to do anything at all. You are for the time like one who is drunk or crazy.

When a man has drank too much, if he have any sense left he will keep out of the way of other people until he is sobered. For he knows he is not fit to do or say anything when he is intoxicated, and that he will only make a fool of himself if he tries.

That is common sense and prudence; and many men, even when drunk, have enough common sense and prudence left to follow this course. But very few have when under the passing drunkenness of anger. Most angry people do not know enough to hold their tongues. They ought to. They ought to have learned by experience. Well, then, this being the matter, the fault of angry people is plain enough. It is this: that they do not try to guard themselves against this temptation in the only way they can— **that is, by remembering and acting on these words** of St. James which I read to you from the Epistle of to-day: "The anger of man worketh not the justice of God." It always works injustice; that is, it always makes a mistake and does what is wrong. It has not sense enough to do what is right.

The only way to avoid the sin, then, is the one that St. James gives. Be slow to anger. Don't trust it, however sure you may be that it advises you rightly. It is a fool; don't listen to it. Wait till you get cool, till reason can have fair play.

I say this is the only way you can avoid this sin. I mean that nothing else will cure you of it unless you do this. Confession and Communion, prayer, penance, and other things, will help you; but this is indispensable. You know when you are under the influence of anger well enough. When you are, hold your tongue and hold your hand. You may have to do or say something afterwards, but very seldom there and then. God will not be likely to give you grace that is not needed; and you will not have the grace to do what is right when your duty is to do nothing, and wait till the temptation passes by. Remember that you are a fool when you are angry, if you do not want to act like one and be sorry for it afterwards.

Fifth Sunday after Easter.

EPISTLE. *St. James i. 22-27.* Dearly beloved: Be ye doers of the word, and not hearers only, deceiving your own selves. For if a man be a hearer of the word, and not a doer, he shall be compared to a man beholding his natural countenance in a glass. For he beheld himself, and went his way, and presently forgot what manner of man he was. But he that hath looked into the perfect law of liberty, and hath continued in it, not becoming a forgetful hearer, but a doer of the work : this man shall be blessed in his deed. And if any man think himself to be religious, not bridling his tongue, but deceiving his own heart, this man's religion is vain. Religion pure and unspotted with God and the Father, is this : to visit the fatherless and widows in their tribulation; and to keep one's self undefiled from this world.

GOSPEL. *St. John xvi. 23-30.* At that time : Jesus said to his disciples : Amen, amen I say to you, if you ask the Father anything in my name, he will give it you. Hitherto you have not asked anything in my name. Ask, and you shall receive: that your joy may be full. These things have I spoken to you in proverbs. The hour cometh when I will no more speak to you in proverbs, but will show you plainly of the Father. In that day you shall ask in my name : and I say not to you, that I will ask the Father for you. For the Father himself loveth you, because you have loved me, and have believed that I came forth from God. I came forth from the Father, and am come into the world ; again I leave the world, and I go to the Father. His disciples say to him : Behold now thou speakest plainly, and speakest no proverb. Now we know that thou knowest all things, and that for thee it is not needful that any man ask thee. In this we believe that thou camest forth from God.

SERMON LXXIII.

Amen, amen I say to you, if you ask the Father anything in my name, he will give it you.—St. John xvi. 23.

WHAT a wonderful promise this is—that everything we ask of Almighty God, who is the Father of mercies, shall be granted to us, if we ask it in the name of his only-begotten Son, our Lord and Saviour Jesus Christ! Does our Lord really mean all he says? Do people get all they pray for? Does it not seem to us sometimes that we pray in vain—that God seems to shut his ears against our cry, and has no regard to our tears and supplications? Yes, it does often *seem* so, but it is not really so. God's ways are not always our ways to reach the end we desire. And our own experience will tell us that it is very seldom it would be the best for us if God took us at our word. The real reason why we do not obtain the answer we wish to many of our prayers is, first, because we do not ask, as we ought, in the name of Jesus Christ. What is it to ask in his name? It is to ask in the name of Him who came on earth, not to do his own will, but the will of his Divine Father. Oh! how seldom we pray for favors and blessings according to the will of God. Our blessed Lord, on the night before he was crucified, foreseeing his death, and bowed to the earth in his agony, ended his prayer with the words. "Not as I will, but as thou wilt." That is not our way. When we are in sorrow and trouble we think

God should will as we will, and we are disappointed and discouraged because we do not get well of our sickness, or that calamity we feared comes, or poverty sticks to us, or the conversion of those we pray for is denied, or we do not obtain the employment we seek, or we have to give up hope of getting that farm we set our heart upon. Who is the judge, after all, about granting prayers? Who else but God, who not only has the power to grant or refuse them, as he chooses, but also has the perfect knowledge whether it would be best for us to receive a favorable answer or not? He who prays in the name of Jesus, prays with implicit trust in God's goodness and wisdom, and if he has not mistaken his own will for the will of God, will feel and should feel just as contented, no matter which way God answers his prayer.

The second reason why we do not always get what we pray for is because we are constantly asking for things which we dare not presume to ask in the name of Jesus Christ. We know in our heart of hearts that it is a petition he would not offer to his Divine Father for us. If we had to write that petition down we would neither begin nor end it with the words, "In the name of Jesus." It is our pride that is praying, our worldly ambition, our lusts and our selfish desires. We do not put the name of Jesus to our prayer, because the spirit of Jesus is not in it. Charity is wanting. We want to be happy, even if others are suffering. We want money, even if our brethren starve. We desire high places and the success of our undertakings, even if our neighbor and his interests go to the wall. Alas! it is self that prays the loudest and the oftenest and makes the greatest show.

Now, dear brethren, let us learn to bring all our prayers up to the right standard. No matter what we ask for, let it be always according to the will of God, and that alone. Then our prayer will surely be granted, for the will of God, no longer opposed and hindered by our will, accomplishes just what is best for us. If we do not get just what *we* think best, it is because God, in his divine generosity, chooses to give us something better, or takes a wiser way to do it than we knew of.

If I were to advise you how to always pray in the name of Jesus, I would say, Add always these words to every prayer you make: "So may God grant it, if my salvation be in it." God grants no prayer that does not have that end in view. His divine love for us constantly regards that, even if we forget it. Pray, then, with confidence and perseverance, but have a care to pray always with and for the will of God. Then in heaven we shall see, if not here, how not a single true prayer we ever made was left unanswered.

SERMON LXXIV.

Amen, amen I say to you, if you ask the Father anything in my name, he will give it you.—St. John xvi. 23.

These are the words of Christ, taken from the Gospel of to-day; we cannot doubt them for a moment. They are the words of him who is the infallible Truth, who can neither deceive nor be deceived.

And yet how seldom do we act as if we really believed them! How seldom do you, my brethren, ask anything of the Father in the name of Christ with real confidence that you will receive what you ask for

Many people say prayers, but few really pray. That is, many say over certain forms of prayer which they know by heart or read out of their prayer-books; many even feel bound to say some particular set of prayers every day, for the scapular which they wear, or for some other reason; but if you should ask them what they are praying for, what particular thing they wish to obtain from God when they say these prayers, few would be able to tell you, unless, indeed, they happened to be making a novena for some special object.

So, I say, it does not seem as if we Christians believed what our Lord tells us in these words. For surely, if we did, almost all our prayers would be petitions for some particular thing which we wanted, instead of mere devotional exercises. And why? Because we are always in want of something, and we must certainly believe that Almighty God has the power to give us what we want; should we not, then, be always praying for what we want, did we fully believe that he has the will to give it to us?

Is it, then, really true that God will give us all good things which we ask in prayer? Yes, it certainly is; that is exactly the meaning of these words of Christ. All good things, I say; for it is only good things which we can ask in his name. And if God would give us bad things which we should ask for, our Saviour's promise would be a curse, not a blessing as it really is.

No; God will not answer bad prayers—that is, prayers for what is bad. People sometimes make such prayers and expect him to answer them. They pray for vengeance on those who have injured them; they pray that others may suffer as much as they have made them suffer, and the like. Or they pray for something which seems to them good, but really is not so—that they may get rich, for instance, when riches will only be an occasion of sin to them. The prayer seems to them good, but it is not; perhaps even those prayers for vengeance may seem so. But God knows better, and will not, as he says in the Gospel of to-morrow, give us a stone when we ask for what seems to be bread. If anything, he will give better, instead of worse, than what we ask.

But really most things that Christians would think of praying for are not bad; but you do not pray for them, because you think that if they are good for you, you will get them, if you try, whether you pray or not. Now, that is the great mistake which our Lord wishes to correct. When he says, "If you ask the Father anything in my name, he will give it you," that means, also, that if you do not ask he will not, or at least not in such abundance.

Try, then, to bring this truth home to yourselves and make it practical: that if you want anything the way to get it is to ask it from God, not forgetting, of course, to work for it as well as to pray; for no one prays in earnest who does not do that. And the way not to get it is not to ask for it.

Pray, then, for what you want; and of course, before praying, find out what you do want. You want, for instance, to be kept from sin; but what sin? What is the one you are most inclined to? Examine your conscience and find out. Then your prayer will really mean something, especially if it be accompanied by good and strong resolutions against your besetting vices.

If you know what you want, and pray for it in

Christ's name and in earnest, using all other means to get it, it shall, if it be good, be yours. That is the lesson of our Lord's words in the Gospel of to-day.

SERMON LXXV.

Amen, amen I say to you, if you ask the Father anything in my name, he will give it you.—ST. JOHN XVI. 23.

These words must be true, my brethren, for it is the Eternal Truth who has spoken them. And yet I dare say you cannot see how they are. You have often, perhaps, asked God for something which you wanted, and put our Lord's name to your prayers, and yet you have not got the thing on which your heart was set.

Well, let us see what is the matter; why it is that our experience seems to contradict our faith. It may be that, though the words seem plain, we do not understand them aright.

Perhaps we are under a mistake as to what is meant by asking in the name of Christ. Let us consider what is really the common and natural sense of asking for anything in somebody else's name. What should we ourselves mean by it?

Suppose I say to one of you: "If you ask Mr. So-and so for such a position or employment in my name you will get it," what do I mean? I mean that his regard for me is such that, if you have my name to support you, he will give it to you for my sake.

Well, now, this is, as it seems to me, what our Lord means by his promise. The sense of it is: "The Father loves me so much that if you have my name to support your prayers—that is, if I wish that you should have what you ask for—he will give it to you for my sake."

What it comes to, then, is this: If we ask the Father for anything *really* in the name of Christ—that is, if our Lord really endorses our prayer—we shall have it.

"Well," perhaps you may say, "it seems to me that does not amount to much. Will not God give us what our Lord approves of, any way, whether we ask it or not? I don't see what we gain by praying, if that is all."

There, my friends, you labor under a great mistake. The Father wants Christ's name, but he wants your prayer, too. Some things, it is true, you have got without praying; but there are many which you have not got, but which you might have had if you had added your own prayer to the name of our Lord.

I do not believe, for instance, that you ever asked in his name to be rich. And yet it is quite possible that you might have done so. If he knew that it would be good for yourself and others for you to have money, if he knew that you would make a good use of it, he would have put his name to your request. So you might, perhaps, have been much richer than you are; perhaps it was only the prayer for it on your part that was wanting. If it could have been made in the name of Christ—that is, with his approval—it would have been effectual.

It is very likely that he would, for good reasons, have refused to give his name to such a prayer. Still it would be worth while to try. It is always worth while to try praying for anything that is not in itself bad ; we may be able to get Christ's name for it, who knows ? And if we do not pray for what we want we will not be nearly so likely to get it.

There are some things, though, that we can be sure to have his name for, and which are besides much better than worldly goods. Those are the virtues with which our souls ought to be adorned—our true riches, the riches of the soul. Pray for these, then, with full confidence that he will endorse your prayer.

But when you pray for them work for them too. He will not give you either spiritual or temporal riches if you sit still and fold your hands, and wait for them to drop into your lap. A prayer which is not in earnest is no prayer at all ; and no prayer is in earnest if the one who makes it is not trying to get what he wants in every way open to him.

Now, I hope you see that our Lord's promise is a real and true one ; for by it we can get many, very many things which otherwise we never can have. And I hope you see that it is a most generous one ; for by it we can have everything that is really good. Could you possibly ask anything more ?

Sunday within the Octave of the Ascension.

EPISTLE. 1 *St. Peter iv.* 7–11. Dearly beloved: Be prudent, and watch in prayers. But before all things have a mutual charity among yourselves: for charity covereth a multitude of sins. Using hospitality one towards another without murmuring. As every man hath received grace, ministering the same one to another, as good stewards of the manifold grace of God. If any man speak, let him speak as the words of God. If any man minister, let it be as from the power which God administereth: that in all things God may be honored through Jesus Christ our Lord.

GOSPEL. *St. John xv.* 26–*xvi.* 4. At that time: Jesus said to his disciples: When the Paraclete shall come whom I will send you from the Father, the Spirit of truth, who proceedeth from the Father, he shall give testimony of me. And you shall give testimony, because you are with me from the beginning. These things have I spoken to you, that you may not be scandalized. They will put you out of the synagogues: yea, the hour cometh that whosoever killeth you, will think that he doeth a service to God. And these things will they do to you, because they have not known the Father, nor me. But these things I have told you, that when the hour of them shall come, you may remember that I told you.

SERMON LXXVI.

Charity covereth a multitude of sins.—1 ST. PETER iv. 8.

THOSE words are from the Epistle appointed for this Sunday, and St. Peter, when he wrote them, meant that a man who gets his heart full of charity is sure to be truly penitent for his sins, no matter how many they may have been, and will thus win the mercy of God and receive full pardon for them. St. Peter's words are quite a popular saying. You will hear all sorts of people quote them with evident satisfaction and belief in their truth. But do they all mean just what I have said *he* meant ? I am not so sure that they do. I fear that some think that giving a few dollars to the poor (which they call charity) is a convenient way of throwing a cloak over a multitude of sins—covering them up, as it were—and hiding them rather than getting rid of them. I know the Scripture says also that "almsgiving redeems the soul from death," and tells the sinner to "redeem his sins with alms and his iniquities with works of mercy to the poor." But the Catholic doctrine is that charity must prompt the almsgiving in order to work the miracle of pardon. It is not the money or the clothing, the food or the fire, given to those who need, which compounds for sins and buys pardon at a cheap rate ; but the virtue of divine charity, a Christ-like love of God and of our neighbors, that wipes out the judgment of condemnation and cleanses the guilty stains from the soul. The giving of alms to the suffering poor is certainly one of the first things that a sinner who is trying to get back, or has already got back, the love of God will set himself to do ; and it is the very sacrifice of his goods for God's sake and for God's love that proves he wants to have done with his sins, and that he is anxious to do penance for them. It would be the gre test folly in the world for a man to give alms *for his sins,* if he was not trying to do so for the love of

God. It is all very well and very benevolent to help a poor wretch with food and raiment because we do not like to see a fellow human being suffer. But thieves, and adulterers, and drunkards, and Easter-duty breakers, and all sorts of sinners who have no intention whatever of stopping their sinful career will do that; and when they say, "Charity covereth a multitude of sins," they are very well content to have their benevolence accounted as a set-off to their sins. But mere benevolence is not charity, and to think it is would be a very great mistake. St. Paul says that a man may distribute all his goods to feed the poor, and yet not have charity. So then, dear brethren, if you want your almsgiving to be profitable to your own soul as well as helpful to your suffering neighbor, stop your sins and begin to be, first of all, a little generous with God. Give him what he is constantly knocking at the door and begging for—your heart, your love. Then you will have the charity that covereth a multitude of sins, even before you give the poor a cent. Get into the love of God, and then the love of your neighbor for God's sake will follow of itself. You will then feed and clothe and comfort the poor, not only because you pity them, but because you love them. Then will God love you and forgive you your sins.

Now that we have a just idea of charity, you see how it is to be exercised in a great many more ways than in almsgiving. You will easily forgive your neighbor his offences against you; you will hold no spite or revenge in your heart. If he has disgraced himself you will not go and tell all your acquaintances of it, but will jealously hide it and excuse it, and help him out of his trouble. Thus the charity you have will not only cover a multitude of your own sins, but a multitude of your neighbor's sins as well. When you forgive in charity you will forgive out and out, as God does, and hold no grudge afterwards. O my dear Christians! try to learn this lesson and lay it to heart. Strive after this divine love; pray for it; ask Our Blessed Lady and all the saints to help you obtain it; your salvation depends on it. I say it again: your salvation depends on it. "Charity covereth a multitude of sins." Yes; but nothing else will cover even *one* sin. Without the love of God there is no contrition; without contrition there is no absolution; without absolution you are lost! Think well on this.

SERMON LXXVII.

Before all things, have a mutual charity among yourselves; for charity covereth a multitude of sins.—1 St. Peter iv. 8.

What does St. Peter mean, my brethren, by these words? How does charity cover a multitude of sins?

Well, it covers our own sins, of course—that is, it helps us to obtain their forgiveness, and it atones for them when they have been forgiven. There is no better way to obtain mercy from God than to show it to others.

But then all the virtuous acts which we can do have the same effect to some extent; so I think that the sins which St. Peter speaks of are not our own merely, but also those of others. And it is a special effect of charity to cover the sins of others; it seems, then, that it is charity as shown in this way that the apostle here urges on us.

It is not a very common kind of charity, either,

this of covering other people's sins. Some, indeed, seem to think that the sins of their neighbors ought not to be covered. They do not appear to understand that every one has a real right that his sins should remain unknown; that it is not only uncharitable but unjust to mention them to those who do not know them already. No; as soon as they hear a piece of news to any one's disadvantage they are not easy till they have told it to their whole circle of acquaintance; the idea of covering it up, of not letting it go any farther, of saving their neighbor's character never occurs to them. If they feel pretty sure that it is true, that is enough to remove all scruple about telling it.

But this telling about people's sins is a sin, as I have said, not only against charity but against justice. Charity goes a good deal farther than that. It covers sins not only from other people's eyes, but even from our own.

That is what St. Paul says about it. He says: "Charity thinketh no evil"—that is to say, it does not see sin in other people; it puts the best construction on their actions. How rare it is to find any one who thoroughly practises charity of this kind!

For instance, somebody tells something about you which you know to be false; do you put the best construction on this? No, you put the very worst you can. You say to yourself: "He, or she, did that out of malice. He knew very well that what he said was not true, and said it to slander me, out of pure spite." You never stop to think that he may be laboring under a false impression—may really think that what he says is true, and that he is, moreover, justified in saying it. You never make any allowance for the passion he may be under which has blinded his judgment; you never think of the provocations he may have had, or may at least fancy that he has had. The utmost you do is to say: "Well, I do not wish him any evil; I forgive him the injury he has done me." And if you have said that, which ought to be a matter of course, you look upon yourself as a great Christian hero.

Try to learn, then, that charity means more than forgiving sins. It means *excusing* them—finding out, if possible, some reason which may show that what seems to be a sin was not really so. You are ready enough to excuse your own sins; to say, "I could not help it," or "I did not mean any harm." Why don't you say the same thing for somebody else? Throw the veil of charity over the faults of others—if they have sinned it will do you no good to know it—and take it off from your own, which you ought to know a great deal better than you do. By the charity of covering other people's sins from your own eyes you will cover your own from the eyes of God.

SERMON LXXVIII.

Before all things, have a mutual charity among yourselves; for charity covereth a multitude of sins.—1 ST. PETER iv. 8.

NOTHING is more frequently or more forcibly commanded by our Lord and his apostles than fraternal charity. Mind well the text: "*Before all things,*" says St. Peter, "have a mutual charity among yourselves." In fact, if you give a little attention to your daily thoughts, words, and deeds, you will find that the burden of your daily sins is uncharitableness in one form or another. It was want of fraternal charity that brought about murder on the very morning of this world's life. Hatred came between the first two brothers of our race, and the result was the murder of the innocent Abel. A preacher who lived some three hundred years ago—they had a quaint way of telling plain truths in those days—said in a sermon, and was willing to wager, that the first thing that Adam and Eve did after eating the apple was to quarrel, to have a downright good dispute, which was only continuing, in another way, the first sin. Samson slew a thousand Philistines "with a jawbone, even the jawbone of an ass." How many reputations are destroyed in a like manner!—for a wise man knows how to hold his tongue. What a heaven on earth our homes and our social circles would be, if a constant mutual charity was kept up between husband and wife, brothers and sisters, and acquaintances! "With charity," said St. Gregory, "man is to man a god; without charity man is to man a wild beast."

It may seem rather bold of St. Peter to say that charity should be had *"before all things"*; but he gives a good reason for his assertion, and a very consoling one it is for us: "for charity covereth a multitude of sins." We all have, God knows, a multitude of sins on our souls; anything that will take them away, rid us of them, cover them up from God's sight, is of the greatest possible benefit to us. Now, this is just what charity does. How? It is said that love is blind; charity blinds us to the defects and sins of our neighbor—in fact, covers them up either by excusing, or by bearing patiently, or by forgiving the sins and offences of others. "Charity," says St.

Paul, "is patient, is kind, charity envieth not, thinketh no evil, rejoiceth not in iniquity, beareth all things, endureth all things." But in thus covering the sins of others how does charity cover our own? Remember your "Our Father": "Forgive us our trespasses, as we forgive those who trespass against us." Here is a contract between you and God; you stake the forgiveness from God of your sins on your forgiveness of the sins of others. If, therefore, from a motive of charity you cover the sins of others, God will cover your sins; they will stand no more before him and against you.

"Well, well, dear father," it is often said to us, "forgive, yes; but I will never forget." My dear friend, you remind me of the beggar who, seeing a gentleman put his hand in his pocket, fervently exclaimed, "May the blessing of God follow you," and then, seeing that it was the smallest of coins that was handed to him, added no less fervently, "and never overtake you!" To *forgive really* is to forget. We are to forgive as God forgives; that is the bargain, is it not? Now, God forgets our sins; they are for ever wiped out of his memory. Remembrances of offences are temptations that you must hunt down as you would impure thoughts; you must try to forget, else you do not forgive. Next Sunday we celebrate the descent of the Holy Ghost. The Holy Ghost is the spirit of love, the outcome of the mutual charity of the Father and the Son. Pray to him that he may put in your hearts the true virtue of Christian charity.

Feast of Pentecost, or Whit-Sunday.

Epistle. *Acts ii.* 1–11. When the days of the Pentecost were accomplished, they were all together in the same place : and suddenly there came a sound from heaven, as of a mighty wind coming, and it filled the whole house where they were sitting. And there appeared to them cloven tongues as it were of fire, and it sat upon every one of them. And they were all filled with the Holy Ghost, and they began to speak with divers tongues, according as the Holy Ghost gave them to speak. Now there were dwelling at Jerusalem, Jews, devout men out of every nation under heaven. And when this voice was made, the multitude came together, and was confounded in mind, because that every one heard them speak in his own tongue. And they were all amazed and wondered, saying : Behold, are not all these who speak, Galileans ? And how have we every one heard our own tongue wherein we were born ? Parthians, and Medes, and Elamites, and inhabitants of Mesopotamia, Judea and Cappadocia, Pontus and Asia, Phrygia and Pamphilia, Egypt and the parts of Libya about Cyrene, and strangers of Rome, Jews also, and proselytes, Cretes and Arabians : we have heard them speak in our own tongues the wonderful works of God.

Gospel. *St. John xiv.* 23–31. At that time: Jesus said to his disciples : If any one love me, he will keep my word, and my Father will love him, and we will come to him, and make our abode with him. He that loveth me not, keepeth not my words. And the word which you have heard is not mine, but the Father's who sent me.

These things have I spoken to you, remaining with you. But the Paraclete, the Holy Ghost, whom the Father will send in my name, he will teach you all things, and bring all things to your mind, whatsoever I shall have said to you. Peace I leave with you; my peace I give to you: not as the world giveth do I give to you. Let not your heart be troubled, nor let it be afraid. You have heard that I have said to you: I go away, and I come again to you. If you loved me, you would indeed be glad, because I go to the Father: for the Father is greater than I. And now I have told you before it come to pass: that when it shall come to pass, you may believe. Now I will not speak many things with you. For the prince of this world cometh, and in me he hath not anything. But that the world may know that I love the Father: and as the Father hath given me commandment, so I do.

SERMON LXXIX.

The Holy Ghost, whom the Father will send in my name, he will teach you all things.—St. John xiv. 26.

To day, my dear friends, as you know, we celebrate the descent of the Holy Ghost upon the apostles. It was, of all the wonderful works that God has wrought for the salvation of men, in one way the most extraordinary and miraculous; for it was an immediate and evident change, not in the material world, but in the spiritual—that is, in the souls of those upon whom the Holy Spirit thus came. In a moment they became entirely different men from what they had been before.

What was this change which was worked in the souls of the apostles? It was, as we commonly regard it, an infusion of supernatural courage and strength. Before they had been hiding themselves, hardly daring to appear in public, still less to preach the Gospel, or even to profess themselves Christians; but now they came forth boldly, ready not only to be known as followers of Christ, but also to suffer all things for his sake.

There was, however, another change worked in them in that moment; and it is the one which our Lord predicted in the words which I have taken from the Gospel of this day. "The Holy Ghost," said he, "will teach you all things."

What was the meaning of this promise, and what was its fulfilment? Did our Lord mean that the Holy Ghost would teach the apostles all the truths of natural science; that they should become great chemists, geographers, or mechanics; that they should know how to construct steam-engines or telegraphic cables? By no means. These things are in themselves of little importance, and would have had no direct bearing on the work to which St. Peter and his companions were called. No; the things which the Holy Ghost was to teach them, and did teach them on the day of Pentecost, were spiritual things—those things which concerned the salvation of their own souls, and of the other souls which were committed to their charge. In an instant they became learned in the mysteries of the kingdom not of nature but of grace; they became in a moment great saints and doctors of theology. They knew at once what others, superior to them in natural gifts, have not been able to acquire after long years of study and prayer. They were miraculously prepared to do the work of infallible founders and teachers of the Church of God.

It was a wonderful promise of Christ to them, and wonderful was its fulfilment. But are we merely to admire it in them, or have we too a share in it?

We have a share in it. Yes, though the promise in its fulness was only made to them, all of us, even the humblest, can claim it for ourselves. The Holy Ghost will teach us also all spiritual things, if we will only listen to his voice—not suddenly or miraculously as to them, but none the less surely. He has already taught to millions of the faithful children of the church, though they were ignorant of that natural science which the world values, what the most learned and able men have died without knowing.

He will teach us all things, but we must listen to his voice. Where, then, is that voice to be heard?

First, it is to be heard in the voice of the church itself, which speaks in his name and by his power. You can hear it in the words of your Holy Father the Pope, the successor of the apostles, and in those of your bishop and of your pastors. You can also hear it in good books, published with the authority and approval of the church. Lastly, you can hear it in your own souls. The Holy Ghost is always speaking there, but it is with a gentle and low voice; and if you would hear it pride and passion must be still. It is in silence and in prayer that you will learn those things which he has to teach you. Listen, then, to the voice of God, of the spirit of wisdom, of understanding, of counsel, and of knowledge, which you have received in Confirmation, and which dwells in your souls; and our Divine Lord's promise shall certainly be fulfilled in you.

SERMON LXXX.

If any one love me he will keep my word.—St. John xiv. 23.

THERE are some people who have a great deal of what they call devotion, and there are others who seem to have very little or none at all. The hearts of the first are filled, one would think, with the love of God. They are never so happy as when at church, assisting at Mass or some other service, or on their knees before their altar at home. They say as many prayers every day as would make up the office which a priest is bound to recite, or perhaps even more. Some other people, on the contrary, find it a hard matter to say any prayers. Their minds wander, they cannot tell why. They do not care much about coming to church; they come, though, for all that. But it is all uphill work with them; and they think they are in a very bad way, and are tempted to envy those who seem to be getting along so much better.

But is it certain that those whom they are tempted to envy are, in reality, in so much better a state? No, I do not think it is. Of course it is a good sign for any one to like to pray. It is much better to have a taste for that than for the pleasures of the world. But it does not certainly follow that one who likes to pray really loves God very much. He may like it because he is paid for it; that is, because he gets rewarded for it in a way that others do not. He may like it in the same way that a child would like the company of any one who would give him candy. If the supply of candy stops his affection is gone. If, instead of getting candy, he is asked to go on an errand, his feeling will be very different.

So one may like to pray because he or she has in

prayer a pleasure which would be attractive to any one, even to the greatest sinners. The pleasure may come merely from one's having a lively imagination, and getting what seems to be a vision of heaven when on one's knees or in church. But ask such a person to do something for the one who gives him this pleasure—that is, God—and there will perhaps be a great change. If our Lord, instead of giving candy, proposes him an errand—if he asks a girl, for instance, instead of going to Mass or to Communion, to stay at home and help her mother—the shoe, it may be, will begin to pinch immediately.

The others, who have little of what is called devotion, may stand this trial much better. They may be willing not only to give up prayer, which they are not so fortunate as to like, but other things which they really do, if it is the will of God. They pray because it is God's will, and because they know it will bring them nearer to him, and they will do anything else that he wishes them to do for the same reason.

Now, do not misunderstand me. I do not mean that all those who do not like to pray are better than those who do; far from it. But I do mean that real devotion which is the same as a true love of God, is what our Lord sets before us in the words of to-day's Gospel which I have read. "If any one love me," he says, "he will keep my word"; that is, "he will do what I want him to." "You are my friends," he says in another place, "if you do the things that I command you." That is true devotion, to have our will the same as God's will; to be willing to sacrifice everything for him, even the pleasure we may find in bad society.

So I mean that a person who has none of what is called devotion, but who does what he understands to be God's will, and avoids what is contrary to it, is much more acceptable in his sight than one who has what is called devotion, and gives up God's will to satisfy it. Thus, for instance, any one of you, my brethren, who has not been to Holy Communion since Lent began, and who really wants to please God, will go this week, before the time of the Easter-duty runs out, and not wait for Corpus Christi, which comes in the next week. That is just now a special good example; try and remember it. If any one wants to commit a mortal sin, let him put off his Easter-duty till Corpus Christi and the Forty Hours, for devotion's sake.

Real devotion is to remember God's words and obey them at any cost. This is the true way, as he also says in to-day's Gospel, to induce him and his Father to really come to us and make their abode with us; and to have the Holy Ghost, who proceeds from them, enter into our hearts, though we may not feel his presence, as the apostles did on the first Pentecost day.

SERMON LXXXI.

Let not your heart be troubled, nor let it be afraid.—St. John xiv. 27.

Our Lord spoke these words to his apostles before his Passion, but they were not to have effect till after his ascension into heaven. It was not his will that they should have the courage and confidence to which he here exhorts them till that time which we celebrate to-day, when the Holy Ghost came upon them and fitted them for the great work to which they were appointed. Even while our Lord was with them after his resurrection, and still more after he had ascended and left them to themselves, they were anxious and fearful, not daring to call themselves his disciples or to risk anything for his sake. But when they received the Holy Ghost all this was changed. They confessed Christ openly; all their doubts and fears were gone; and "they rejoiced," as we read in the Acts, "that they were accounted worthy to suffer reproach for the name of Jesus. And they ceased not every day, in the temple and from house to house, to teach and preach Christ Jesus."

Now, we ought to imitate their conduct after Pentecost, and not that before. For we have not the excuse that they had before that time. We have received the Holy Ghost, as they did. He has not come on us visibly in fiery tongues, but he has come just as really and truly in the sacrament of confirmation which we have received. There is no reason for us to be troubled or afraid; when the Holy Ghost came into our hearts he brought courage and confidence with him; he brought them to each one of us, as he did to the holy apostles.

And he gave this courage and confidence to each of us for the same reason as to them, because we have all to be apostles in our own way and degree. We have not all got to preach Christ publicly, as they did, but we have all got to speak a word for him when the proper occasion comes. We have not all got to die for Christ, as they did, but we have got to suffer something for the sake of our faith in him, and that quite often, too, it may be. We have a real duty in this matter; we shall be rewarded if we fulfil it, and punished if we do not. It was not for his apostles only but for each one of us that those words of his were meant: "Every one that shall confess me before men, I will also confess him before my Father who is in heaven; but he that shall deny me before men, I will also deny him before my Father who is in heaven."

And yet how often must it be acknowledged, to our shame and disgrace, that Christians do deny their Lord and Master before men! I do not mean that they deny their faith, and say they are not Catholics when they are asked; this, thank God! though it does happen, is not so very common. But is it not common enough to find young Catholic men and women with whom one might associate for years and never suspect them to be Catholics, and, in fact, be quite sure that they were not?—and this not merely because they do not parade their religion, but because they do not defend it when it is attacked; because they agree with, and even express, all sorts of infidel, heretical, false, and so-called liberal opinions, that they may not give offence; or even, perhaps, without any sort of need, but only to win favor for themselves by falling in with the fashion of those with whom they associate.

And how often, again, do Christians, even if they do stand up for their faith, cast contempt on it in the eyes of the world by acting and talking just as if it had no power over their lives, and was never meant to have any! They curse, and swear, and talk immodestly, just as those do who do not profess to believe in God and Christ, and even, perhaps, worse. Or if they do not go so far as this, they laugh at profanity and impurity, and make companions of those who are addicted to these vices; and this they do, not becáuse they really wish to do or to sanction such things, but merely from a miserable weakness that prevents them from facing a little contempt and unpopularity. What would they do, if called on to shed their blood for Christ, who cannot bear even to be laughed at a little for being practical Catholics? They are like cowardly soldiers who run away from a battle at the first smoke from the enemy's guns.

You know what a shame it is for a soldier to be a coward. And now try to remember, dear Christians, especially on this holy day, that a Christian has got to be a soldier, and that if he is a coward he disgraces himself and his cause. The Holy Ghost is given to us in confirmation that we may not be weak and cowardly, but strong and perfect Christians, and *true* soldiers of Jesus Christ. If you have not yet received him in this way make haste to do so; if you have, make use of the graces which he has given you. Do not let your hearts be troubled or afraid; there is nothing to be afraid of, for God is on your side. Do not fear but rather count it a joy to suffer a little persecution for his name.

Trinity Sunday.

EPISTLE. *Rom. xi.* 33-36. O the depth of the riches, of the wisdom, and of the knowledge of God! How incomprehensible are his judgments, and how unsearchable his ways! For who hath known the mind of the Lord? Or who hath been his counsellor? Or who hath first given to him, and recompense shall be made to him? For of him, and by him, and in him, are all things. To him be glory for ever. Amen.

GOSPEL. *St. Matt. xxviii.* 18-20. At that time: Jesus said to his disciples: All power is given to me in heaven and on earth. Go ye, therefore, and teach all nations: baptizing them in the name of the Father, and of the Son, and of the Holy Ghost: teaching them to observe all things whatsoever I have commanded you; and behold I am with you all days, even to the consummation of the world.

LAST GOSPEL. *St. Luke vi.* 36-42. At that time, Jesus said to his disciples: Be ye merciful, as your Father also is merciful. Judge not, and you shall not be judged. Condemn not, and you shall not be condemned. Forgive, and you shall be forgiven. Give, and it shall be given to you: good measure and pressed down, and shaken together and running over, shall they give into your bosom. For with the same measure that you shall measure it shall be measured to you again. And he spoke also to them a similitude: Can the blind lead the blind? do they not both fall into the ditch? The disciple is not above his master; but every one shall be perfect, if he be as his master. And why seest thou the mote in thy brother's eye, but the beam that is in thy own eye thou considerest not? or how canst thou say to thy brother, Brother, let me pull the mote out of thy eye, when thou thyself seest not the beam in thy own eye? Thou hypocrite, cast first the beam out of thy own eye, and then shalt thou see clearly to take out the mote from thy brother's eye.

SERMON LXXXII.

Teach all nations: baptizing them in the name of the Father, and of the Son, and of the Holy Ghost.—ST. MATT. xxviii. 19.

THE mystery of the Most Blessed Trinity is one of those wonderful truths of our holy faith which form the foundation of the Christian religion. He who does not believe in the Trinity cannot call himself a Christian; neither can any one be a Christian unless he is baptized in the name of the Father, and of the Son, and of the Holy Ghost. We are taught to make acts of profession of this mystery oftener than of any other. We do so every time we make the sign of the cross; and there are very few Catholics who do not make that sign more than once every day. Every one should know what is meant by the Trinity.

There is but one God, who is the infinite, eternal, almighty, all-wise, all-good, and all-just Being who created all things that exist.

But God, who is one in his Divine Being, is a Trinity in person. That is, he is three persons. These persons are named Father, Son, Holy Ghost. God is, then, Father, and he is Son, and he is Holy Ghost. These three persons are the same God. So, if there were three men praying to God, one praying to the Father, a second to the Son, and the third to the Holy Ghost, they would all be praying to the same God. How there can be more than one person in one being is a mystery to us, because we have no knowledge of any other being but God who has more than one person. But now this truth is revealed to us, we know, by our faith, which is divine knowledge, that there are three persons in God, and are sure also that God must, as a Divine Being, have three persons, because God cannot be other than he is. Let us help our minds to understand this by a comparison. Suppose a tower built in such a shape that it has three sides. Now, there are *three* distinct sides and only *one* tower; and whichever side we look at we see a distinct side which is not either of the other two sides, but we always can say, I see the tower. So, no matter which person of God we regard, it is always the same God.

Our holy faith teaches us that God the Father is the Divine Person who created all things, as we say in the Creed: "I believe in God, the Father Almighty, creator of heaven and earth." It furthermore teaches us that God the Son is the Divine Person who redeemed us by becoming man and dying on the cross, as the words of the Creed declare; and again it teaches us that God the Holy Ghost is the Divine Person who sanctifies us and is the source and giver of all grace. These truths are revealed to us, and we believe them, as we do all mysteries, for the reason we give when we make an act of faith: "O my God! I believe all things taught by the holy Catholic Church, because thou, who canst neither deceive nor be deceived, hast revealed them to her."

The Catholic Church is the voice of God to us, and when we hear her we hear God. She lives, and speaks, and acts by the Holy Ghost through Jesus Christ, our Saviour, her Divine Head. The reason some very wise people, very learned in different kinds of science, do not believe in the Trinity and other mysteries of religion as we do is because they do not hear the voice of God in the Catholic Church. It is not by science that we know the Trinity to be true, but by divine faith.

This divine faith is a gift of God, which we are bound to nourish in our souls with profound gratitude and humility, for it is a sad truth that this faith may be lost.

Catholics lose their faith by their sins, and chiefly by the sin of pride. All heretics and apostates show this in their conduct and in their words. They adhere to their own opinions and refuse to submit to the divine teaching of the church. O dear brethren! let us fear this sin of pride more than all other sin—a temptation, too, that is very apt to come up when we are ridiculed by unbelievers for our faith. Then is the time to confess the truth boldly, for if we deny our Lord before men he will deny us before the face of his Father in heaven.

Let us keep our faith by purity of life and humility of heart; for, as says the *Imitation of Christ*: " What doth it avail thee to discourse profoundly of the Trinity, if thou be wanting in humility, and consequently displeasing to the Trinity? If thou didst know the whole Bible by heart, and the sayings of all the philosophers, what would it profit thee without the love of God and his grace?"

SERMON LXXXIII.

In the name of the Father, and of the Son, and of the Holy Ghost.—St. Matt. xxviii. 19.

To-day, my dear brethren, the church celebrates the greatest of all the mysteries of our religion: the mystery of the Holy Trinity; of the one God in three Divine Persons—the Father, the Son, and the Holy Ghost.

We all believe it; we must believe it if we would be saved. But no one of us can perfectly understand it. St. Patrick, you know, is said to have illustrated it to his converts by showing them the shamrock with its three leaves on one stem; but, of course, he never pretended that this was a perfect explanation of it. No perfect explanation of it can be given to us.

And why not? Is it because it really has no explanation? No, but because we are not able to understand the one which might be given. Explain the solar system to a child of five years: will he understand you? It is something the same with us and this greater mystery of God.

Some people, especially at the present day, who consider themselves very wise, say to themselves and to others: "Oh! this doctrine of the Trinity cannot be true." Ask them why not, and they will say: "Because we cannot understand it; it seems to us to be nonsense."

Well, what does their argument amount to? Just to this: "If the doctrine were true we should understand it; but we don't understand it, therefore it is not true."

"If it were true," they say, "we should understand it." And why? "Why, of course, because we are so wise that we can understand everything. It is well enough for stupid people, like those benighted Romanists, to believe what they don't understand, but such a proceeding would be quite below our dignity and intelligence. It is quite absurd to suppose that there is any mystery so deep that we cannot see to the bottom of it."

Now, I do not want to accuse these worthy people of any one of the seven capital sins; they are, no doubt, as good as they are wise. But there is something in what they say that looks just a little bit like one of those sins; like the first and most deadly of them all: that is, the sin of pride. And there is not much doubt that pride has in some form or other had something to do with all heresies; so I am afraid that those who deny the Holy Trinity are not quite free from it.

You think so, my brethren, I have no doubt. But, after all, are you not perhaps guilty of a little of the same sin yourselves? You believe in the Holy Trinity, it is true, but are there not some other things which you do not fully believe, though you ought to, and for very much the same reason?

God has given you the gift of faith; and you are willing to believe what you know to be of faith, even if it be beyond your reason, especially if it be something, like the Holy Trinity, beyond the reason of any one else. But are you not sometimes rather unwilling to believe other matters of religion, for which there is good authority, just because you, with your present lights, do not quite see through them? That is just the trouble with the heretics of whom I have spoken; is it not so with you, too, perhaps?

Do you not say even about some of these matters: "Oh! I do not think the same about that as the priests do; they are welcome to their opinion, but I claim the right to mine"? It may be some question of morals; then you say: "The priests say so-and-so is not right; but I don't see any harm in it. I have got a conscience of my own."

Did it ever occur to you that as God knows more, and has told more to his church about himself than you could have found out, so he may have enlightened it rather more about some other matters in its own sphere than he has enlightened you, even though they are not of faith? And even setting that aside, is it not possible that those who have studied a subject know more about it than those who have not?

I think there is only one answer to these questions. Try, then, to have the same humility which you have about the doctrine of the Holy Trinity in other things too. You believe that the officers of a ship know a little more about her position and proper course than you do; make the same presumption in favor of those who are in charge of the bark of St. Peter. It is only reasonable to think so; only showing a little of the same common sense which you show in other things.

SERMON LXXXIV.

Why seest thou the mote in thy brother's eye, but the beam that is in thy own eye thou considerest not ?—St. Luke vi. 41.

THESE words, my dear brethren, are taken from the Gospel of the first Sunday after Pentecost, which is always read at the end of Mass on this day. Of all those which our Divine Lord spoke during his ministry on earth, there are none more practical, none which have a more immediate bearing on our daily lives.

There is nothing which shows the perversity of our fallen nature more clearly than the common habit, in which even many persons who are pious in their way continually indulge, of criticising and commenting on the actions and character of others.

Some people, indeed, seem to think that there is no harm in talking about the character and conduct of their neighbors, as long as they do not say anything which is not true. This is a great mistake; one hardly needs to stop and reflect for a moment to see that it is a grievous injustice to speak of a sin which another person has actually committed, if it be not known, or at least certain soon to be known in some other way, by the one to whom we speak. So there are many who have sense enough not to make this mistake and who do hold their tongues about the secret sins of others. But there are comparatively few who seem to realize that it is against charity, though not against justice, to speak even of well-known and evident faults of one's neighbors, when there is no good object to be gained by so doing; and, in fact, even to think of them and turn them over in one's mind, for which there can never be any good object.

It is to such as these—and there are hosts of them—that our Lord's words are addressed. He does not himself answer the question which he asks in the text; but there is not much difficulty in our answering it ourselves.

"Why," then, "seest thou the mote in thy brother's eye, but the beam in thy own eye thou considerest not?" The two always go together. You will always find that just in proportion to a person's watchfulness about others' faults is his carelessness about his own. Why, I say, do you do so? Let us try to find out.

Are you so sensitive about your neighbor's faults because they offend God? No, I do not believe that is the reason. If it were you would be a great deal more troubled about your own than you are. If you really cared for God's honor in the matter you would go to work on your own sins, which you really can amend, and not on those of your neighbors, which you only carp at but do not even try to correct. Do not pretend, then, that your habit of finding fault with others comes from a desire that God may be better served. Such a pretence would be only hypocrisy. It is especially to such pretenders that our Saviour says: "Hypocrite, cast first the beam out of thy own eye; and then shalt thou see clearly to take out the mote from thy brother's eye."

Are you so sensitive about your neighbor's faults, then, because they offend yourself? No, I do not think that can be the reason either—or, at least, not the whole reason; for you are nearly as apt to speak of them when they do not concern you at all. You even take trouble to find out about those which do not come under your own observation. I know that we all have a weakness for noticing unpleasant things when they occur, and passing over those which are agreeable as a matter of course; we complain of the weather when it is bad, and give no thanks when it is fine; we grumble when we have a bad dinner, and say nothing about a good one. But this does not explain the matter entirely, for most of the faults which you notice in others do not hurt you in any way.

No; the fact is, it is simply a vice in yourselves which makes your neighbor's faults so glaring in your eyes. And that vice is the great vice of pride. You are trying to exalt yourselves, at least in your own mind, above others, and the easiest way to do it is to try to push them down. This is at the bottom of all this uncharitableness which is the staple of so many people's thoughts and conversation.

There is, therefore, only one real remedy for it, only one which strikes at the root of the whole thing: that is to cultivate the virtue which is the opposite of pride, the great virtue of humility.

I said just now that as a person is watchful about his neighbor's faults, so is he careless about his own. Well, the rule works both ways. If you will be careful about your own you will not notice those of other people. For you will acquire this virtue of humility. You will appear so bad in your own sight that others will appear good in comparison. And then, when you have cast out this beam of pride from the eye of your own soul, you will indeed be fit to correct others, and not till then.

Second Sunday after Pentecost,

AND SUNDAY WITHIN THE OCTAVE OF CORPUS CHRISTI.

EPISTLE. 1 *St. John iii.* 13-18. Dearly beloved : Wonder not if the world hate you. We know that we have passed from death to life, because we love the brethren. He that loveth not, abideth in death. Whosoever hateth his brother, is a murderer. And you know that no murderer hath eternal life abiding in himself. In this we have known the charity of God, because he hath laid down his life for us : and we ought to lay down our lives for the brethren. He that hath the substance of this world, and shall see his brother in need, and shall shut up his bowels from him : how doth the charity of God abide in him? My little children, let us not love in word, nor in tongue. but in deed and in truth.

GOSPEL. *St. Luke xiv.* 16-24. At that time: Jesus spoke to the Pharisees this parable : A certain man made a great supper, and invited many. And he sent his servant at supper-time to say to them that were invited that they should come, for now all things are ready. And they began all at once to make excuse. The first said to him : I have bought a farm, and I must needs go out and see it ; I pray thee, have me excused. And another said : I have bought five yoke of oxen, and I go to try them ; I pray thee, have me excused. And another said : I have married a wife, and therefore I cannot come. And the servant returning, told these things to his lord. Then the master of the house, being angry, said to his servant: Go out quickly into the streets and lanes of the city, and bring in hither the poor and the feeble, and the blind and the lame. And the servant said: Lord, it is done as thou hast commanded, and yet there is room. And the lord said to the servant: Go out into the highways and hedges, and compel them to come in, that my house may be filled. But I say unto you that none of those men that were called shall taste my supper.

SERMON LXXXV.

A certain man made a great supper, and invited many.—St. Luke xiv. 16.

If there could be any question about what kind of a "great supper" our Lord meant in the parable all doubt is removed by reading the Gospel, which tells us that some one of the persons to whom he was speaking had just said: "Blessed is he who shall eat bread in the kingdom of God." We know how to interpret the parable. The "great supper" is the divine banquet of Holy Communion, in which we receive the Body and Blood of Jesus Christ. On another occasion our Lord said: "I am the bread that came down from heaven. If any man eat of this bread he shall live for ever, and the bread that I will give is my flesh for the life of the world." The parable of the "great supper" is, therefore, very appropriately chosen as the Gospel for this Sunday in the octave of the magnificent and triumphal festival of Corpus Christi. This festival is also well placed in the calendar of the church, coming as it does, at the end of all the solemn commemorations of the divine life and person of our Lord. For the institution of the Blessed Sacrament is the greatest act of his love; the consummation and fulfilment of his love. "Having loved his own, he loved them unto the end." He is present in this divine mystery because he would be present with us and give himself to us, and unite himself to us in the most intimate manner. He promised that he would live in us, and we in him and be one with him. In the Blessed Sacrament he makes that life and union a reality.

Before the altars of his holy church, therefore, he spreads the holy table for his "great supper," and he invites many to the banquet. Such an invitation, we would think, does not need much urging to bring in the guests—*all* the guests—as quickly and as frequently as he desires. And yet, as he tells us in the parables, and as we see and hear ourselves, there are many who make little of his invitation, and either do not come at all or come with such reluctance or so seldom that it is plain they are acting more from fear of punishment than from a motive of love.

It is true that those who do not come when he calls are far from daring to say that it is not worth coming to, but they act very much as if they thought so. They have other friends who invite them to their feasts, and as they think more of these friends than they do of Jesus Christ, and relish their food more than they do his, they send in their excuses to him. These excuses are paltry enough. One has bought a farm and must go and see it; another has purchased five yoke of oxen—this is just the time he must go and try them; a third has just got married, and so on. Any excuse for not coming to Communion seems good enough for some Catholics, who want to keep friends and company with the world, the flesh, and the devil, and eat their dishes of avarice, lust, and pride. I don't wonder they stay away; for let a man get his heart full of avarice, or burning with lust, or puffed up with pride, the very idea of Holy Communion is wearisome and distasteful to him.

But there is a dreadful warning in the parable. *The excuses are not taken;* and he who sets forth the banquet declares that none of such men shall eat of his supper; and he makes that threat in anger. Woe, then, to those Easter-duty breakers who heard the invitation and came not! They have incurred the anger of the Lord. To pass by the Easter duty out of contempt for it, or because one is unwilling to give up the sins that he knows make him unfit to make it, is to commit a mortal sin. And when I see some persons who know their duty, and have every opportunity, neglecting their Easter Communion for years, and appearing to be perfectly hardened against every appeal and argument made to them, I am always fearful lest the Lord is not only angry with them, but that he is carrying out his threat that he will never invite them again, and that they will die some day without absolution and without Communion. Oh! if there be any such here let them hasten to beg pardon with deep contrition for their past neglect, and earnestly seek for admission to the heavenly banquet. Perhaps it may not be yet too late even for them. I know it is the eleventh hour, but the Lord invites some to come even at the eleventh hour. *But they must not wait longer!* At midnight the door will be shut, and the only answer they will get then is: "It is too late; I know you not!" God grant that such a curse of banishment from the eternal Communion of heaven shall never be addressed to one of us !

SERMON LXXXVI.

And they began all at once to make excuse.—St. Luke xiv. 18.

Notice the words, my brethren. Our Lord does not say that these men whom the master of the house invited to supper all happened to have an excuse, but that they began all at once to make one. They gave various flimsy reasons why they could not come—reasons that anybody could see would not have prevented them from coming if they had wanted to, but were merely given in order to avoid telling the plain truth, which was that they did not care a straw for the one who had invited them or for the supper that he proposed to give.

Well, now, what did our Saviour mean by this story which I have read you in the Gospel?—for he certainly did not tell it simply for the amusement of his disciples. It was a parable, and had a spiritual signification, or more than one. I think there cannot be much doubt in our minds about one of them, at least. We cannot help seeing that the supper means the rich banquet to which all of us are invited, and which has been commemorated in the great solemnity of Corpus Christi, through which we have just passed. God himself is the master of the house, and he has invited all of us his friends—that is, all of us who have come by holy baptism into the fold of his church—to come to this great feast, the feast of his own Body and Blood. Not once only but many times he has invited, nay, commanded, you all to come and taste of this supper, which is himself—to receive him in Holy Communion.

And what have you done—many of you, at least? You have done exactly what these men did of whom the parable tells us. You have, as soon as the words of invitation came to you, immediately set about to see if you could not find some way of avoiding compliance with them. You have begun all at once to make excuses—excuses as silly as those which the men made in the parable.

"Oh!" you say, "I have not got time to approach the sacraments worthily. It's all very well for women, who can run to church whenever they want, but I have got my business to attend to; if I neglect it my family will starve." Humbug! I say—as transparent humbug as that stupid story which the man whom our Lord speaks of had about his farm. "I have bought a farm," says he, "and I must needs go out and see it." That excursion to his farm was got up just to dodge the invitation, which he did not care to accept. It is the same with you. Your business is not so important that it will keep you from the theatre or the liquor-store, but as soon as the service of God is mentioned it becomes urgent all at once.

Or perhaps you do not plead any particular business, but you make an excuse like that of the man who said he had married a wife, and therefore could not come. You say: "Piety is very good for priests and religious; but I am living in the world, and can't be good enough to go to Communion." Humbug! I say again; you know very well that there have been plenty of people, who have lived in a much brighter world than is ever likely to be open to you, who have not only made good communions, but made them frequently, and become saints by doing so. Kings and queens have given the lie to your excuse. Are you more in the world than St. Henry, Emperor of Germany ; St. Louis, King of France ; the two Saints Elizabeth, of Hungary and Portugal ; and St. Margaret, Queen of Scotland, whose feast we kept last Tuesday ?

Don't make any more foolish excuses, then ; our Lord, who has invited you to his banquet, will not be deceived by them. Acknowledge the truth, that if you do not come to his supper it is because you do not care for it, or for Him who gives it.

But do you dare to say this ? I hope not. Do not say it, then. Do what is far better. Come when he calls you. Come, that you may not offend him, as those ungrateful men of whom the parable tells us offended the master of the house. Come, that he may not say to you, as the master of the house said : "Those men who were called shall not taste my supper," not even when they shall desire it at the hour of their death. Come, that your inheritance in the kingdom of heaven may not be taken away from you, and others called in to take the places which you have refused. Come and show love and not base ingratitude to Him who has taken so much pains to prepare this feast for you ; this feast which is not only the greatest gift that he can give you now, but also a pledge of the kingdom which has been prepared for such of you as are faithful, from the foundation of the world.

SERMON LXXXVII.

And they began all at once to make excuse.—St. Luke xiv. 18.

When men are in sin and do not wish to give it up the answer which they commonly make to an invitation of God is an excuse. Excuses! Yes, there are plenty of them. But from what do these men of whom our Lord speaks in this parable wish to be excused? Is it from something painful and humiliating? No, strange to say, it is from a great privilege; it is from a wonderful feast in which men receive the Food of Angels and are made one with God; it is from the feast of the Blessed Sacrament, in which our Blessed Lord offers his own Body and Blood. What! is it possible that one who has the faith and is possessed of reason can slight such a gift from the God who has redeemed him? Listen to the excuse of one: "I have bought a farm." What is a farm? It is dirt. His excuse, then, is that he does not want the Bread of Heaven, because he is occupied with dirt. In a word, he prefers dirt to God. But another man has this excuse for spurning the heavenly banquet: "He has bought five yoke of oxen," and he wants "to go and try them." He declines the company of the saints and angels because he prefers that of oxen. He had rather be with the brutes, because he is much like them himself. His body rules his soul, and he is too much of an animal to care anything about a feast which furnishes only good for the soul.

But we hear yet another excuse. Here is a man who "has married a wife, and therefore cannot come." What does this mean? Does he pretend that the holy sacrament of matrimony is keeping him away? But this is not the shadow of an excuse. Ah! if he would speak out his mind clearly he certainly would have an excuse. He means that he cannot come because he is wallowing in the mire of sin. He is too filthy to come. He would have to purify himself. He cannot put on the wedding garment of divine grace and wallow with the swine, so he thinks that he will leave the Body and Blood of Jesus Christ to others and stay where he is.

You see, brethren, what it is to offer an excuse when God invites or commands; and these are only fair samples of the excuses which all sinners who seek to justify their conduct make. But what do such excuses denote? They are sure signs of impenitence. Men often make hypocrites of themselves by their excuses. Some even make bad confessions by covering their guilt with an excuse; and a great many show their imperfect sorrow for sin in this way. On the other hand, the man who is sincerely sorry for his sins fears nothing so much as to excuse a fault. He would rather accuse himself of too much than to excuse himself for the least fault. Excuses such as are mentioned in this parable may justify men before the world, but never before God. When our souls come before the Divine Judge all their disguises shall be torn off. Eternal justice shall then reveal all; it shall weigh every motive; it shall judge every act.

But what does our Divine Lord say of those who now refuse his invitation to this heavenly banquet? He says: "None of those men who were called shall taste my supper." Those who now receive the sweet invitation of our Blessed Lord to approach the altar will at the hour of death wish for that divine food, which they now treat with so much contempt; but God may then say to them: "You did not come when I invited you, and now you shall not taste my supper."

Third Sunday after Pentecost.

EPISTLE. 1 *St. Peter v.* 6–11. Dearly beloved : Be you humbled under the mighty hand of God, that he may exalt you in the time of visitation. Casting all your solicitude upon him, for he hath care of you. Be sober and watch ; because your adversary the devil, as a roaring lion, goeth about seeking whom he may devour. Whom resist ye, strong in faith : knowing that the same affliction befalleth your brethren who are in the world. But the God of all grace, who hath called us unto his eternal glory in Christ Jesus, when you have suffered a little, will himself perfect, and confirm, and establish you. To him be glory and dominion for ever and ever. Amen.

GOSPEL. *St. Luke xv.* 1–10. At that time : The publicans and sinners drew near unto Jesus to hear him. And the Pharisees and the Scribes murmured, saying: This man receiveth sinners, and eateth with them. And he spoke to them this parable, saying: What man among you that hath a hundred sheep : and if he shall lose one of them, doth he not leave the ninety-nine in the desert, and go after that which was lost until he find it ? And when he hath found it, doth he not lay it upon his shoulders rejoicing : and coming home call together his friends and neighbors, saying to them : Rejoice with me, because I have found my sheep that was lost. I say to you, that even so there shall be joy in heaven upon one sinner that doth penance, more than upon ninety-nine just who need not penance. Or what woman having ten groats, if she lose one groat, doth not light a candle and sweep the house and seek diligently until she find it ? And when she hath found it, call together her friends and neighbors, saying: Rejoice with me, because I have found the groat which I had lost. So I say to you, there shall be joy before the angels of God upon one sinner doing penance.

SERMON LXXXVIII.

Rejoice with me, because I have found my sheep that was lost.
—St. Luke xv. 6.

I AM sure you have often heard related, if you have not yourselves known, examples of the singular affection which parents show towards the worst behaved child they have, the " black sheep of the flock," as their neighbors call him, or her, as the case may be—some wretched, ungrateful, dissipated son whose disgraceful life and cruel treatment of them fairly breaks their hearts; or some disobedient, wild daughter who is led off and gets ruined. While they are in the height of their bad career the parents are very apt to act as if they wished every tie between them broken. No one dares mention the name of their lost child to them. Instances have been known where the angry parents have blotted out the name of the dishonored one from the record in the family Bible where it was written on the day when he was brought back an innocent child from the font of baptism, and when they have taken the little lock of flaxen hair cut from their darling's head, and kept so many years as a treasure, and have scattered it to the winds. But what do we see? There comes a time when things are at their worst, when their poor lost one has reaped the bitter fruits of his disobedience and is in utter misery and despair; then the hearts of the parents are softened; they yearn to see their poor child once more, and all on a sudden there is a reconciliation, all is forgiven and forgotten; the one who was dead has come to life again, and the lost one is found. The parents will not hear one word said against him, but on the contrary, in word and action, say to all their friends: Rejoice with me, because I have found my child that was lost.

Now, if we examine into any such a case we shall almost certainly discover that the penitence of the bad child bears no comparison to the greatness of the parents' affection or to the magnanimity of their forgiveness. Very few such repenting sinners are deserving of the joyful pardon they receive. Mercy is always a mystery, and pardon ever a miracle. So it is with God and his divine forgiveness of repenting sinners. Our Lord tells us there is joy in heaven over their return. Did you ever know any such case whose repentance you thought was worthy of such celestial rejoicings? Very, very few, I am sure. And how many forgiven sinners, do you think, realize that God loves them so much as that—so much that, when he has brought back to his love and obedience one so unworthy, he should tell all his holy angels of the happy event and bid them rejoice with him? Not many. This truth however, is a most important one which our Lord wishes us to learn. It is the greatness of his mercy and the depth of his love. To tell the honest truth, it is the revelation of God's mercy and love that will bring hardened sinners back, which will win and convert them when nothing else will. We often see the proof of this on our missions, when we find the hardest cases, the most abandoned and hopeless sinners, coming to confession after the sermon on the mercy of God. And who does not know that an appeal made to sinners by showing them the crucifix, where they see their Lord and Saviour dying for his great love, with arms outstretched to receive them back, is an argument few of them can withstand? The sermon of the Cross is one the holy church is always preaching—the sermon of love and mercy.

Well, dear brethren, learn this lesson from the Gospel. When you find the burden of sin heavy on you, and your conscience tells you that you have wandered far from God, go before a crucifix and let the love and mercy of your crucified Lord preach to you.

There is nothing helps one so much to overcome the horror and shame of going to confession as a few minutes' prayer on one's knees before a crucifix. Are you in temptation and danger of losing God? Kiss the feet of a crucifix and you are saved. Do you want to win and save those who have sinned against you? Preach to them the sermon of mercy and love, in your own way, and, like God, you will win them and convert them, and rejoice with your friends that you have found the lost one again.   B.

SERMON LXXXIX.

Be sober, and watch.—1 St. Peter v. 8.

THESE few words of the Epistle, my brethren, contain a most important lesson for us. We may indeed say that of all the innumerable souls which have been lost, and which are going down every day into hell, far the greater part have come to this terrible end for neglect of this warning.

There is a proverb, with which you are all familiar, that hell is paved with good intentions. What does this mean? Does it mean that a good intention in itself is a thing which leads to hell? Of course not. But it means that the kind of good intentions which people are too apt to make are signs rather of damnation than of salvation, as they should be.

What is this kind of good intention? It is one which stops just there, and which the one who makes it does not take the means to carry out. Sometimes we call them by a stronger name than intentions. We call them purposes, even firm purposes of amendment. They are the kind of purposes which a great many people make when they repent, or think they repent, of their habitual sins.

A man comes to confession with a fearful habit of sin—of profane swearing, for instance. It has been on him for years. He has learned it in his youth, perhaps, from wicked parents or companions. He has almost become unconscious of it, and it seems to him no very important thing; it may be that he would not even mention it, did not the priest question him pretty closely. But when the priest does warn him about it he makes up his mind in a certain way that he ought to stop it, and makes a kind of purpose to do so. It is to be feared, however, that this is one of the purposes or intentions with which hell is paved. And why? Because it stops just there. It has no effect at all. It is all gone before he gets out of the confession-box. He will swear just as much to-morrow as he did to-day. He does not, probably, even remember his purpose, at any rate only till the time of his Communion; or if, perchance, he does remember it, he does not take the means to carry it out. And what is that means above all others? It is to watch against his sin. This he does not do. He does not keep on his guard to avoid those horrible oaths which have become a fixed habit with him. He does not watch himself, and, of course, falls again as he did before.

Now you see, perhaps, the importance of St. Peter's warning in the Epistle. Most of you who will be lost will be lost on account of habitual sins like this I have spoken of, not on account of occasional and unusual ones. It may be a habit of impure thoughts or words, of drunkenness, or something else; but it is a habit of some kind that will cause your damnation. The habit is a disease of your soul; you must get rid of it, if you wish to have any well-grounded hope of salvation. And you cannot get rid of it without watching as well as praying. "Watch," says our Lord, "that you enter not into temptation."

Yes, a bad habit is a disease of your soul, a weak spot in it which you must guard. It is there your enemy is going to enter. What does St. Peter go on to say? "Be sober, and watch," he says, "for your adversary, the devil, as a roaring lion, goeth about seeking whom he may devour." Very well; the devil is not such a fool as to neglect your weak points. So it is those which you must watch and guard.

If, then, you would be saved, keep before your mind all the time your habitual sins. Be on your guard against them continually, just as a man going on slippery ice is all the time careful how he places his feet. Repeat your resolutions frequently; make them practical and definite. Say to yourself, "Next time I am provoked I will keep down that profane word; next time such an object comes before my eyes

I will turn them away; next time such a thought occurs I will instantly repel it." Be on the lookout for danger, as a sailor is for rocks or icebergs in his course. Pray, of course, earnestly and frequently, but watch as well as pray. If you do you will save your soul; if you do not you will lose it.

SERMON XC.

There shall be joy in heaven upon one sinner that doth penance, more than upon ninety-nine just who need not penance.—St. Luke xv. 7.

I DO not think, my brethren, that there is any parable in the Gospel which comes more home to your own experience than these which you have just heard about the lost sheep and groat. I am sure you have all of you lost something at some time or other; and I am sure, too, that, even though it was not very valuable, you began to think it was when it was lost, and hunted for it high and low. It seemed to you that you cared more for it than for any other article of your property, and that you did not mind much what became of your other things as long as that was missing.

That, of course, was not really the case. For, although you seemed to give all your thoughts and energy in searching for the lost article, you cared just as much all the time for what you meanwhile left at home or unnoticed. And if, while you were hunting up one thing, another should get lost, you would start out after that with just as much anxiety as you did for the other.

So our Lord spends his time, not only now and then

but always, chiefly in hunting after what he has lost, and lets what he has got shift a good deal for itself. Always, I say; for he has always lost something. He keeps losing things all the time. The sheep keep straying away from his fold continually. As soon as one is brought back another has gone, and he has to set out in pursuit of it. And meanwhile the sheep in the fold do not seem to get as much care and attention as they think they deserve for their obedience and general good behavior.

Now, this is an important thing for the sheep to understand, both for those who have not strayed away and for those who have. Those who are faithful must be contented with his absence, and those who are not should thank him and reward him for his labor for them.

Those who need no penance—that is, those who remain habitually in the state of grace—are apt to say: "Why is it that religion does not give me more happiness? Why is it that I have so little devotion and that God seems so far away?" Well, the reason is because he is away. He is off hunting for sinners. He is giving them his chief attention and his choicest graces because they need them. The just can get along with the sacraments, which are always open to them, and with the other ordinary means of salvation.

Or you say, perhaps: "Why is it that the best preachers and confessors among the fathers are out on the mission, so that we seldom or never see or hear them?" Well, that is for the same reason. Our Lord sends them out on the hunt in which he is so much interested. Surely you will not find fault with him. You will not deprive him of his greatest joy— that of bringing sinners back—for the sake of offering him a little more devotion, which he does not care so much about. No, you will rather be faithful, and do your duty in the place where he has put you, and be very thankful that you are not among the lost, and perhaps one among them who will never be found.

And surely those who have strayed away and whom he is seeking, when they come to think of it, will try to give him the consolation which he takes so much trouble to secure. They will not let him spend all his time on them and get nothing for it in return. No, they will not hide from him any longer; they will give themselves to him, never to stray again; and be the occasion of a joy in heaven which shall not be merely for a moment, but which shall last for evermore.

Fourth Sunday after Pentecost.

Epistle. *Rom. viii.* 18–23. Brethren: I reckon that the sufferings of this present time are not worthy to be compared with the glory to come, that shall be revealed in us. For the expectation of the creature waiteth for the revelation of the sons of God. For the creature was made subject to vanity, not willingly, but by reason of him that made it subject, in hope: because the creature also itself shall be delivered from the servitude of corruption into the liberty of the glory of the children of God. For we know that every creature groaneth, and is in labor even till now. And not only it, but ourselves also, who have the first-fruits of the spirit, even we ourselves groan within ourselves, waiting for the adoption of the sons of God, the redemption of our body, in Christ Jesus our Lord.

Gospel. *St. Luke v.* 1–11. At that time: When the multitudes pressed upon Jesus to hear the word of God, he stood by the lake of Genesareth. And he saw two ships standing by the lake: but the fishermen were gone out of them, and were washing their nets. And going up into one of the ships that was Simon's, he desired him to thrust out a little from the land. And sitting down, he taught the multitudes out of the ship. Now when he had ceased to speak, he said to Simon: Launch out into the deep, and let down your nets for a draught. And Simon answering, said to him: Master, we have labored all the night, and have taken nothing: but at thy word I will let down the net. And when they had done this, they enclosed a very great multitude of fishes, and their net was breaking. And they beckoned to their partners that were in the other ship, that they should come and help them. And they came, and filled both the ships, so that they were almost sinking; which when Simon Peter saw, he fell down at Jesus' knees, saying: Depart from me, for I am a sinful man, O Lord. For he was wholly astonished, and all that were with him, at the draught of the fishes which they had taken. And so were also James and John, the sons of Zebedee, who were Simon's partners. And Jesus saith to Simon: Fear not, from henceforth thou shalt be taking men. And when they had brought their ships to land, leaving all things, they followed him.

SERMON XCI.

And sitting down, he taught the multitudes out of the ship. —St. Luke v. 3.

THE ship, as the Gospel tells us, was St. Peter's, and our Lord continues to teach his divine doctrine from the same ship. This ship of St. Peter is the Catholic Church. Its captain is the Pope, the Vicar of Jesus Christ. He not only guides the ship in its ordinary course, but knows also what special orders to give when particular dangers threaten it. The plain duty of every Catholic is, therefore to receive with obedience the teaching of the Pope, and in times of danger to be on the alert and obey quickly, without hesitation and with perfect confidence. There is no fear for the ship herself, no matter what storms may arise. The danger is for those who are in her, and each one's safety depends upon his prompt obedience. There are some Catholics who appear to think that because the ship is always safe they are safe too, no matter how they behave. Alas! this is often a fatal mistake. Christ teaches by the mouth of Peter, and their salvation depends upon their listening to what is taught, and learning the lessons of faith and morality which fall from his lips. But what do we see? We see many who remain so ignorant of their religion that they ought to be ashamed to call themselves Catholics. There is plenty of instruction given, but they take no pains to hear it. Year in and year out they never come to a sermon or instruction. They never think of reading a good religious book or a Catholic newspaper. They have time to go to some immoral play at the theatre, they read the trashy, beastly stuff that is served up daily and weekly to pander to depraved appetites such as theirs, but of their sublime, true, and holy religion, which should be a light to their minds and a comfort to their hearts, they know next to nothing. They let their children grow up in the like ignorance, who are swift to follow the bad example set before them. Now, the chief duty of a Catholic is to learn what his religion teaches, and it is a grievous sin to neglect the opportunities one has to acquire that knowledge. The devil is busy scattering the seed of false doctrine, and keeping his agents at work telling all sorts of lies about God and Jesus Christ and the Catholic Church, and it is not possible for one to keep his faith pure unless he takes care to learn all he has the chance to learn of the truths of his holy religion.

Then, again, see how anxious people are nowadays that their children should have what is called "a good education." What is the teaching of Christ from the ship of Peter on this subject? It is that **without religion education cannot be good.** Our faith, as well as our experience, tells us that an education with religion left out is apt to prove rather a curse than a blessing to a child. Pride, conceit, loose morals, love of money, disobedience to parents and clergy—these are the things we see plenty of in the lives and habits of children who have received a "good education" with religion left out.

There is another thing which is often the subject of much wonder to me. From time to time the bishops and priests find it necessary to warn their people against certain prevailing vices, or to denounce certain secret societies as anti-Christian, or to make regulations which are required to secure the proper administration of the sacraments—for instance, the publication of the bans of marriage—and there are found Catholics who set themselves in opposition to these counsels and laws of their pastors with a pertinacious obstinacy such as one would not expect to see except in a downright heretic. The conceit of these people is truly marvellous. They talk and act as if the whole Catholic Church belonged to them, and their priests were a miserable set of hirelings who can be persuaded to connive at anything they choose to pay them for. What is the reason of this? I'll tell you. It is due to their ignorance. The better instructed a Catholic is the more docile and humble he is. He hears Christ teaching when he hears the instructions of his pastor, and he rejoices to follow his counsels. "He that heareth you heareth me," said our Lord. God send us Catholics who love their religion well enough to make them desirous of being well instructed in its doctrine!

SERMON XCII.

I reckon that the sufferings of this present time are not worthy to be compared with the glory to come.—Rom. viii. 18.

BRETHREN, if we wish to rejoice in the next world we must suffer in this. There is no escape from suffering here if we reckon on happiness hereafter. And there are good reasons for this. One is because we must atone for sin. Do not our own sins, little or great, continually cry out for penance? And if we give not suffering willingly they threaten to crucify us in spite of ourselves. And there are the sins of others, of heathens, and heretics, and bad Catholics—all these demand atonement, and, as it was not beneath the dignity of the Son of God to die for them, so, if we are Christians more than in name, we shall be ready to suffer with our blessed Lord for the sins of the world. Another reason why we must suffer is that we may not become attached to the joys of this world, for we must leave them all some day or other. And, besides, God demands a heart quite undivided; he wants all our love, and not what is left after we have expended our chief affections on created things. And yet another reason for suffering is that we may merit more happiness in heaven. The Christian has a kind Father in heaven, who notes every pang, and sigh, and tear, and who will know how to reward.

So one would think that a wise man would seek sufferings rather than avoid them; would thank God for the afflictions of his providence, and would look upon the troubles of this life—the loss of health, the loss of reputation, the loss of money—would look upon all this as God's way of elevating our life here on earth and of increasing our happiness hereafter; and that it would be true wisdom to voluntarily deny ourselves the joys of this world, reckoning rather upon those of the future life as the apostles did. Yes, brethren, patient suffering is the very A B C of the Christian religion. What are Christ's blessings? Blessed are the poor; blessed are they that mourn; blessed are you when they persecute and revile you. Truly his religion is a religion of the cross.

But what kind of Christians must we think ourselves since we all hate to suffer? We reckon fondly upon the joys of *this* life; those of the life to come may take care of themselves. Although we have a lifetime of horrid sins in our memory, and know that we have not done any penance, still we not only refuse to suffer willingly, but we speak and act as if God were a cruel tyrant thus to send upon us sickness, and poverty, and disgrace. And as to suffering in union with our Lord Jesus Christ for the sins of the world, such a generous thought never enters our mind at all; nor do we think of mortifying the rebellious passions, nor of the merit of sacrifice, nor of anything except to enjoy this world, to cling to this poor, fleeting world and its deceptive joys.

Brethren, let us strive to obtain a wiser and stronger spirit in regard to suffering. I know that we may not hope to become heroes all at once, but may in time if we begin without delay; and the only way to begin is by prayer. You complain of the company of wicked and unpleasant people; but instead of snapping at them and quarrelling, offer your annoyance to God and pray him to assist you. Are you in poverty? Instead of giving way to weariness and despair, think of Jesus and Mary at the humble cottage at Nazareth; think of the poor, wandering life of our Lord while he preached the Gospel, and beg him to give you some of his own patience. Are you afflicted with incurable illness? Remember that God has sent you this for your own good and will know how to recompense you. Instead of making your friends miserable by your impatience, think of Christ upon the cross, and of your sins which crucified him.

St. Teresa had for her motto these words: "*Either to suffer or to die.*" Oh! that we had only a little of the heroic spirit of the saints. Then we could welcome every dispensation of divine providence, whether of pleasure or of pain, and should be able to say with St. Paul: "I have learned in whatsoever state I am to be content therewith. I know both how to be brought low and how to abound . . . both to be full and to be hungry, both to abound and to suffer need; I can do all things in him who strengtheneth me" (Phil. iv. 11–13).

Fifth Sunday after Pentecost.

Epistle. 1 *St. Peter iii.* 8–15. Dearly beloved : Be ye all of one mind, having compassion one of another, loving brotherhood, merciful, modest, humble : not rendering evil for evil, nor railing for railing, but on the contrary, blessing : for unto this are you called, that by inheritance you may possess a blessing. "For he that will love life, and see good days, let him refrain his tongue from evil, and his lips that they speak no guile. Let him decline from evil, and do good : let him seek peace, and pursue it : because the eyes of the Lord are upon the just, and his ears unto their prayers : but the countenance of the Lord against them that do evil things." And who is he that can hurt you, if you be zealous of good? But if also you suffer anything for justice' sake, blessed are ye. And be not afraid of their terror and be not troubled ; but sanctify the Lord Christ in your heart.

Gospel. *St. Matt. v.* 20–24. At that time : Jesus said to his disciples : I say to you, that unless your justice abound more than that of the Scribes and Pharisees, you shall not enter into the kingdom of heaven. You have heard that it was said to them of old : Thou shalt not kill. And whosoever shall kill shall be guilty of the judgment. But I say to you, that whosoever is angry with his brother, shall be guilty of the judgment. And whosoever shall say to his brother, Raca, shall be guilty of the council. And whosoever shall say, Thou fool, shall be guilty of hell fire. Therefore if thou offerest thy gift at the altar, and there shalt remember that thy brother hath anything against thee, leave there thy gift before the altar, and first go to be reconciled to thy brother, and then come and offer thy gift.

SERMON XCIII.

Unless your justice abound more than that of the Scribes and Pharisees, you shall not enter into the kingdom of heaven. —ST. MATT. v. 20.

THE Scribes and Pharisees were very particular about keeping the *letter* of the law, and prided themselves mightily on this kind of "justice." But Jesus Christ says that unless *our* righteousness exceed theirs we shall not save our souls. Here, then, he teaches us that we must keep the *spirit* of the commandments as well as the letter. And to show what he means by the *spirit* of the law, he quotes the commandment which forbids murder. "Now, it is not enough," he says, "that you refrain from committing murder; you must equally refrain from the passion of anger—anger, that is, which destroys charity, and breeds ill-will, hatred, and revenge; for those who give way to these malicious feelings shall be arraigned at my judgment-seat side by side with murderers." Among those who heard him was St. John, his apostle; and St. John says: "He that hateth his brother *is* a murderer."

Again, our Lord tells us that the spirit of the Fifth Commandment includes lesser sins than anger—that to call our brother contemptuous names, to provoke and irritate him by hard words (except, of course, in the case of just rebuke), is a grave violation of this law as he would have us Christians understand it.

The words which follow—addressed to those who

were in the habit of going into the temple to lay their gifts before God's altar—apply with even greater force to *us*. *We* come before God's altar when we come to hear Mass, and we come with the profession, at least, of offering a gift—that worship which is the tribute of our faith and love. There is one thing, then, which our Lord requires before he will receive our offering: that " our brother have" not "anything against us." In other words, we must be in perfect charity with our neighbor. If *we* have anything against *him*, we must forgive him there and then "from our hearts." If *he* have anything against *us*, we must either have already done our best towards reconciliation and reparation, or at least be prepared and determined to do it at the very first opportunity.

Now, it may be we are not in the state of grace when we come to hear Mass, but, on the contrary, laden with mortal sins. Well, we still have the right to hear Mass—nay, are bound to hear it; and, further, we can still offer a gift, and a very acceptable gift—an earnest prayer for contrition and amendment—a cry for mercy and deliverance. Our Lord once said to St. Mathilda: "However guilty a man may be, however inveterate the enmity of his heart against me. I will patiently bear with him whenever he is present at Mass, and will readily grant him the pardon of his sins if he sincerely ask it." Clearly, then, dear brethren, there is but one thing that can keep even a poor sinner from coming before God's altar with an acceptable gift—viz., the want of charity to his neighbor; that is, either the refusal to say from his heart: " Forgive us our trespasses *as we forgive* those who trespass against us"; or, equally, the refusal to seek reconciliation or make reparation for wrongs of his own doing. Now, in either case there is a brother who "has something against us," and that brother is Jesus Christ himself, who calls all men his brethren without exception, and especially our fellow-Catholics, having given to all his Sacred Heart and the love of his Blessed Mother.

B.

SERMON XCIV.

He that will love life and see good days, let him refrain his tongue from evil.—1 St. Peter iii. 10.

THE words of the blessed Apostle St. Peter teach us that the good, peaceable man is the happiest, that God rewards a kind heart even in this life. Yes, the kindly-spoken man is a happy man. He has no quarrels on his hands. You cannot make him quarrel. Though he be strong and active, yet he is incapable of using his strength to injure his neighbor. Say a sharp, bitter thing to him, and instead of feeling insulted, he will laugh it off, and tell you to be good-natured, or will act as if *he* had offended *you*. And the good, peaceable man is no slanderer or tale-bearer. When he hears anything to his neighbor's detriment he is sorry; he buries it in his kind heart, and tries to forget it. If his friends quarrel among themselves, he is the ready and successful peacemaker. If death, sickness, or misfortune of any kind afflicts his neighbor, he is the kind and skilful comforter. What do people think of such a man? Everybody loves him. And is not that happiness? Why, if a dog loves you it gives you joy, and the affection of many friends makes this world a paradise. So the good, peaceable man has that element of a lovely life and good days.

I need not say that the good, peaceable man is happy in his family. How children love a kind parent! How they enjoy home when he is there, with his happy laugh and innocent jest! His wife is proud of that husband, and blesses God for such a father for her little ones. There is no bickering, jealousy, or ill-will in that home, but charity and joy the whole year round.

And the good, peaceable man is happy in his own self-respect. Without presumption he may say with the apostle: "I owe no man anything." He owes no man any grudge. He has inflicted sorrow upon no man. He has deprived no man of honor or of goods. He who is not at war with his neighbor is at peace with himself. His conscience is at peace, and a peaceful conscience is a soft pillow. So that by his kind words and deeds he really loves his life, as St. Peter says, and has provided himself with good days.

But besides all this, God watches over the good, peaceable man. "He that loveth his neighbor hath fulfilled the law," says the Scripture. Our Lord loves those who love his children, and he is one who can make his friends happy. Did he not promise a reward for even a cup of cold water? And are not kind words often of more worth than bodily refreshment? God loves the good, peaceable man, and the love of God is enough to make any one happy.

So the next time you complain and say, "Oh! why am I so miserable? what ails me or my family, or my neighbors, that I am always in hot water, and can scarcely call one day in ten really happy?" just ask yourself: "Am I a peaceable, good-natured man?" Anger, hatred, and ill-will poison one's food as well as kill the soul, disturb one's sleep as well as perplex the conscience. To be happy you must be loved; and who will love one who hates? A sour face, a bitter tongue, a bad heart, gain no friends. A harsh voice, a cruel hand, a selfish heart, turn wife and child into enemies. So the suspicious man is unhappy; he breeds treason and jealousy among his friends. The touchy man is unhappy; you shun his company, for you fear to offend him. The critical man is unhappy; he is over-zealous about others and careless of himself. And, brethren, I might continue the sad litany, and to every unkind act, or thought, or word I could answer, It makes men miserable.

Come, brethren, let us all try and be good-natured. Let us be so for the love of our Lord, who made and loves us all, and died to bind us all together in one happy household.

Sixth Sunday after Pentecost.

EPISTLE. *Rom. vi.* 3–11. Brethren: We all, who are baptized in Christ Jesus, are baptized in his death. For we are buried together with him by baptism unto death: that as Christ is risen from the dead by the glory of the Father, so we also may walk in newness of life. For if we have been planted together in the likeness of his death, in like manner we shall be of his resurrection. Knowing this, that our old man is crucified with him, that the body of sin may be destroyed, and that we may serve sin no longer. For he that is dead is justified from sin. Now if we be dead with Christ, we believe that we shall live also together with Christ: knowing that Christ rising again from the dead, dieth now no more, death shall no more have dominion over him. For in that he died to sin, he died once: but in that he liveth, he liveth unto God. So do you also reckon yourselves to be dead indeed to sin, but alive to God in Christ Jesus our Lord.

GOSPEL. *St. Mark viii.* 1–9. At that time: When there was a great multitude with Jesus, and had nothing to eat, calling his disciples together, he saith to them: I have compassion on the multitude, for behold they have now been with me three days, and have nothing to eat. And if I send them away fasting to their own houses, they will faint in the way, for some of them came from afar off. And his disciples answered him: From whence can any one satisfy them here with bread in the wilderness? And he asked them: How many loaves have ye? And they said: Seven. And he commanded the people to sit down on the ground, and taking the seven loaves, giving thanks, he broke, and gave to his disciples to set before them, and they sat them before the people. And they had a few little fishes, and he blessed them and commanded them to be set before them. And they did eat and were filled, and they took up that which was left of the fragments, seven baskets. And they that had eaten were about four thousand: and he sent them away.

SERMON XCV.

Taking the seven loaves, giving thanks, he broke and gave to his disciples to set before them.—St. Mark viii. 6.

ON this and on other occasions our Lord Jesus Christ blessed the food that was to be eaten. In imitation of his divine example we are taught to give thanks and bless ourselves and our food at meals. This pious practice is commonly called grace before and after meat. The word "grace" is English for the Latin word *"gratias,"* which means thanks, taken from the thanksgiving to be said after meals. There are two prayers to be said, therefore: the first, a blessing to be invoked upon ourselves and upon the food prepared; and the second, a thanksgiving to be said after we have eaten it. The first is as follows: "Bless us, O Lord, and these thy gifts which we are about to receive from thy bountiful hands, through Christ our Lord. Amen."

When we say the words, "Bless us, O Lord," we should make the sign of the cross on ourselves. When we say "These thy gifts," we should make the sign of the cross over the table. The thanksgiving is said thus: "We give thee thanks, Almighty God, for all thy benefits, who livest and reignest for ever and ever. Amen." And it is also proper to add: "May the souls of the faithful departed, through the mercy of God, rest in peace." Th Catholic practice is also to say these prayers standing.

In religious communities the blessing and grace are much longer, consisting of versicles and sentences from Scripture appropriate to the ecclesiastical season or festival; the Lord's Prayer is said and the "Te Deum" is said.

This is a pious practice which ought to prevail in all Catholic families. The children should be taught to do it from the time they can bless themselves and lisp the words. Yes, everything we eat and wear ought to be blessed first before we use it. The sign of the cross and asking God's blessing is to acknowledge, as we are in duty bound, the source of all that is given to us, and to sanctify it to our own use, and also to make a good intention in using it. To act otherwise—to hurry to table and eat and drink without a thought of God or a word of religion, as I have seen so many do—is to act like a heathen or a beast.

And this practice is not only for those who have a table set before them supplied with every luxury in the way of food, but it is especially good for those whose poverty compels them to sit down to scanty and common meals. The rich certainly ought to bless their bountifully-supplied tables, lest they prove to them the dangerous occasion of intemperance and gluttony, but the poor should remember the miracle of to-day's Gospel, when our Lord blessed and gave thanks over seven loaves and a few little fishes, and with that small store satisfied the hunger of four thousand people. God is ever a kind, loving Father, and will not forget the cry of those who put their trust in him. Such was the trust of the poor man who had nothing but a little porridge to set before his family at dinner when he said: "God be good to us, and make this trifle of porridge go far enough for a poor man with a wife and seven children."

This makes me think of two classes of people who I wish could be obliged to bless with the sign of the cross what they give and receive as nourishment. I mean the liquor-seller and the drunkard. The grocery-keeper, the butcher, the baker could do it, and why not the liquor-seller? You know the result if they did. the one would soon give up the business, and the other would soon give up drinking.

But do not forget, as some do, to return thanks— to say the *grace* after meals. Thank God for what you have received from his bounty. Again I say, act like a reasonable being and a Christian in this, and not like a heathen or a beast. You who are parents should see to the carrying out of this instruction. If you have not done so yet, begin to-day. Let the father say the prayer and make the sign of the cross over the table, and if one of the children come late don't give him a morsel to eat till he has said his blessing. In all things remember you are Christians, "giving thanks always for all things in the name of our Lord Jesus Christ to God and the Father."

SERMON XCVI.

Know you not that all we who are baptized in Christ Jesus are baptized in his death.—ROM. vi. 3.

THESE are strong words, brethren, too strong, I fear, to be accepted in their full meaning by many of us; for we are quite too apt to mitigate the strong doctrine of Christ. Those great maxims of penance, of poverty, of obedience, of perfection, which the saints understood in their plain reality, we are very anxious to understand in a figurative sense, or to apply to somebody else besides our guilty selves. But let us look fairly and frankly at these strong words of St. Paul. How are we baptized in Christ's death? By being guilty of the sins which delivered him up to his enemies. Did he not die on account of mortal sins, and have we not committed mortal sins—violated God's most sacred commandments, and done it often—and wilfully, and knowingly, and habitually done it? Then the innocent blood of the Lamb of God is upon our hands, and nothing but penance can ever wash it off. And what sort of a penance? So thorough, so heartfelt, so practical that the apostle says it must condemn and put us to death with Christ; a penance so thorough that our Lord himself tells us that it must produce a new being in us: "Unless a man be born again he cannot enter into the kingdom of heaven." So you see that St. Paul, in the words of our text, has given us the very charter of Christian penance; just as he explains it a little further on: "Knowing this, that our old man is crucified with Christ, that the body of sin may be destroyed."

Behold, therefore, brethren, the plain statement of the greatest of all the practical duties of the Christian; to make reparation to God for his sins in union with the sufferings and death of Jesus Christ. They tell us that our only hope of restored innocence is in participation in the crucifixion—its shame, its **agony, and** its death.

Oh! that we could fully realize the necessity of penance. Oh! that the terrible form of Christ upon the cross could be ever in our eyes as it is ever above our altars. Oh! that the awful cries of Jesus' death agony could be ever sounding in our ears. Then we should be Christians indeed. Then the profound hatred of sin, the Christian duties of fasting and prayer, the holy offices of helping the poor and instructing the ignorant, the devout reception of God's grace in the sacraments ; in a word, all the yearly round of a good Catholic life would have its true meaning. If we appreciated that Christ died for our sins, we should not have to drag ourselves so reluctantly to confession, we should not grumble at the fast of Lent, we should not strive to creep out of the duty of paying our debt of penance to God by this or that all too ready excuse, but we should take Christ for our example and his cross for our standard, and long for stripes and even death as the wages of sin. We should appreciate the wisdom of what the old monk of the desert said to the novice when asked for a motto: "Wherever you are, or whatever you are doing, say often to yourself : I am a pilgrim." Yes, a pilgrim ; a banished son wearily waiting till his Father shall call him home ; a convicted traitor working out the years of his banishment. I know, brethren, that this sounds like a melancholy doctrine. Yet is it not true? And to know the truth is the first beginning of peace in the heart. And listen to the joyful side. Hear it stated by the apostle in this very epistle : "For if we have been planted together in the likeness of his death, in like manner we shall be of his resurrection." Yes ; if we die to our old selves and to sin, we shall rise with our Lord Jesus Christ to everlasting glory. He sprang forth from the grave filled with joy, triumphing over sin; and so shall we rise if we are buried with him in penance. And what is the world's joy compared to the joy of paradise? What care we for a few years of labor and waiting here, when we think of the countless ages of the kingdom of heaven! You have heard, brethren, that St. Peter of Alcantara led a very penitential life; well, shortly after death he appeared to one of his friends surrounded with heavenly light and his face beaming with joy, and he exclaimed: "Oh! happy penance which has gained for me so great a reward." Brethren, let us do penance while we can, and leave it to a good God to provide us with happiness, and he will give us joys which will never fade.

SERMON XCVII.

That as Christ is risen from the dead by the glory of the Father, so we also may walk in newness of life.—ROMANS vi. 4.

THE words of the Epistle to-day carry us back to Easter-tide, and give us a renewal of the lessons of Easter. St. Paul tells us that as Christ is risen from the dead and dieth no more, so we also should die indeed to sin, and rise again to newness of life through Jesus Christ our Lord. And as the Gospel relates how our Lord miraculously fed the multitudes in the wilderness, the church to-day seems to speak with especial force to those who have let the Easter-time go by without fulfilling the precept of yearly Communion, without seeking that heavenly food without which our souls must surely die of starvation. To to all sinners the church appeals to-day, bidding them at least now to rise from the death of sin and walk in newness of life.

The circumstances attending our Lord's resurrection teach us how we, too, should rise from the dead. An angel descended from heaven, and a mighty earthquake shook the holy sepulchre. And so the grace of God descends into our hearts, moving us to penance, and as with an earthquake our hearts must tremble with the fear of God and true sorrow for our sins. And then as the angel rolled away the stone from the mouth of the tomb, so divine grace will assist us in removing every obstacle in the way of our repentance—the slowness and dulness of our minds and wills, our spiritual sloth, the false shame that may keep us back from a good confession. Arise, and, God's grace urging you, make one mighty effort, and the stone will speedily be rolled away.

Around the grave of our Lord stood the watch of Roman soldiers, guarding the seal that had been set upon the stone. Satan, perhaps, has set his seal upon your heart, and the devils watch around it for fear you should break loose from their bondage. But if you are determined to rise from the death of sin they will be as powerless to hinder you as the Roman soldiers were to prevent the resurrection of Jesus. When he rose from the dead he left behind him the grave-clothes and linen bandages with which his body had been bound. And this teaches us that we should leave behind us our evil habits and inclinations, and no longer remain slaves to our passions. Lazarus could not walk freely after his resurrection until he had been freed from his grave-clothes.

Your grave-clothes are the habits of sin you have contracted, the cravings of your sensual appetites, the love of sin that lingers in your hearts. Cast off these thongs that bind your souls, that you may walk freely in newness of life. When the women came to seek the body of Jesus the angel said to them: "Why seek you the living among the dead? He is not here, but is risen." If, risen from the death of sin, Satan should again seek to gain possession of you; if your former bad companions should try to bring you back to your old ways; if the voice of passion should strongly lure you to leave the path of right, you can answer: "Why seek you the living among the dead? My soul is not here; but is risen—risen from the dead. It dieth no more; death hath no more dominion over it." Crucify, then, my dear brethren, the old man within you, that the body of sin may be destroyed, and that you may serve sin no longer. "Let not sin reign in your mortal bodies, so as to obey the lusts thereof," but "reckon yourselves to be dead indeed unto sin, but alive to God, in Christ Jesus our Lord." As our Lord had compassion upon those who listened to his words, and fed them with the loaves and fishes, so will he also have mercy upon you, if you hearken to his voice now calling you to penance, and will feed you with his own most precious Body and Blood.

Seventh Sunday after Pentecost.

EPISTLE. *Rom. vi.* 19-23. Brethren: I speak a human thing, because of the infirmity of your flesh. For as you have yielded your members to serve uncleanness and iniquity, unto iniquity ; so now yield your members to serve justice, unto sanctification. For when you were the servants of sin, you were free from justice. What fruit therefore had you then in those things, of which you are now ashamed ? For the end of them is death. But now being made free from sin, and become servants to God, you have your fruit unto sanctification, and the end everlasting life. For the wages of sin is death : but the grace of God, everlasting life in Christ Jesus our Lord.

GOSPEL. *St. Matt. vii.* 15-21. At that time: Jesus said to his disciples: Beware of false prophets, who come to you in the clothing of sheep, but inwardly they are ravenous wolves. By their fruits you shall know them. Do men gather grapes of thorns, or figs of thistles ? Even so every good tree yieldeth good fruit, and the bad tree bad fruit. A good tree cannot yield bad fruit, neither can a bad tree yield good fruit. Every tree that yieldeth not good fruit, shall be cut down, and shall be cast into the fire. Wherefore by their fruits you shall know them. Not every man that saith to me, Lord, Lord, shall enter into the kingdom of heaven : but he that doeth the will of my Father who is in heaven, he shall enter into the kingdom of heaven.

SERMON XCVIII.

Beware of false prophets, who come to you in the clothing of sheep, but inwardly they are ravenous wolves.—St. Matt. vii. 15.

A PROPHET is a teacher, and a teacher who assumes to have more than ordinary knowledge. He is one who claims to speak from authority, and demands a hearing on the score of his being inspired directly by the all-wise God, or as being commissioned to speak in the name of God. When such true teachers speak to us we are bound, of course, to listen to them, to receive their words with humility and obey them implicitly.

It is the way of God with men. We are taught all we know. Now, if all teachers were true teachers, all men would believe alike and there would be no error in the world. But because there have been and are many false teachers, there are many false religions and innumerable lies of all kinds which thousands believe to be truths. For one to be sure, therefore, that what he believes is true, he must not be simply content with the fact that *he* sincerely believes it, but he must know that his teacher is a true teacher.

Those who are not Catholics wonder how it is that we feel so certain of the truths of our faith. Their wonder would cease if they were to become Catholics, as it does happen with all converts; for then they would know, as we know, *how it feels to be sure of one's teacher.* That is our inestimable privilege and inexpressible joy—that we know our teacher is true, and that a false teacher is instantly detected, no matter how carefully and cunningly he has put on his sheep's clothing. The disguise is never thick enough to hide the wolf's teeth and claws.

I do not say that a Catholic may not be deceived and be misled by these wolves in sheep's clothing, else our Lord would not have told us to beware of such, and the history of all heresies proves that many can be deceived by them. But that is their fault. They go out of the fold where all is light and clear, and where a wolf is found out in a moment, and they wander about in places and in company where there is no light of divine faith. To tell the truth, the false teacher finds his victims already misled and enticed away by their own passions and pride. He finds they have already begun to believe a lie, and he has only to encourage them in it. What do I mean by wandering outside the fold? I mean imitating the talk and following the example of those whose principles are false; who say: "Religion is a matter of choice"; "It does not matter what a man believes so long as he is good"; "Education is the business of the state"; "Religion has nothing to do with science"; and also immoral principles such as these: "A man cannot help his nature"; "A young man is expected to sow his wild oats"; "We are in the world and must go with it," and such like.

When a Catholic talks that way he is fair game for the first false teacher that comes along.

Then one wanders outside the fold and is caught by the wolves when he ventures into forbidden secret societies. These wolves have got the sheep's clothing of charity and brotherly love on. It is a wonder that there can be found Catholics silly enough not to feel the wolf's claw the first time they are taught the secret-society grip. "Charity and brotherly love" forsooth! They had better say, "We swear to love ourselves, and to look out for number one," for this is what all the twaddle of these secret brotherhoods amounts to. Avoid them. Their leaders are false teachers, their principles are false, and their association is dangerous to both faith and morals.

Beware of the false newspaper prophet. Everybody reads the newspapers, and too many, alas! think they have the right to read any newspaper that is printed. That is what the false newspaper prophet says when he offers for sale his filthy, licentious, and lying sheet. Beware of him! His talk is corrupting and demoralizing.

Do you wish, dear brethren, to make sure of not being deceived by these wolves in sheep's clothing? Then obey with humility and docility the shepherd of the flock. When he cries, "Wolf! wolf!" then be sure that there is a wolf. Defer to his judgment. *His* preaching, you know, is true. Follow that, and not even the devil himself can deceive you.

SERMON XCIX.

Every tree is known by its fruit.—St. Luke vi. 44.

THE great lesson taught us to-day by the offices of the church is that the Christian life of faith must show itself in good works. Faith is the foundation, but a building must not stop with the foundation; more stones must be added continually until it rises complete in all its parts, according to the plan of the architect. So we must not be content with the foundation of faith, but, by co-operating with the graces

God is always giving us, must be always striving after the model set before us by the Divine Architect, our Lord Jesus Christ, always adding virtue to virtue, until at last we shall appear before the God of gods in Sion to receive the reward of our good deeds. Faith is the root, but the root must grow into a tree, and put forth not only leaves and blossoms, not only pious thoughts and fine words, but the fruit of good deeds, the fruit of a life spent in conformity to the maxims of our holy faith.

Our Lord tells us that a tree is known by its fruit. For there is no good tree that bringeth forth evil fruit, nor an evil tree that bringeth forth good fruit. So the earnestness of our faith will be known by our lives. If we find that our lives correspond to what our faith teaches us, we may be sure that our faith is living and not dead. "By their fruits ye shall know them." Alas! how many who call themselves Catholics make their lives an argument against the faith in the hands of its enemies, who point at us the finger of scorn, and loudly proclaim that, by our Lord's own test, we fail. And then we have the careless and the lukewarm, who, while they are not an open scandal, yet fall far short of the test our Lord proposes. In them we see plenty of leaves, and even blossoms, but the fruit is sadly wanting, or, at best, is but worm-eaten and rotten through a lack of earnestness and a pure intention. They, perhaps, will talk about their faith as though they were the most zealous Catholics in the world; but if we look into their practice we find it very different from what their language would lead us to expect. How many, for instance, are ready enough to defend in argument the doctrine of the

Real Presence who never think of making a visit to the Blessed Sacrament, nay, who rarely approach the Holy Communion, and perhaps have not made their Easter-duty!

Well, I fear it will always be so. Fine words are cheap and good resolutions are easily made, but it is another thing to keep them. But listen to our Lord's warning: "Every tree that yieldeth not good fruit shall be cut down, and cast into the fire." Our eternal welfare depends upon our deeds. Our faith alone will not save us. It is necessary, indeed; for just as the root is to the tree the source of all its life, so faith is what gives to our good works their merit before God. But unless it bears the fruit of good works it is worthless and dead.

"Not every one that saith unto me, Lord, Lord, shall enter the kingdom of heaven: but he that doth the will of my Father who is in heaven, he shall enter into the kingdom of heaven." That is to say, not every one who professes the true faith shall be saved, but those only who shall bring their wills into conformity with the will of God. It is not enough to acknowledge God as our Lord and King, if his holy will is not fulfilled in us and by us. If we would enter into life eternal we must keep the commandments of God and his church. And we also do the will of God by suffering it; that is, by enduring with patience all the trials and crosses he may send us, for these are his holy will for us as much as his positive precepts. There is often more merit in patiently suffering than in great deeds that would astound the world. This is the way to fulfil the prayer so often on our lips: "Thy will be done on earth as it is in heaven." Strive, then, both in doing and in suffering, to make real for yourselves this holy petition, that God may not have to say of you, as he said of the Jews of old: "This people honoreth me with their lips, but their heart is far from me."

SERMON C.

The wages of sin is death.—ROMANS vi. 23.

THIS is a truth plain enough to the thoughtful; but there are some, alas! who think about it only when it is too late. The wages have not yet become due, and the sinner, thinking only of his present pleasures, goes on unmindful of that time when the terrible wages will have to be paid in full.

Death, says St. Paul, is the wages. Tell a man that if he goes to a certain place or performs a certain act the penalty will be death, and he cannot be persuaded to go to that place or perform that fatal act. On the other hand, he will do anything to save himself from such a fate. But the death of which St. Paul speaks is not to be compared with that of the body, for it is the soul. The wages of sin is, then, a spiritual death. If we could see before us in one vast pile a number of bodies corrupted by death, what a revolting spectacle it would be! But if we could see the dead souls of so many around us, who seem to be so full of life, as God beholds them, we should be far more horrified. There are some who, as they sit in their houses, walk in the streets, are engaged at work, or even as they are on their knees in church, have with them only wretched corpses of souls. Who will reap this terrible wages of sin? We have all sinned, therefore we must all reap some of its wages. By the sin of one man "death has passed unto all men, in whom all have sinned." Death is the most dreadful temporal calamity with which we are acquainted; yet it is the wages which the whole human race have to pay for the sin of one.

But the penalty of that second death, which is eternal, is the most terrible wages of sin; and yet our holy faith teaches us that one mortal sin is enough to cause the instant death of the soul. But the man who lives in mortal sin abides in death. Every sin that he commits plunges his soul deeper into the abyss of death, till at last he receives the full wages of his crimes in the flames of hell. How shall we escape this terrible penalty? Our blessed Lord, by his death, received the wages due to us on account of sin. Through the infinite merits of his death our souls may be brought to life, if we will truly repent and sin no more. St. Paul says: "As in Adam all die, so also in Christ all shall be made alive." But we cannot hope to escape the bitter wages of sin, unless we cease to sin. If we live in sin, and, as generally happens to such, die in sin, we shall not be helped by the death of Christ, but shall receive more bitter wages for our sins than if Christ had not died for us. We shall then, in addition to our other crimes, be guilty of the death of our Blessed Redeemer; for, as St. Paul says: "By our sins we crucify Jesus Christ afresh."

There are, also, wages which have to be paid for sins forgiven. Though the eternal guilt is remitted, the infinite justice of God has yet to be satisfied. We shall all of us have to receive the wages of our forgiven sins in penance and sufferings in this life and in purgatory till the last farthing has been paid.

This ought to make us fearful about our past sins, and to make us dread nothing so much as to fall into sin again. The words of the text, "For the wages of sin is death," should be continually in our minds when we are tempted to sin, and, knowing the terrible consequences which must follow every sin, we shall rather endure any temporal evil than to incur the terrible misfortune of having offended God.

Eighth Sunday after Pentecost.

EPISTLE. *Rom. viii.* 12-17. Brethren : We are debtors not to the flesh, to live according to the flesh. For if you live according to the flesh, you shall die. But if by the spirit you mortify the deeds of the flesh, you shall live. For whosoever are led by the spirit of God, they are the sons of God. For you have not received the spirit of bondage again in fear: but you have received the spirit of adoption of sons, whereby we cry, Abba (Father). For the Spirit himself giveth testimony to our spirit, that we are the sons of God. And if sons, heirs also : heirs indeed of God, and joint heirs with Christ.

GOSPEL. *St. Luke xvi.* 1-9. At that time : Jesus spoke to his disciples this parable : There was a certain rich man who had a steward : and the same was accused unto him, that he had wasted his goods. And he called him, and said to him : What is this I hear of thee ? Give an account of thy stewardship : for now thou canst not be steward. And the steward said within himself : What shall I do, because my lord taketh away from me the stewardship ? To dig I am not able, to beg I am ashamed. I know what I will do, that when I shall be put out of the stewardship, they may receive me into their houses. Therefore calling together every one of his lord's debtors, he said to the first : How much dost thou owe my lord ? But he said : A hundred barrels of oil. And he said to him : Take thy bill and sit down quickly, and write fifty. Then he said to another : And how much dost thou owe ? Who said : A hundred quarters of wheat. He said to him : Take thy bill and write eighty. And the lord commended the unjust steward, forasmuch as he had done wisely: for the children of this world are wiser in their generation than the children of light. And I say to you: Make to yourselves friends of the mammon of iniquity, that when you shall fail they may receive you into everlasting dwellings.

SERMON CI.

Make to yourselves friends of the mammon of iniquity, that when you shall fail they may receive you into everlasting dwellings.—St. Luke xvi. 9.

WHAT is this mammon of iniquity of which, or with which (for that is the true sense of the words), we are to make friends for ourselves? It is the money or other property that God has given us to use in this world. We have only to read a few verses more to see that this is what it means; for when our Lord said immediately afterwards, "You cannot serve God and Mammon," the evangelist tells us that "the Pharisees, who were covetous, laughed at him."

It is called the mammon of iniquity or injustice, because it is the cause of almost all the injustice in the world.

We have, then, to make friends for ourselves with the money or other temporal means which God has entrusted to us.

This is what the steward of whom the Gospel tells us did. He was entrusted by his master with the management of an estate. He was to take care of it in his master's interest, not in his own, for it did not belong to him; as we are here to use our property in God's interest, for he is our Master, and what we have really belongs to him and not to ourselves.

The steward was not faithful to his master; he wasted his goods; so he was discharged from his office and had to give an account of his stewardship, as we also shall have to give an account of ours to our Master when we are discharged from it—that is, when we come to die. Then he began to think how he could make use of the means that had been committed to him to provide for himself in the new state of life upon which he had to enter. He had not much time to make his arrangements, but he hit upon a very good plan. In that we do not resemble him, for with all our lifetime to make our arrangements in, and the certainty that we shall have some time to be discharged from our stewardship, and give an account of it before the judgment-seat of God, we too often make none at all. As our Lord says: "The children of this world are wiser in their generation than the children of light."

The steward, I say, hit on a good plan; and that was to obtain the favor of his master's debtors by taking something off the bills which they had to pay, that they might in return contribute something to his support and save him from the necessity of working or begging for the remainder of his life. In this way he made friends for himself with the money which had been committed to him, in order that these friends might receive him into their dwellings when he was turned out of his own.

This is the part of his conduct which we have to imitate. We have to imitate the steward by making friends with the means which our Lord has given us —friends who will be of service to us in the new life upon which we have so soon to enter, the life which comes after death.

But who are these friends to be? Generally people try to buy the favor of the rich and the great. But these are not the friends who are going to be of use to us in the next world.

No, the poor, not the rich, are the ones whose friendship will be of use to us there. In this life they will not help those who help them, because they cannot; but they will in the next. If you help them the blessing which they give you is not only a blessing when you receive it, but it is treasured up for you, long after you have forgotten it, in God's eternal memory.

He is preparing in heaven beautiful and glorious mansions for these friends of yours, who are also friends of his, to make up for the miserable ones in which they have lived on earth. There are others like them which he is preparing for us all. He has gone to get them ready. "In my Father's house," said our Lord, " there are many mansions. . . . I go to prepare a place for you."

These mansions are being prepared for you, but whether you enter into their possession depends very much on how you treat the poor, to whom they more properly belong. Be charitable, then, to them, for they have the keys of the homes which you will shortly have to seek.

And in your charity to the poor remember one who is always poor, at least in this country of ours. I mean God's holy church. She is a very great beggar, and a very tiresome one, I know—always asking you for more; it seems as if she would never be satisfied, and I do not believe she ever will. But then she is a good friend of yours, and what you give to her is, like what you give to other poor people, more for your own good than for hers. For it is chiefly by her help that you are to reach those everlasting dwellings which our Lord promises to you. If you did not do anything for her it certainly would be hard for you to be saved; for it is through her that the means of salvation come. The more liberal you are to her the more liberally will those means be given to you; and if you think you have enough of them, and are quite sure of heaven with what you have got, certainly that is not the case with everybody; and you know we ought to love our neighbor as ourselves.

These, then, God's poor and his church, are the best friends you can make with the temporal means that he has given you, for they are the ones who can provide for you in that eternity which is coming so soon. Imitate the prudence of the steward, and you will not only make friends as he did, but you will also please your Master, which he did not, and obtain from Him who is your best friend an eternal reward.

SERMON CII.

Give an account of thy stewardship.—St. Luke xvi. 2.

THERE is nothing said against the ability of this steward. On the contrary, he gives every evidence of being a shrewd business man. His investments had probably been prudent, and his debtors reliable men. The fault for which he is held blamable is carelessness. He had not kept his accounts squared up. If the master had waited for the regular time of enquiring into his accounts, or had given him a little notice of his intention to do so, he would, in all probability, have found everything in excellent order, and have praised his steward for his good management. But he came upon him unawares, when he had many debts outstanding and his books were in disorder. This, in a business man, is inexcusable; and whenever we hear of a similar case we always condemn the unfortunate man, and say, "It served him right; he should have attended to his business." Little do we think, indeed, how our own words may some day stand witness against us. The application of the Gospel is too plain to need any explanation, but there is one point I would impress upon you particularly this morning: our carelessness. We are all stewards of our own souls, and concerning the care we have taken of them, the use to which we have put the many opportunities of merit, the investment, as it were, we have made of the innumerable graces offered us, we shall have to render a strict account, and at what moment we know not. We know that we have many debts, and that it would go hard with us if we had to meet them at once; we know that we have not straightened up our accounts for a long time, and that everything is in disorder. Yet we go on in the same careless way day after day and month after month. Sometimes we get messages and warnings from our Lord; a mission is preached, we meet with temporal reverses, or we are thrown on a bed of sickness and think our Lord is about to ask us for the account of our stewardship, and we make a hurried compromise with our sins, the best we can do under the circumstances. But no sooner do we find the account is not really required than we fall back into the former careless way of conducting the business of our soul. Indeed, it is strange that women who are such good housewives, and men who give such careful attention to the temporal things of this life, are so utterly negligent when it comes to that which is the most important of all—the business of their soul. One would think they had no faith. The foolish excuses they make!—they are too much mixed up with the world to be pious, they have to attend to their family, and the like. As though they were not to save their soul in this world; as though the attending to their soul and the care of their family were two separate and distinct things! And then, when God, seeing that prosperity is not good for them, sends them reverses, they neglect their soul more than ever, and fail to see that if they had looked after their soul they might have been even better off in this world's affairs. Take a warning, then, my brethren, from the lesson of to-day's Gospel; keep the accounts of your soul in order, for you know not the time when the Master will say: "Give an account of thy stewardship." And let not those who make their Easter duty think the lesson does not apply to them, but let not a single month pass by without rendering an account to God.

SERMON CIII.

Make to yourselves friends of the mammon of iniquity, that when you shall fail they may receive you into everlasting dwellings.—St. Luke xvi. 9.

Every Christian knows our Lord does not intend to encourage men to love that which is entirely worldly. In fact, his caution often repeated, his most important warning to men, is that they do not love too much the riches of this world. He even tells us it is impossible for a rich man to enter the kingdom of heaven unless God himself keep that man from loving his money and possessions more than he ought to do. This is what too often makes riches a mammon of iniquity. The words can also be taken to mean riches gained by fraud, robbery, or unjust dealing of any kind. Men of the world will say this is all the words can mean. God, however, has more to say about it. In his mind these words include all that a man may gain from motives which are impure and mean in the sight of God. Now, the duty of every man is to look at everything as God looks at it. He must find out God's opinion of what is right or wrong, and make that opinion the law of his own life. The words "mammon of iniquity" mean, therefore, not only riches and possessions gained unjustly, but also that honor, esteem of men, that social position, or that high office gained by sinful actions or from bad motives. What, then, is a man to do who has offended God in this way? If he has gotten unjustly money or property he must restore it, be it much or little. But, one may say, "I will lose my reputation if I give it back. I shall be found out." This is not true in most cases. A man can restore privately. He can see that the one he has wronged gets back again that which belongs to him. He is not obliged to tell him who took it from him. If it cannot be done by himself without losing his good name, let him tell his confessor about it. He will manage it for him. The priest is ordained and instructed in order to help him in this as well as in other difficulties. Moreover, what sort of a good name is that which that man knows is a false one? If not dead to sincerity of spirit that man must feel like a hypocrite. He must feel that he is not even the shadow of an honest man so long as he is called by a name he does not deserve. He must sometimes long to be again a truly honest man. Let him restore, and then he will be again an honest man. He will then have that peace which is more to him than wealth or honor of this world. At least let him tell the priest about it. He makes a great mistake who stays away from confession because he has done wrong. The confessor can help him when he cannot help himself. He can make it easy for him to do right when it seems hard. Another will say: "I have taken a little from this one and a little from that one. I do not know the people I have wronged." Then give what is gained unjustly to the poor. The law of the land, as well as God's law, will not permit a man to keep that which he has gained dishonestly. The one who restores in this manner adds good works to his act of restitution. He relieves God's poor; he clothes the naked and feeds the hungry; he gains the prayers of the poor, whom God has promised to hear always. These prayers bring blessings on his head, true sorrow for sin into his soul, and secure for him the grace of a happy death. Riches of injustice thus used will make friends who will get for him by their prayers an everlasting habitation in heaven. What other things are included in the riches of injustice? All that is valued by pride, ambition, self-love, vanity. All that man loves in this world because it makes him appear to be above his fellow-men. The proud, ambitious, selfish, and vain man has robbed God of the glory and honor due to him alone. He has worked for himself alone, and forgotten God, except to use God for his own private benefit. This man will often make bad confessions and communions in order to appear to be good. But what riches of injustice has he gained? He has gotten a pleasant manner, a sweet smile, a habit of talking respectfully to every one whose praise is pleasing to him, who can bring him custom or give him a vote for office. These things, good in themselves, are made bad by the motive in his heart. Let this man change his motive and all will be right. He must use these same manners and smiles for God's sake. He must show that respect to every one, high or low, rich or poor. He must do this for the love of God and love of all men, for God's sake. This man, also, will then have gained the prayers of the poor by repairing in this way sins of pride, ambition, and self-love. He will find he has gained friends with the riches of injustice who will cause him to be received into everlasting habitations.

Ninth Sunday after Pentecost.

EPISTLE. 1 *Cor. x.* 6–13. Brethren: We should not covet evil things, as they also coveted. Neither become ye idolaters, as some of them: as it is written: "The people sat down to eat and drink, and rose up to play." Neither let us commit fornication, as some of them committed fornication, and there fell in one day three and twenty thousand. Neither let us tempt Christ: as some of them tempted, and perished by the serpents. Neither do you murmur: as some of them murmured, and were destroyed by the destroyer. Now all these things happened to them in figure; and they are written for our correction, upon whom the ends of the world are come. Wherefore let him that thinketh himself to stand, take heed lest he fall. Let no temptation take hold on you, but such as is human. And God is faithful, who will not suffer you to be tempted above that which you are able; but will make also with temptation issue, that you may be able to bear it.

GOSPEL. *St. Luke xix.* 41–47. At that time: When Jesus drew near Jerusalem, seeing the city, he wept over it, saying: If thou also hadst known, and that in this thy day, the things that are for thy peace; but now they are hidden from thy eyes. For the days shall come upon thee: and thy enemies shall cast a trench about thee: and compass thee round, and straiten thee on every side, and beat thee flat to the ground, and thy children who are in thee; and they shall not leave in thee a stone upon a stone: because thou hast not known the time of thy visitation. And entering into the temple, he began to cast out them that sold therein, and them that bought, saying to them: It is written: "My house is the house of prayer"; but you have made it a den of thieves. And he was teaching daily in the temple.

SERMON CIV.

My house is the house of prayer. But you have made it a den of thieves.—St. Luke xix. 46.

WHAT made our Lord so severe with these people of whom the Gospel tells us, who were selling and buying in the temple? He was usually gentle and mild, not violent, as on this occasion. He was generally content with reproving what was wrong; here he resorted to force—that force which no one could resist, and which he could always have used if he had chosen; by which he could have destroyed all his enemies in a moment, if he had seen fit to do so. And he not only made these buyers and sellers leave the house of God, but he drove them out in confusion, and also, as we read elsewhere, overturned the tables and chairs which they had used.

Well, one reason for his severity probably was that those who sold were making an unjust profit out of the necessities of those who bought; for the things which they were selling were such as had to be offered by the people for the sacrifices of the temple, and could not well be obtained by them anywhere else. But I think his principal motive was to impress on his followers, and on us who were to come after them, a lesson which we are very apt to forget. He wanted to teach it to us in such a way that we could not forget it: and therefore he made use of this extraordinary means.

This lesson is contained in the words which he quotes from his prophet Isaias: "My house is the house of prayer." These words were true of the temple in which he then was, but they have a more special reference to the temples in which he now dwells, in which he dwells continually, which he did not in that temple, magnificent as it was.

You know, or ought to know, what these temples are. They are our churches, where he is all the time, in his Real Presence, in the Blessed Sacrament. These are the temples of which that in Jerusalem was only a figure or type.

The church is the place for prayer. That is the lesson for us, and we were, as I have said, the ones whom he chiefly wanted to instruct. For prayer— that is, for acts of religion of all kinds—and for nothing else. It is the place to think of God and to speak to him, and not to do anything else, innocent though it be.

It is not a place to talk or laugh in. You know that well enough, and would not, I suppose, laugh or talk; at any rate not much in church, especially if Mass was being celebrated or if there were a good many people there. But perhaps that would be because you would be afraid of what these people would say or think of you; for there are persons who, sometimes when nobody seems to be looking, do not scruple to have quite a nice little conversation, which might just as well be put off till some other time, if, indeed, there was any need for it at all.

The church is not a place to stare around in, or to see what is going on, except at the altar. And yet there are persons who come to it, especially if there is to be a wedding or some other event of general interest, simply for this purpose and for nothing else. Perhaps they will kneel down a little while for form's sake; but they did not enter God's house to pray for themselves or for anybody else, but only to gratify their worldly curiosity by seeing how people look or behave, and to have something to talk about, possibly to make fun about afterwards, if not, indeed, at the time.

And that reminds me of another thing. The church is not the place to see what kind of clothes people have on, or to show off one's own good clothes. It is a place to be well dressed in, as far as one's means will properly allow; but that is in order to give honor to God, not to win it from one another. It is the place to dress neatly, but not showily; not in such a way as to attract the eyes of others, and draw their thoughts from those things on which they should then be employed.

And this again suggests something else; that is, that our thoughts, as well as our words and actions, belong specially to our Lord when we are in his presence, before his altar. Let us take particular care about this. If we take care of our thoughts our words and actions will take care of themselves.

And let us remember that when we spend our time in church unworthily we are stealing something from God. What is this that we are stealing? It is the time and the honor that he has a right to expect from us. It is because of these thefts that he can truly say to us: "My house is the house of prayer; but you have made it a den of thieves." This seems strong language; but do we not deserve it if we take from our Lord the little that he claims as his own? He may have called those who sold in the temple thieves, because they were cheating their neighbors; but is it not as bad to cheat him? Let us, then, be sorry for this cheating of ours, and try to make restitution in the time that is to come.

SERMON CV.

God is faithful, who will not suffer you to be tempted above that which you are able.—1 Cor. x. 13.

SOME people seem to think that their sins are principally God's fault. A great many of you, my dear friends, who are listening to me now have frequently, I have no doubt, said as much. Of course you will say, and very rightly too, that such a charge against the good God is a horrible blasphemy; but, for all that, you have often been guilty of it.

You will, I think, want me to prove this before you will fully believe it. Well, it is very easy to do so. Have you never, when you accused yourself of some sin, said that you could not help it? You got in a passion, for instance, perhaps quite frequently, and spoke angry words, which of course you were sorry for afterwards; but you say that at the time you could not help it.

What follows, then, if what you say is true? Why, in the first place, it follows, of course, that it was not your fault that you sinned; that in fact it was no sin for you at all, for if a person really cannot help doing a thing he is not to blame for it. But it was a sin; you acknowledge that; so if it was not your sin it must have been somebody else's. And that somebody else must have been **Almighty God**. He was answerable for the sin by not giving you the grace to avoid it. That is what it amounts to when you say that you could not help committing sin.

This horrible blasphemy, which then certainly is implied by the words, "I could not help it"—this blasphemy, which makes God the author of sin and responsible for it, is what St. Paul denies in the words from the Epistle of to-day which I have read to you. He says: "God is faithful"; he does give you enough grace. "He will not suffer you to be temp ed above that which you are able"; he will not let you have a temptation so strong that, with the grace which he gives you, you cannot resist it.

There are some things which one cannot help, but sin is not one of them. If a hot coal falls on one's hand one cannot help feeling pain from it; and in the same way one cannot help feeling the fire of temptation with which God is sometimes pleased that we should be tried. But sin, which is the giving way of the will to temptation, one can always help. Sin, the giving way to temptation, is like holding the hot coal in your hand after it has fallen there.

You do not want to hold the coal in your hand; but you do want to give way to temptation, because there is something pleasant in that. It is more pleasant to give way than to resist it; if it were not it would not be a temptation. It relieves your mind to say that angry word when you are provoked. It is hard often to resist temptation; that is the amount of it. But it is not impossible.

Never say, then, when you accuse yourself of anything with which your conscience really reproaches you, that you could not help it. Do not say it, unless you wish to blaspheme God and throw the blame of your sin upon him. Remember that he is faithful, and does not suffer you to be tempted above what you are able; and say, rather, "It was hard to help it; I was very much tempted, but I could have resisted, and I am very sorry that I did not."

I know that is what you mean very often when you say, "I could not help it." Say, then, what you mean, for it will help you very much the next time. It will put you in mind of what you must know to be the truth—that is, that you could have kept from sin; and when you are convinced of this you will, if you are in earnest, use all the means you have to do so. Above all you will see that one great reason why it was so hard to resist temptation was that, though you had grace enough to do so, you did not have enough to make it easy; and you will pray hard to get that abundant help which God will give to all who continually ask it from him.

Tenth Sunday after Pentecost.

Epistle. 1 *Cor. xii.* 2–11. Brethren: You know that when you were heathens, you went to dumb idols, according as you were led. Wherefore I give you to understand, that no man, speaking by the Spirit of God, saith Anathema to Jesus. And no man can say, The Lord Jesus, but by the Holy Ghost. Now there are diversities of graces, but the same Spirit: and there are diversities of ministries, but the same Lord. And there are diversities of operations, but the same God, who worketh all in all. But the manifestation of the Spirit is given to every man unto profit. To one, indeed, by the Spirit, is given the word of wisdom: to another, the word of knowledge according to the same Spirit: to another, faith in the same Spirit; to another, the grace of healing in one Spirit: to another, the working of miracles: to another, prophecy: to another, the discerning of spirits: to another, divers kinds of tongues: to another, interpretation of speeches: but all these things one and the same Spirit worketh, dividing to every one according as he will.

Gospel. *St. Luke xviii.* 9–14. At that time: To some who trusted in themselves as just, and despised others, Jesus spoke this parable: Two men went up into the temple to pray: the one a Pharisee, and the other a publican. The Pharisee, standing, prayed thus with himself: O God! I give thee thanks that I am not as the rest of men, extortioners, unjust, adulterers, nor such as this publican. I fast twice in the week: I give tithes of all that I possess. And the publican, standing afar off, would not so much as lift up his eyes towards heaven; but struck his breast, saying: O God! be merciful to me a sinner! I say to you, this man went down to his house justified rather than the other; because every one that exalteth himself shall be humbled: and he that humbleth himself shall be exalted.

SERMON CVI.

Two men went up into the temple to pray: the one a Pharisee, and the other a publican.—St. Luke xviii. 10.

There are not supposed to be any Pharisees nowadays, and the word "publican" is getting rather old-fashioned; so perhaps, before applying this parable to our own times, we had better understand who the Pharisees and the publicans were.

The Pharisees, in our Lord's time, were a very religious class among the Jews, very strict and correct in their belief, and with very strict consciences, too—strict, at least, about some things, particularly about such things as concerned their reputation for piety. About other matters they were sometimes rather too easy and charitable—easy and charitable, that is, to themselves; for it is quite possible that they might have criticised others for faults not very different from their own, as when this Pharisee in the Gospel called the poor publican standing in the corner an extortioner, or robber, as perhaps the word is better rendered; forgetting, it may be, some little transactions which, if rightly understood, might have fixed as bad a name on himself.

These publicans, on the other hand, were not in any way a religious set of people; they did not pretend, like the Pharisees, to be so, nor were they in point of fact. They were called publicans because they collected the public taxes; they were blamed by the people, and with good reason, for extorting money unjustly from the poor. Their business was really, in those times, a proximate occasion of sin; this was the reason why St. Matthew, who was a publican before our Lord called him to be an apostle, never went back to his business again, as St. Peter did to his innocent occupation as a fisherman. The publican of this parable also, no doubt, had either made up his mind to give up his sinful life or was endeavoring to do so.

Both of these men, the Pharisee and the publican, were sinners. In that they were alike; the difference between them was that the publican acknowledged that he was a sinner and was trying to amend his life, while the Pharisee thought that he was perfect, or that, if he had any faults, they were such as no one could avoid, and which his Maker would readily overlook, especially in a person of his exalted piety.

Now, I said in the beginning that there were not supposed to be any Pharisees nowadays: but I think that we shall find that there are some people of this kind, even among us Christians; and perhaps, if we go down very deep into our own consciences, we shall even find that we are Pharisees ourselves.

Some of these Pharisees make excellent confessions. They show a care in their examination of conscience equal to that of the saints; they have the most accurate knowledge of every fault, and are willing to go into every detail, if they are permitted to do so. This delicacy of perception of sin is a quality which certainly commands our admiration; but there is a circumstance which prevents this admiration from being quite unlimited. This circumstance is that the faults which they are so keenly alive to are not their own. They are those of other people with whom they live, or of whom they hear through some person of the same sort of sensitive conscience that they themselves have.

The world, in the eyes of these sensitive people, certainly has a melancholy aspect. Everybody is doing wrong, and nobody is doing right—nobody, that is, except themselves. They, thank God! are not so bad. They are innocent sufferers, enduring a continual martyrdom at the hands of these wicked people who live in the same house or close by. Their only consolation here below is to tell their friends how much they suffer, and how much others suffer, from these sinners. Others, it is true, may deserve it, but they themselves certainly never have. They wish that they were dead and out of reach of their persecutors. The most curious thing is that one of their great causes of annoyance is the way that other people will carry stories; this is the story that they spend their lives in carrying.

Perhaps you think this picture is overdrawn. I hope it is. And I do not believe that many people are such thorough Pharisees as these whom I have described. But there is too much, a great deal too much, of the Pharisaic spirit about us all.

And not nearly enough of the spirit of the publican—of humility, contrition, and purpose of amendment. How shall we acquire this spirit? By looking into our own conscience, unpleasant as it may be, and letting those of our neighbors alone. If we sincerely examine our own hearts we shall not thank God that we are not like others, but rather pray to him that we may, before we die, have something like the perfection that many others have already reached; and ask him, as the publican did, to have mercy on us sinners—on us poor sinners, who are trying to be so no more.

That is the way, and the only way, that we sinners can get into the company of the saints; not by fancying ourselves there already. If we wish, then, to reach that blessed company, let us start on this way at once, for there is no time to lose.

SERMON CVII.

Every one that exalteth himself shall be humbled; and he that humbleth himself shall be exalted.—St. Luke xviii. 14.

ONE does not need to be a Christian, my dear brethren, to understand, as it would seem, the truth of these words of our Lord. Everybody knows that a man who is all the time praising himself, or who even shows that he has a pretty good opinion of himself, loses by it in the opinion of others. He does not even get as much credit for ability or virtue as he really deserves, besides being considered as stuck up and conceited, which everybody feels to be a defect. In fact, a man who is evidently very proud makes himself ridiculous.

And, on the other hand, one who is modest and unassuming generally is supposed to be more clever than he really is. People sometimes get a reputation for learning and depth of thought by simply holding their tongue—so convinced is the world that a really great man will not make a parade of his greatness.

But this lesson of worldly prudence is not the real meaning of our Saviour's words. He does not wish to show us how to get a reputation for learning or for anything else. This would be merely encouraging and helping our vanity and pride. What he wishes to teach us is humility. He wants us to humble ourselves really; not to pretend to do so, that we may be more esteemed by the world.

Why, then, if that is the object, does he promise us that if we humble ourselves we shall be exalted? That, it would seem, could be no inducement to a man who had real humility. Such a man would not want to be exalted, you will say. Ah! there is where you are mistaken. Every humble man, every really good man, does want to be exalted. The saints, who are the models of humility for us, wanted it more than any one else in the world.

This may sound strange, but it is undoubtedly true. For what is it to be exalted in the true sense of the word?

It is to get near to God, who is the Most High. And the more one loves God the more does he wish to be near him; so all those who love God wish to be thus exalted and the saints more than all, because they love God more than any one else.

And this exaltation, which comes from being near to Almighty God, is what he promises, in these words of the Gospel, to the humble and refuses to the proud. This was what he gave to the publican and refused to the Pharisee; for he gave the publican his grace and his friendship, but the Pharisee failed to receive it on account of his pride. "This man," says our Lord, "went down to his house justified rather than the other"—that is, nearer to God, and therefore more exalted.

The humble, then, will be raised into the friendship of God, and the proud will not. Nor can they come near him in any other way. He is too high above us for us to come near him except on his own terms. You cannot get near Almighty God by making the most of your natural powers, any more than you can get near the stars by going on the roof of your house. Some people in old times thought to scale the heavens by building a high tower; but God confounded their pride, and the tower of Babel is a byword for human folly and presumption to this day.

Let us, then, my dear brethren, not follow their example. Let us seek truly to be exalted, but in the way that he has appointed, in the way that his saints have chosen, and especially the way of Our Blessed Lady, the nearest to him and the humblest of all. And, in fact, if we really wish for this true exaltation it must needs be in this way; for if we really wish to be near God it must be for the love of him; and if we love him we must often think of him; and if we often think of him we must be humble; for how can the creature be proud who often thinks of the Creator of heaven and earth?

SERMON CVIII.

Every one that exalteth himself shall be humbled; and he that humbleth himself shall be exalted.—St. Luke xviii. 14.

It is a blessed and a happy moment, a sort of turning-point in life, my brethren, for any one of us when he wakes up to the conviction that he is nothing extraordinary after all. That is, if there is such a moment; for sometimes this conviction dawns on one gradually.

Almost every one begins life with the other idea. Not that he has it himself at the start, but his friends have it for him. Almost every baby is considered, as you know, to be the finest and most beautiful one that ever was seen. Perhaps he does not quite come up afterward to the expectations of his fond parents; but at least he is remarkable in some way. He is a very clever boy, or a very good boy, or, at any rate, he could be if he wanted to; he has got it in him; he is much finer in some respects, perhaps in a great many, than the common run. He is going to turn out a great man; he is much more likely to be President of the United States than any other boy of his age.

And by the time he has got to man's estate he has a good deal of the same opinion himself. He does not like to have it even hinted that he is at all below par in anything; or if it is plain, even to himself, that he is, then it is a thing of no consequence, or he could excel in it if he chose to. The sorest points are of course those in which his choosing would make no difference. The less said about these the better.

Well, you know all this is what we call pride. Almighty God has mercifully arranged it so that it is generally knocked out of us to some extent as we travel on through the world; but still a good deal of it remains.

It is a thing that gives us a great deal of trouble of mind, and which generally keeps us back a great deal from really excelling in anything. It is a thing, therefore, which it is good to get rid of as soon as we can; and of course, therefore, you all want to know how to do this. I think the Gospel story of to-day throws some light on this point.

The way to do it is the way of the publican, and the way not to do it is that of the Pharisee. And the way of the publican is that of common sense, too.

What is it? It is to look at and consider our defects, and not our strong points. The publican might have talked like the Pharisee, too. He might have said: "I am a much better fellow than that old Pharisee. I am a good, hearty, generous soul. I treat my friends to the best I have got; and if I do cheat sometimes a little in business I make up for it in charity; and I don't make a show of the good I do and put on a pretence of religion like those canting hypocrites."

And so he might have gone on to the end of the chapter. But he didn't. No; he just went off in a corner all by himself and said: "O God! be merciful to me a sinner." He did not think about his virtues, but about his sins; and when he asked the Lord to be merciful to him he meant that he wanted to amend his life, and was going to do it with the help of God, and imitate the Pharisee, whom he really thought better than himself; for you see he did not think of the sins of the Pharisee, but of his virtues.

I say that his way was of common sense. It is the way we all follow when at work on anything except ourselves. We look at the defects in our work, and not its excellences; and if we have very good sense it seems to us pretty much all defects.

Humility, then, after all, is only common sense. And I think you ought to see pretty well one reason at least why, as our Lord says, he that exalteth himself shall be humbled, and he that humbleth himself exalted. The one who exalts himself, who stops to look at his virtues, is all the time running down, and losing even the little virtue that he admires; while he that really humbles himself is constantly getting better. So humility is necessary for progress. It is so in the things of this world even, and much more so in our spiritual affairs.

Eleventh Sunday after Pentecost.

Epistle. 1 *Cor. xv.* 1–10. Brethren: I make known unto you the gospel which I preached to you, which also you have received, and wherein you stand: by which also you are saved, if you hold fast after what manner I preached to you, unless you have believed in vain. For I delivered to you first of all, which I also received: how that Christ died for our sins, according to the Scriptures: and that he was buried, and that he rose again the third day, according to the Scriptures: and that he was seen by Cephas, and after that by the eleven. Then was he seen by more than five hundred brethren at once, of whom many remain until this present, and some are fallen asleep. After that he was seen by James, then by all the apostles. And last of all, he was seen also by me, as by one born out of due time. For I am the least of the apostles, who am not worthy to be called an apostle, because I persecuted the church of God. But by the grace of God I am what I am: and his grace in me hath not been void.

Gospel. *St. Mark vii.* 31–37. At that time: Jesus going out of the borders of Tyre, came by Sidon to the sea of Galilee, through the midst of the territories of Decapolis. And they bring to him one that was deaf and dumb; and they besought him to lay his hand upon him. And taking him aside from the multitude, he put his fingers into his ears, and spitting, he touched his tongue: and looking up to heaven, he groaned, and said to him: Ephpheta, which is, Be opened. And immediately his ears were opened, and the string of his tongue was loosed, and he spoke right. And he charged them that they should tell no man. But the more he charged them so much the more a great deal did they publish it. And so much the more did they wonder, saying: He hath done all things well; he hath made both the deaf to hear, and the dumb to speak.

SERMON CIX.

He hath made both the deaf to hear, and the dumb to speak.—
St. Mark vii. 37.

Our Saviour, in his ministry on earth, no doubt cured a great many deaf and dumb people. The story of this particular cure has been preserved for us on account of the peculiar and significant way in which he performed it. The memory of it is renewed every time that a child is baptized in the Catholic Church.

In the ceremonies of baptism the priest, who represents our Lord in this as in all other sacraments, touches the nostrils and the ears of the infant or adult with his thumb moistened with the saliva of his mouth, saying this same word, "Ephpheta"—that is, "Be opened."

Now, the child or grown person who is brought to baptism is not, as a general thing, deaf or destitute of any of the senses, and the priest does not, in performing this ceremony, work what we should commonly call a miracle, as our Lord did in the cure of this deaf and dumb man. But in baptism what we may call a miracle, because it is so wonderful, though so common, is worked ; or rather not one miracle but many. One of them—the one represented by this action of the priest, and also by that of our Saviour in the Gospel—is the opening of the spiritual senses by the words which come from the mouth of God.

This opening of the spiritual senses is a much greater blessing than the opening of the bodily ears. But, unfortunately, most of us who are baptized do not preserve this great grace. As we grow up, instead of seeing and hearing better and better all the time with our spiritual eyes and ears, as we do with our bodily ones, we are too apt to lose the use of them altogether. They get covered over and choked up with the dust of this world; and, after a while, though having eyes we do not see, and having ears we do not hear.

So there are a great many deaf and dumb people besides those who are commonly called so. These deaf and dumb people, however, often talk a good deal, and hear, as it would seem, pretty much everything that is to be heard. But there is only a very little of all the immense amount of talk that comes from their mouths that is of any use to themselves or to their neighbors, and that which they happen to hear that might be of use to them seems to go in at one ear and out at the other.

What is it that the spiritual ear ought to hear? It is the voice of God. The Holy Ghost is all the time speaking to us, either by his own inspirations in our hearts, by our guardian angels, by the voice of the clergy who preach with his authority and in his name, by good books, or by some other means. But we do not listen to his voice; we do not let it reach the ears of our soul, though it may those of our body; and so those ears of the soul, from want of practice, get so deaf that they cannot hear it, though it sound ever so plainly.

And so, becoming deaf, we become dumb also. You know that is always the way. When a person cannot hear at all he is apt to forget how to speak. This is the case with people who become deaf to God's voice. First they do not try to hear it, either because they are careless, or because they do not want to; they stifle his inspirations; they never think of such a thing as reading a spiritual book, and if they listen to sermons it is only to criticise the preacher, not to hear the word of God, which they could find in any Catholic sermon, if they chose. And so, not hearing his voice, their spirit loses its tongue; they forget to pray to him, or, if they do pray, it is only with the lips and not with the heart; they forget to say anything for him or about him to their neighbor; and, worst perhaps of all, they forget to go to confession. That is where their tongues are specially tied. Sometimes they even imagine that if they should go to confession they would have nothing to tell.

To be spiritually deaf and dumb is a great deal worse than to have no bodily senses at all. A man may live without those senses just as with them; but when he is spiritually deaf and dumb, it means that his soul is dead. If, then, you are in this state, or falling into it, rouse yourself while there is time, and beg of our Lord to open your ears that you may hear his voice plainly, for it will not speak to you much more; and to loose your tongue, that it may give glory to his name before you die.

SERMON CX.

He hath made both the deaf to hear, and the dumb to speak.
—St. Mark vii. 37.

THERE are a good many people, my dear brethren, who are afflicted with a deafness and dumbness a great deal worse than that of the poor man whose cure is recorded in to-day's Gospel. You all know several such people, I think; perhaps you are acquainted with quite a number; it may be even that you are such yourselves. The trouble with the poor man whom our Lord cured was only in his body; the trouble with these people of whom I speak is in their souls. He was deaf and dumb corporally; they are deaf and dumb spiritually. Who are these unfortunate people? They are those who are in the state of mortal sin; who are living day after day in that state, and have been, perhaps, for years. Their souls are deaf; for God is calling to them continually to repent, and they refuse to hear him. Their souls are dumb; for they have had for a long time a confession to make, and that confession is not yet made.

As I said just now, you all know such people. They are easily known. They are the people who let Easter after Easter go by without approaching the sacraments. Their life may be evidently bad; or perhaps, on the other hand, it may seem to be pretty good. They go, it may be, quite regularly to Mass, and observe some of the other laws of the church. But there is one which they neglect, and that is the one which shows their true character. That is the precept of the yearly confession. When it comes to that either they are honest enough to say: "I cannot make up mind to give up my sins, so it will be no use for me to go to confession," or they are dishonest enough to make some wretched excuse, such as: "I have too much reverence for the sacraments to receive them without due preparation, and I have not time to prepare," or, "I am sure I don't know what I would have to say to the priest; I can't think what you people are bothering him for all the time."

My dear brethren, people that make excuses of this kind are like ostriches. These birds, it is said, when pursued, hide their heads in the sand to avoid being seen, leaving their whole bodies exposed. Excuses like these never deceived anybody yet, and never will. Everybody knows that if a man refuses to go to his confession when the church requires him to do so, the reason is that he is living in a way that his conscience reproaches him for, and that he does not choose to live in any other way. Everybody knows that if a man's conscience is really clear he will be very willing to go to the priest and tell him so; and everybody knows that everybody has time to prepare.

No, the fact is that these Christians who live in the state of sin and neglect of their duties are, if not already quite deaf and dumb spiritually, at least rapidly becoming so. Every day the voice of the Holy Ghost is sounding more and more faintly in their ears; every day, instead of bringing them nearer to a good confession, puts them farther away from it. Every day the cure of their spiritual deafness and dumbness is getting more and more difficult, and needing more of a miracle of God's grace to accomplish it. They are like travellers who lie down to rest in the Alpine snows and wake only in the next world.

If any of you, my dear brethren in Christ, who are now here and listen to my voice, which is another call from him to you, are in this fearful state, or are falling into it, may he work that miracle and bring you back to your senses! But whether he is to work it or not depends very much upon yourself. Rouse yourself, then, and ask him to do so while you are yet able.

For a time is coming, and that soon, but too late for you, when he will make you hear and speak indeed, whether you will or no; when the thunders of his eternal judgment shall sound in your ears, and when you will have to confess your sins, not to one man in secret, but before all men and all the angels and saints; and not with the hope of forgiveness, but with the certainty of condemnation. God grant that you may save your soul before that dreadful day, and be able to say with thankfulness, not with terror and despair: "He hath made both the deaf to hear and the dumb to speak."

SERMON CXI.

And taking 'm aside from the multitude.—St. Mark vii. 33.

I SUPPOSE there is no trouble more common to people in the practice of their religion, whether they are particularly pious or not, than distractions at prayer. One's thoughts, perhaps, are pretty well under control while employed in the usual duties of the day; but as soon as the time comes to get on one's knees before

God, away go the thoughts over everything under the sun except the words which are in the prayer-book. It really is quite discouraging sometimes; it appears as if our Lord did not want to speak to us or to have us speak to him.

But we know that this is not so. How, then, shall we account for our not hearing his voice, and not being able to say anything worth his hearing, when we set out to pray? How is it that we are so deaf and dumb in his presence?

There are various reasons, no doubt, my brethren, but there is one common to almost all people living in the world; and I think it was this which our Saviour wished to suggest to us when he took the deaf and dumb man aside from the multitude, as we read in to-day's Gospel, before he would work his cure.

He could have cured the man where he was; but he took him aside from the multitude, he got him away from the crowd in which he was, to show us, as it seems to me, that we cannot be cured of our spiritual deafness and dumbness, that we shall never be able to hear God or to speak to him as we should, till we, too, come out of the crowd.

This living all the time in a crowd is really the most common and most fatal obstacle to prayer, at least with those who are really trying to serve God. It is not always that there are so very many people around us; we may make a crowd, a multitude for ourselves out of a very few. The crowd is not so much one of people as of ideas coming from the people and things which we meet with in our daily life. We talk too much; we look around and notice things too much; we read the papers too much—too much for our profit in any way, but especially for acquiring the spirit of prayer.

What wonder is it that it is so hard to pray, and that there are so many distractions? One kneels down at the end of the day and tries to say some evening prayers. There is not a single thought in his or her head like those which are in the prayer-book. And why not? Because there is no room for any. The poor head is packed full of all sorts of other ones coming from the events of the past day or week. All the people one has seen, all the foolish things they have said, the gossip they have retailed, even the clothes they have worn, or perhaps the stories or squibs and the useless and trifling news one has seen in the paper, take up the mind; there is a multitude of reflections and echoes from the sights and sounds of the day, which hide the face of God and drown his voice. It is in vain to say that one cannot help it. Of course one cannot separate one's self from these things altogether. Those who live a life of prayer in the most secluded convent, even the hermits of the desert, have sources of distraction around them and in their past lives. But what is the need of having so many of them? Why not hear less talk and gossip, see fewer people and things, read less useless trash, cultivate silence a little more, and make a little solitude within ourselves, even when we cannot have it outside? If we will not do this, if we will distract ourselves needlessly out of the time of prayer, what wonder if we are distracted in it?

Come out of the multitude, then—the multitude of people that surround you, and of unnecessary thoughts, words, and actions, and see if your spiritual deafness and dumbness will not get better. You will hear a good deal from God, and be able to say a good deal to him that seems impossible now, if you will get a little away from this crowd, and from the noise it makes.

Twelfth Sunday after Pentecost.

Epistle. *2 Cor. iii.* 4–9. Brethren : Such confidence we have, through Christ towards God. Not that we are sufficient to think anything of ourselves as of ourselves ; but our sufficiency is from God. Who also hath made us fit ministers of the new testament, not in the letter, but in the Spirit. For the letter killeth ; but the Spirit giveth life. Now if the ministration of death, engraven with letters upon stones, was glorious, so that the children of Israel could not steadfastly behold the face of Moses, for the glory of his countenance, which is done away : how shall not the ministration of the Spirit be rather in glory ? For if the ministration of condemnation be glory, much more the ministration of justice aboundeth in glory.

Gospel. *St. Luke x.* 23–37. At that time : Jesus said to his disciples : Blessed are the eyes that see the things which you see. For I say to you that many prophets and kings have desired to see the things that you see, and have not seen them : and to hear the things that you hear, and have not heard them. And behold a certain lawyer stood up, tempting him, and saying : Master, what must I do to possess eternal life ? But he said to him : What is written in the law ? how readest thou ? He answering, said : "Thou shalt love the Lord thy God with thy whole heart, and with thy whole soul, and with all thy strength, and with all thy mind : and thy neighbor as thyself." And he said to him : Thou hast answered right : this do, and thou shalt live. But he, willing to justify himself, said to Jesus : And who is my neighbor ? And Jesus answering, said : A certain man went down from Jerusalem to Jericho, and fell among robbers, who also stripped him, and having wounded him, went away, leaving him half dead. And it happened that a certain priest went down the same way, and seeing him, he passed by. In like manner also a Levite, when he was near the place and saw him, passed by. But a certain Samaritan being on his journey came near him; and seeing him was moved with compassion. And going up to him, bound up his wounds, pouring in oil and wine: and setting him upon his own beast, brought him to an inn, and took care of him. And the next day he took out two pence, and gave to the host, and said: Take care of him: and whatsoever thou shalt spend over and above, I at my return will repay thee. Which of these three in thy opinion was neighbor to him that fell among the robbers? But he said: He that showed mercy to him. And Jesus said to him: Go and do thou in like manner.

SERMON CXII.

Which of these three in thy opinion was neighbor to him that fell among the robbers? But he said: He that showed mercy to him. And Jesus said to him: Go and do thou in like manner.—St. Luke x. 36, 37.

You would not think it a compliment if one should say that you were a bad neighbor, for that would mean that you were quarrelsome and tale-bearing, that you kept late and noisy hours, that you beat the neighbors' children; perhaps that you would steal something, if you got the chance. So none of us would like to be called a bad neighbor. But let us see how good a neighbor we are, using our Blessed Lord's words read to-day as a text.

As we pass along the road of life here and there

we see a neighbor lying half dead. He is stricken down with sickness; his body tormented with racking pains, burning with fever, and perhaps deserted by all—not one left to give him a drink of cold water. What kind of a neighbor are we to this poor brother of ours? When we hear him moan and cry, and ask for a bite of nourishing food, for a little money to buy some medicine, does our heart soften towards him, do we kindly assist him, or do we pass on as if we saw him not, hard of heart like the degraded Jewish priest or the self-sufficient Levite?

And we come across many a poor creature who has fallen among the worst kind of thieves—viz., those who have stripped him of his good name. Alas! you are often forced to stand by and see and hear your neighbor deprived of his reputation by scandal-mongers. How do you act in that case? Does your heart burn with sympathy for him? Do you raise your voice in his defence? Do you correct your children when they engage in such talk? Do you turn out of your house those notorious backbiters and tale-bearers of your neighborhood when they begin their poisonous gossip? If you act in this way you are a good neighbor, a good Samaritan to an outraged and dying brother. But if you fail in this—if you hold your peace when you could say a good word of praise or excuse; if you permit those subject to you to talk ill of others; if you let your house be made a gossip-shop—then, by your silence and your consent, you are like the priest and Levite of this day's Gospel. And if you join in backbiting, why you are worse yet; you are yourself a robber of your neighbor's dearest possession, his good name.

But O my brethren! what lot so sad as that of

the poor wretch who has fallen into the clutches of Satan and his devils, who has been robbed of God's very grace, his soul killed by mortal sin? The ways of life are full of such poor sufferers. Oh! what pity have you for the poor sinner? What prayers do you offer to God for the conversion of the sinner? What warnings and exhortations do you give him, especially if he be dear to you by ties of blood? What example do you set him? I fear that some of us despise the poor sinner, and feel quite too holy to seek him out, to invite him to hear a sermon, to ask him to come and get the pledge, to try and get him into good company.

Brethren, may God give us grace to be good Samaritans; to have a tender heart and a generous hand for Christ's poor and sick and outcast; to have a charitable word for the saving of our neighbor's good name; and, above all, to be always ready to bind up the spiritual wounds of the sinner by our prayers and example, and to pour healing oil upon them by our exhortations! B.

SERMON CXIII.

THERE are two opposite faults to both of which almost everybody is more or less inclined. The first of these is meddling with other people's business; the second is shirking one's own.

It is rather the second of these than the first which is rebuked in the Gospel of to-day, in the persons of the priest and the Levite who went by without helping the poor wounded man.

Now, in the first place, let me explain what I mean

by shirking one's own business or duties. It is not simply leaving them undone and expecting that they will remain so; but it is putting off what one ought to do one's self on to somebody else, and expecting somebody else to do it for you. So it is, you see, just the opposite of meddling, which is trying to do somebody else's duty for him when he would prefer to do it himself.

Now, this shirking was just what the priest and Levite were guilty of. I do not suppose that our Lord meant to describe them as really hard-hearted men, willing to let the poor man die rather than help him; but they said to themselves, "Oh! this is not my business particularly; there are plenty of other people passing along this road all the time, and I am a little hurried now. I have got a deal to attend to, and there will be somebody coming this way before long. Five minutes or so will not make much difference; and perhaps there is not so much the matter with the man after all. It may be his own fault. Very likely he has been drinking. At any rate, he has got no special claim on me."

This is a very natural state of mind for a person to get into, and how common it is, in such a case as this, we can see from the common proverb that "everybody's business is nobody's business."

There are very many good works that really are everybody's business, that everybody ought to do something towards at least, but which are in great danger of not being done at all on account of this habit of shirking which is so common. And the ones which are most in this danger are those of the kind of which this Gospel gives us an example; that is, works of charity toward our neighbor. People say to themselves, just as the priest and Levite did: "Oh! there are plenty of other people that can attend to this matter a great deal better and easier than I can. I am sure it will be done somehow or other. Such things always are attended to. I don't feel specially called on to help in it."

Well, this might be all very good, if those people did really help in some things generously, and the case before them was one of no very urgent need. Of course we cannot contribute to everything. But the difficulty is that too often we find them shirking, not occasionally, but all the time. If a poor man comes to the door, or a collection is taken for the poor in the church, they say to themselves: "The St. Vincent de Paul Society can look out for those things; I am sure they must have money enough. I shall do my duty if I put a few pennies in the poor-box now and then." If contributions are called for in times of famine or pestilence, they say: "There is plenty coming in to supply all that is wanted; I can see that by the papers. They can get along very well without me." And so it goes all the way through. They do not give anything to anybody or do anything for anybody—that is, nothing to speak of—without getting a return for it. They will go to picnics, fairs, or amusements for a charitable object; but when it comes to doing anything simply for the love of their neighbor, that is left for somebody else.

Let us all, then, my brethren, examine ourselves on this point, and resolve to amend and to do our fair share of the work of charity, which is everybody's business; and not, like the priest and the Levite, pass it on to the next man who comes along.

SERMON CXIV.

But he, willing to justify himself, said to Jesus: And who is my neighbor?—St. Luke x. 29.

The lawyer of whom the Gospel tells us to-day, my brethren, seems to have wanted to be excused from loving everybody, and to find out just how far the circle of his affections must be extended; or, at least, to get our Lord's opinion on that point. The question which he asked was something like that of St. Peter when he enquired how often he must forgive his brother; though I hardly think the lawyer was as much in earnest as the great Prince of the Apostles to know the answer.

Well, our Saviour, as you see, did not answer the question directly, but told a story which is, or should be, familiar to all of you: the story of the good Samaritan. He made the Samaritan give his judgment on the point, and then approved that judgment.

"Which of these three," he asked of the lawyer after telling him the story, "was neighbor to him that fell among the robbers?" That is, "Which of the three seems to have considered the poor fellow to be his neighbor?" "The Samaritan," replied the lawyer, of course, "because he showed love for him." "Very well, then," said our Lord, "adopt his opinion, for it is the right one. Go and do thou in like manner."

And yet what reason had the Samaritan to consider this man to be his neighbor? He must naturally have supposed him to be a Jew, finding him so near to Jerusalem; and the Samaritans had no very neighborly feeling toward the Jews. The Samaritans and

Jews were, in fact, very much like cats and dogs to each other. You may read in the chapter of the Gospel just preceding this how the inhabitants of a certain place in Samaria would not let our Lord into it, simply because he seemed to be going to Jerusalem; and in another of the towns of the Samaritans a woman thought it strange that our Lord, being a Jew, should even presume to ask her for a drink of water. And though this was a good Samaritan who was passing over that road between Jerusalem and Jericho, still he must have had some of the feelings of his people.

The reason why the good Samaritan considered the man his neighbor is, then, plain enough. If he regarded a Jew as his neighbor it was because he regarded every one as such. That was the judgment of his which our Divine Lord approved. Let there be no limit to your charity. Love every one; that is the meaning of his command, just as he told St. Peter to forgive any number of times.

But how few there are who obey this law of his! Some only care for their relations or acquaintances, and regard the rest of the world with the most supreme indifference. Others, on t e contrary, live in a perpetual quarrel with almost every one whom they know, though very willing to be friendly with strangers. Others stop at the limit of their own nation or race; a man who is so unfortunate as to speak a foreign language or have a skin somewhat darkly colored is quite beyond the reach of their benevolence.

It is plain enough that this is all wrong. If we would be like our Lord, and do as he commands, we must get over all these feelings. Above all, we must sink for ever out of sight those hateful standing quarrels which are more after the devil's own heart than anything else which he finds in this world; we must drop at once all that humbug about not wishing any harm to Mr. and Mrs. So-and-so, but being never going to speak to them again. It is not enough to wish no harm to any one; we must wish good to every one, and try to do every one all the good that comes in our way; make up our minds to feel kindly to every one, and to show every one that we are willing and anxious to act as we feel. Of course there must be degrees in affection; we are not required to love every one as much as a father or mother, or a son or a daughter; but that no one must be excluded from it; that we must have a positive love for all; that it will not do even to pass by with indifference a single one of our brethren, however seemingly estranged from us—this is the lesson taught us by the parable of the priest, the Levite, and the good Samaritan.

Thirteenth Sunday after Pentecost.

EPISTLE. *Gal. iii.* 16-22. Brethren: To Abraham were the promises made, and to his seed. He saith not, "And to his seeds," as of many: but as of one, "And to thy seed," who is Christ. Now this I say, that the testament which was confirmed by God, the law which was made after four hundred and thirty years, doth not disannul, to make the promise of no effect. For if the inheritance be of the law, it is no more of promise. But God gave it to Abraham by promise. Why then was the law? It was set because of transgressions, until the seed should come, to whom he made the promise, being ordained by angels in the hand of a mediator. Now, a mediator is not of one: but God is one. Was the law then against the promises of God? God forbid. For if there had been a law given which could give life, verily justice should have been by the law. But the Scripture hath concluded all under sin, that the promise by the faith of Jesus Christ might be given to them that believe.

GOSPEL. *St. Luke xvii.* 11-19. At that time: As Jesus was going to Jerusalem, he passed through the midst of Samaria in Galilee. And as he entered into a certain town, there met him ten men that were lepers, who stood afar off: and lifted up their voice, saying: Jesus, master, have mercy on us. And when he saw them, he said: Go, show yourselves to the priests. And it came to pass that, as they went, they were cleansed. And one of them, when he saw that he was cleansed, went back, with a loud voice glorifying God; and he fell on his face, before his feet, giving thanks: and this was a Samaritan. And Jesus answering, said: Were there not ten made clean? and where are the nine? There is no one found to return and give glory to God, but this stranger. And he said to him: Arise, go thy way, for thy faith hath made thee whole.

SERMON CXV.

And as he entered into a certain town, there met him ten men that were lepers, who stood afar off.—St. Luke xvii. 12.

THE leprosy is a most foul and loathsome disease which attacks the skin and sometimes spreads itself over almost the entire surface of the body. This pestilential disorder, besides the intense suffering it must cause, renders its victim an object of disgust and aversion to those around him. It seems to have been very prevalent in the East in former times, and during the middle ages it was quite common in Europe, where it was brought by the Crusaders returning from the wars carried on for the possession of the Holy Land. A man infected with leprosy was looked upon by the state as dead, and hence the disease was called civil death. The leper was cut off from all intercourse with his fellows, and compelled to live alone or in the company of other lepers. Leprosy, therefore, subjected a man to the most galling sort of exile, since it forced him to part from home and friends, and to tear asunder every tie which binds the heart of man to this earth and to his fellow-men.

The holy Fathers have always regarded leprosy as a strong figure of sin. Sin spreads itself over the soul as leprosy does over the body, tainting and corrupting it, rendering it disgusting in the sight of its

Maker, and forcing him to separate it from himself and the company of his angels and saints. Sin, too, forces the soul into exile from God, its true home, and severs all those endearing attachments which cluster round the thought of home. In this sense all mortal sin is a spiritual leprosy ; but the one sin which deserves the name above all others is the sin of impurity, because it defiles body and soul alike, and is more infectious even than the ancient leprosy of the East. Impurity not only reproduces its pestilential self, but has, besides, the sickening power of engendering a horde of other frightful maladies distinct from, and only less disgusting than, itself. And yet, alas ! impurity is now, as it was in the days of Noe, the crying sin of the world ; a sin that is foreign to no class of society, to no order of civilization ; a sin that each individual has to take constant and wearisome precautions against, if he would not be infected by its virus, which seems to permeate the very air we breathe, and lurk unseen in the meat and drink we take for the support of life.

St. Clement of Alexandria calls impurity the metropolis of vices, by reason, doubtless, of the numberless other vices which are born of it and make their home around it. This leprosy of the soul, impurity, is worse than any leprosy of the body, inasmuch as the death of the soul is an infinitely greater evil than that of the body.

God has at times allowed some of his saints to experience something of the foulness which the sin of impurity inflicts on the soul of the one who commits it. So it was with St. Euthymius and St. Catherine of Siena, who discovered impure persons by the stench which emanated from their presence. It were well, perhaps, if all innocent persons possessed this rare gift of some of God's saints, for they might then easily avoid contracting from others the foul leprosy of impurity. No one, indeed, can look for a grace so extraordinary, but every one who has charge of others, especially of the young, should take every means suggested by wisdom and experience to preserve them from contact with persons already infected with this vile pestilence. A brief conversation with one badly tainted with the leprosy of impurity is oftentimes enough to implant its seeds in young and innocent hearts; and once the seeds are planted, they are hardly, if ever, entirely uprooted.

Leprosy not only attacked persons, but was found also in garments and in houses. So it is with the contagion of impurity, which not only watches its victim from the muddy eye of the libertine, but hides itself also in the folds of the lascivious dress, by which it is scattered abroad, and clings like some noxious vapor to the walls of houses where wanton deeds are done and loose language spoken. From all such persons, and things, and places keep the young and the innocent afar off. Let us remember that those only who love cleanness of heart shall have the King of heaven for their friend; and as we know from Holy Scripture that we cannot be chaste unless God gives us power to be so, let us ask him fervently and frequently for this most royal of all royal gifts, the gift of purity. Let us put aside all pride of heart, which, more than anything else, would provoke Almighty God to leave us to our own weakness and folly. Impurity is the lewd daughter of pride, while humility is the chaste mother of purity.

Finally, brethren, let us all listen to the exhortation of St. Paul, and walk in the love of Christ, and let not fornication and uncleanness be so much as named among us; nor obscenity, nor foolish talking, nor scurrility, but rather giving of thanks (Eph. v. 5-6). B.

SERMON CXVI.

And it came to pass, as they went, they were cleansed.—St. Luke xvii. 14.

You will find people who go to the sacraments pretty regularly sometimes giving rather a strange excuse when they have been away longer than usual. They will say, "My mind was upset," or "I had a falling out with my neighbor"; and they seem to think that of course it was out of the question to go to confession till their minds got right side up again, or till they were thoroughly at peace with themselves and all the world.

And you will find people who do not go to the sacraments regularly, who, in fact, have not been for a long time, and who make a similar excuse for staying away—that is, that they are not in good dispositions to receive absolution. These people also think that they should not go to confession till in some way or another they have got in good dispositions.

It is natural enough, perhaps, that both these kinds of people should think as they do. They want, of course, to make a really good confession. They would not like to receive absolution feeling just as they do now; so they put it off till some time when their dispositions will be improved; but they make a great mistake, and lose a great deal of time by doing so.

The mistake which they make is in not understanding that the preparation for confession which they could make with their present dispositions is the best way for getting them into better ones.

They might learn a salutary lesson from the Gospel of to-day. You will have noticed, if you have listened to it carefully, that the poor men whom our Lord cured were simply told by him to go and show themselves to the priests, and that they set off, with the defilement of the leprosy still upon them, to obey his commands. They might very well have excused themselves by saying that they were not fit to go before the priests; and it would have been very true that they were not. For, according to the law of the Jews, it was only lepers who had already been cured who were to show themselves to the priests; just as now it is only sinners who are penitent who can ask for absolution. The priests of the Old Law could not cure the leprosy, any more than those of the New Law can absolve a sinner before he repents.

But, nevertheless, they went, though it seemed to be of no use for them to go. And what happened to them on the road? Why, it happened, as the Gospel tells us, that as they went they were made clean.

Now, this, as I have said, has a lesson and a meaning for such as now are laboring under any spiritual disease or disorder, be it small or great, which is keeping them from the sacraments. The remedy for them, as for these men of whose cure we read in this Gospel, is to set out to show themselves to the priests; that is, to prepare themselves for confession. If they do they also will be cured on the way.

I will venture to say that if those Catholics throughout the world who now feel themselves in any way indisposed for absolution would go to a church at the next opportunity, kneel down by a confessional, say a few prayers in earnest, examine their consciences, and then go in when their turn should come—and these are surely things that any one can do—far the greater part of them would be in good dispositions for absolution before it was time for the priest to give it. Some time, perhaps when they were on the way to the church, perhaps when they were kneeling and trying to prepare themselves, perhaps not till they were telling their sins or receiving the priest's advice, but some time or other the affection to sin or the temptation which now disturbs the peace of their souls would be taken away.

Why, then, not try such a simple remedy? If you really want to recover the health of your soul set out to make your confession, to show yourself to the priest, whether you feel it or not. If you will believe me, depend on it, it shall also be true for you that your faith shall make you whole.

SERMON CXVII.

Were not ten made clean? and where are the nine?—St. Luke xvii. 17.

How often, my brethren, has our Lord been obliged to ask this question and to make this reproach! Times there have been when your souls were suffering from the leprosy of sin, times when the sight of your defilement, the pangs of a guilty conscience, roused you to a sense of your unhappy state, and you have raised your voice and cried out, "Jesus, Master, have mercy on me." And he, who is goodness and compassion, has looked upon you, and bid you show yourself to the priest, and you have been healed. But have you followed the example of the one grateful leper—have you gone back to thank him? Have you prostrated yourself before him, mindful of the greatness of the favor, and in word and deed, by fervent prayer, by humility, by a new life, shown your gratitude? Or have you, like the nine, gone your way, thankful indeed, but with a momentary, imperfect, unspoken gratitude, because the greatness of the benefit was not dwelt upon?

This ingratitude, which is so common, this forgetfulness, cannot be put before you too strongly or too often. At the coming of Jesus, during a mission or a jubilee, many call out to him to cleanse them; they go to confession and Communion, and for a time are healed of their leprosy. But because they so quickly go their way; because in the bustle of the world they neglect to come back to thank Jesus, their Master and Healer; because they do not separate themselves from and avoid infected persons and places, their old companions, their old haunt of drinking, the occasions of sin whatever they may be, therefore it is that the old malady returns. And as Jesus looks out on the few who come to his feet, to the Holy Communion, he is forced to exclaim in sorrow: "Were not ten made clean? where are the nine?" Alas! that we should so often wound that sensitive, loving Heart, that we should be so remiss in giving a return of thanks, that we should check the divine goodness and turn its very favors into a cause of our own condemnation at the great day of reckoning!

Ingratitude has always been considered, and deservedly, the worst of vices; it touches us more keenly than any other wrong or injury, it moves us with a sense of anger, sorrow, and aversion peculiar to itself, because it is an abuse or a forgetfulness of that which is highest and best in us—our love, and the effects of our love, our kindness. Yet God's benefits are innumerable, his love is infinite, his honor unspeakable, his power almighty. Many who call themselves Christians can find no time to thank him for the blessings of each day; many, whom he has healed from sin, go their way in forgetfulness; even those who do try to make some return, who do keep themselves in his grace and frequent the church and the sacraments, are often niggardly and ungenerous in their efforts. Does his grace move them to some sacrifice of their pride, their convenience, or their means? The kind word, the charitable act come, but oh! so slowly; the poor are dismissed with a trifling alms, the church-collector is an unwelcome visitor. Yet it is by these things we show our gratitude. Let us remember, brethren, that as God is infinitely bountiful himself, so he in turn loves a generous giver, and that his benefits bear a proportion to our return of thanks in words and in actions.

Fourteenth Sunday after Pentecost.

EPISTLE. *Gal. v.* 16-24. Brethren: I say then, walk in the spirit, and you shall not fulfil the lusts of the flesh. For the flesh lusteth against the spirit: and the spirit against the flesh; for these are contrary one to another: so that you do not the things that you would. But if you are led by the spirit, you are not under the law. Now the works of the flesh are manifest, which are, fornication, uncleanness, immodesty, luxury, idolatry, witchcraft, enmities, contentions, emulations, wrath, quarrels, dissensions, sects, envy, murders, drunkenness, revellings, and such like. Of the which I foretell you, as I have foretold to you, that they who do such things shall not obtain the kingdom of God. But the fruit of the spirit is charity, joy, peace, patience, benignity, goodness, longanimity, mildness, faith, modesty, continency, chastity. Against such there is no law. And they that are Christ's, have crucified their flesh with the vices and concupiscences.

GOSPEL. *St. Matt. vi.* 24-33. At that time: Jesus said to his disciples: No man can serve two masters. For either he will hate the one, and love the other: or he will hold to the one, and despise the other. You cannot serve God and Mammon. Therefore I say to you, be not solicitous for your life, what you shall eat, nor for your body, what you shall put on. Is not the life more than the food, and the body more than the raiment? Behold the fowls of the air, for they sow not, neither do they reap, nor gather into barns: and your heavenly Father feedeth them. Are not you of much more value than they?

And which of you by thinking can add to his stature one cubit? And for raiment why are you solicitous? Consider the lilies of the field how they grow: they labor not, neither do they spin. And yet I say to you, that not even Solomon in all his glory was arrayed as one of these. Now if God so clothe the grass of the field, which to-day is, and to-morrow is cast into the oven: how much more you, O ye of little faith? Be not solicitous therefore, saying: What shall we eat, or what shall we drink, or wherewith shall we be clothed? For after all these things do the heathen seek. For your Father knoweth that you have need of all these things. Seek ye, therefore, first the kingdom of God and his justice, and all these things shall be added unto you.

SERMON CXVIII.

No man can serve two masters.—ST. MATT. vi. 24.

WHO is your master? Perhaps you think you are your own master. You may say, "I am a free man in a free country." But think a moment. Is your soul really free? Surely not; for you cannot hinder your thoughts from running backward and forward. Sometimes you think of the past in spite of yourself; you enjoy its sinful pleasures over again in your memory, or you again suffer pain at the bare recollection of past sorrows and trials. Nor can you hinder your soul from rushing into the future. You dream of success; you enjoy in anticipation the pleasures of gratified ambition. Now, why does your soul thus cling to the dead past; why does it strive to fly to the unborn future? Because your soul is a servant. And who is its master? Pleasure. Yes, and pleasure is so powerful a master that we obey and serve even its remembrance, its shadow. Indeed, I might say that we are slaves of pleasure rather than servants.

But this master takes different shapes. Sometimes he calls himself Fashion. Very many otherwise intelligent persons are servants of Fashion. Did you ever spend an hour looking at the drives in Central Park on a pleasant afternoon? There you can see men and women whirled along in carriages fit for kings to ride in, drawn by horses worth thousands of dollars—beasts whose trappings are fastened with gold-plated buckles—and coachmen and footmen dressed in showy livery And why is all this parade? Because those who ride out in that style are servants. The name of their master and lord is Fashion; he demands all this extravagance of them, and they obey him. Follow them home, and you will see them again at his service, spending many thousand dollars in adorning their houses with the costliest furniture and decking their bodies, for Fashion's sake, with rich silks and gold : everything offered up on the altar of Fashion, though the poor of Christ are starving all around them.

And many of the poor are servants. Who is the master of the poor? He is a devil, and his name is Drink. This devil of Drink must have a good share of a poor man's wages of a Saturday night. And as soon as a poor man loses work and loses courage this devil of Drink comes and whispers in his ear : "Be my servant and I will make you happy." And by this lie he entices the poor fellow into one of his dens, and there he makes him drunk, and from the bar-room he sends him home to be a scandal to his little children, and may be to beat his wretched wife.

Others this master sends from that liquor-store to steal, and so to prison and hopeless ruin; others he sends to brothels; many a one he afflicts with frightful diseases and sudden accidents, and so brings them to hell. Sometimes, too, this demon of Drink gathers his slaves together into a mob to murder and plunder, and then to be shot down by soldiers. O brethren! is it not strange that any one should be a servant of this devil, Drink? Yet he has countless slaves, and not only among the poor but in every station in life.

But the strangest thing of all is that the foolish servants of sin and Satan fancy that they can at the same time be servants of Almighty God. They call themselves by Christ's name—Christians. They go to his church now and then; and although they have served Mammon all their days, they yet hope to enjoy God and his happiness for all eternity. Hence Jesus Christ in to-day's Gospel cries out in warning: "*You cannot serve two masters.*" Hence in another place he says: "*Amen, amen I say unto you, that whosoever committeth sin is the servant of sin.*" So we have got to choose. We must be either servants of God or servants of Mammon; we cannot be both at once.

Therefore, brethren, instead of giving our time, and money, and health, and heart, and soul to sinful pleasures, to lust and intemperance, and fashion and avarice—all cruel tyrants—let us have the good sense to enter the service of our blessed Lord Jesus Christ, the Lord and Master who made us, and who redeemed us, and who will judge us; whose yoke is sweet and whose burden is light; whose servants are innocent and happy in this life, and who shall enter him into everlasting dwellings in the kingdom of heaven. B.

SERMON CXIX.

The works of the flesh are manifest. . . . Of the which I foretell you, as I have foretold to you, that they who do such things shall not obtain the kingdom of God.—Gal. v. 19, 21.

The works of the flesh—that is, the various ways in which the desires of the flesh can be gratified—have always been the chief obstacles presented by the world to our salvation. This was specially the case in St. Paul's day, when a corrupt and sensual civilization had been attained which placed the happiness of man in bodily pleasure. And it is also specially the case now more than at any other time since then; for a similar so-called civilization is the boast of the present age, in which the desires and appetites of the body are exalted above those of the soul.

But the temptations of this modern age are more concealed than those of the former one; and on that account they are more dangerous to Christians than those of the time of St. Paul were. Satan has, we may say, learned wisdom by experience. At the present day, instead of shocking us by sins like those of the pagans, which could only repel and disgust those who had even the weakest love of God, he has learned to seduce the faithful by the gradual introduction of amusements and pleasures having the name of being innocent, making them worse and worse as the moral sense of those who engage in them, or who witness them, becomes more and more blunted.

A prominent example of such amusements is to be found in the dances which have become fashionable in the last few years. There can be no question at all that, had they been suddenly presented to our eyes not very long ago, every one, without hesitation, would have pronounced them sinful, and no one would have engaged in them who professed to have a delicate conscience; whereas now it is equally certain that very many people who are careful, and even scrupulous, profess to see no harm in these dangerous recreations.

Let me not be understood to mean that dancing is in itself condemned by the law of God. There is no other harm in it, if it be done in a proper way, than the danger of excess and waste of time to which any amusement is liable. Nor is there any more harm in two people dancing together than in eight standing up in a set; and the particular measure of the music is a matter of no consequence. The harm is in the improper positions assumed in what are called round dances, and which have been lately brought into almost all others. These mutual positions of the parties, these embraces—for that they simply are—are in themselves evidently contrary to modesty and decency. It seems as if no one would have to stop, even a moment, to see and acknowledge this. A very plain proof of it, however, should it be needed, is that every person pretending to be respectable would blush to be detected in such positions on any other occasion, unless united to the other party by very near relationship or marriage.

And let no one say that fashion justifies them. If it did it could justify every other indecency or impropriety. Neither fashion nor anything else can justify what is in itself wrong. Nor is it true that they are not noticed or cared for by those who indulge in them; that they are indulged in only because the dance happens to be so arranged. That may be true for some persons; but there is, unfortunately, very little doubt that many only dance on account of these positions, and would not care about learning or practising this amusement were it not for the opportunity offered by it for them. This is a good enough straw to show which way the wind blows.

The plain state of the case is this: To many these dances are, as one would expect, a remote, or even a proximate, occasion of sin, at least in thought, and sometimes in word and action. To many more they are a sensual excitement bordering on impurity. To many, it is true, they are simply an amusement; but this is due to the force of habit, aided by the grace of God, not to the natural state of the case. But for all they are paving the way—in fact, they have already done so—to things which are more plainly wrong; in fact, they themselves are becoming worse and worse all the time.

One of the works of the flesh of which St. Paul speaks in this Epistle is immodesty. Take away the veil of concealment which the gradual introduction of this sensuous practice has put over your eyes, and see if it does not deserve that name. Do not defend yourselves by saying that some confessors allow it. They only allow it because they are afraid of keeping you altogether away from the sacraments; and they do not wish to do that, if in any way they can satisfy themselves that you have even the most imperfect dispositions with which you can be allowed to receive them. But it is better to be on the safe side. **There is no confessor who would not far rather that** you should abandon this dangerous pastime, that you should cease to set this bad example. There is not one who would not be much consoled should you do so. I beg you, then, to give them that consolation. Give up these dances for God's sake, and for the sake of the salvation of your own soul and those of others. Give them up, and you will receive an abundant reward of grace in this world, and of glory in that which is to come.

SERMON CXX.

No man can serve two masters.—St. Matt. vi. 24.

It is perhaps a little strange, my dear brethren, and not much of a compliment on the part of Christians to the wisdom of Him whose disciples they profess to be, that so great a part of them should spend their lives in trying to do what he so solemnly declares to be impossible. It is curious that so many, so very many, of them should never have made up their minds which shall be their master, Almighty God or the devil, but should be hopefully trying to serve both.

Some there are—nay, many, if you take their absolute number—who have truly gone over, once for all and in real dead earnest, to God's side. They keep up a constant battle with temptation; if by weakness and surprise they fall for a moment, they pick themselves up again instantly by a sincere repentance and confession, and begin the fight again. They live in the grace and friendship of their Creator, and they are willing not only to be his friends but to be known as such; they are not ashamed to be pious, but would be very much ashamed to be anything else.

On the other hand, there are not a few who were put on God's side by baptism, but have gone over entirely to the camp of his enemy; who have sold themselves body and soul to the devil. These wretched traitors have denied their faith, and now perhaps even blaspheme or ridicule it ; they give free rein to their favorite vices, whatever they may be ; they have abandoned prayer, and have openly and even boastingly taken the road which leads to hell. You all know of such. In these days of apostasy many of you have such among your acquaintance. They have got Satan's mark on their foreheads, and they do not care to conceal it.

But there is a very common kind of Christian who does not answer to either of these descriptions or belong to either of these parties, but is trying to get the advantages of both—to serve both masters, God and the devil, and get paid by both. He fulfils part of the divine law ; he goes to Mass, sometimes at least ; perhaps he does not eat meat on Friday ; and now and then, it may be once a year, or on the occasion of a mission or jubilee, he puts in an appearance at a confessional and tells about the sins he has committed. He goes to Holy Communion, and seems to come over really and entirely to God's side. Well, perhaps he does come over, for a little while at least, a few days or weeks ; but the chances are very great that he never really means to quit the other side for ever; or, it may be, at all. In his mind impure thoughts, words, and actions, drunkenness, and the pleasures of the devil generally, are a kind of necessity of life ; he has no idea of really quitting them at once and for ever. His idea is to make a sort of a compromise with God ; to do his " duty," as he calls it—that is, to keep in what he imagines to be the state of grace for a few hours or days now and then, and afterward go on as before. He wants to serve the devil during life, and yet be acknowledged as God's servant at the end ; in short, he tries to be the servant of two masters.

Are there not many of you here, my friends, who have lived in this way all your lives, and mean to all the rest of the time that God spares you in this world ? There are even many who have this intention on whose tongues the traces of his Body and Blood are yet fresh. How do I know ? Because they are not resisting temptation ; because they have not left the occasions of sin ; because, instead of calling on God continually in prayer, they go on wantonly blaspheming his holy name ; because the immodest jest is ready to come at any moment to their lips ; because, instead of showing dislike to impiety in others, they acquiesce in it and applaud it ; because, in short, they have not even begun the battle by which alone they can be saved.

Brethren, this is not the way to live ; this is not the way to prepare to die. If you will not be God's servants during life, the devil will claim you at the hour of your death, and get you, too, in spite of the last sacraments which you may receive. "Ha!" he will say to you, "you tried to serve two masters, did you ? What a fool you were ! You were mine all along. You tried to give God a share of your heart; know now, since you would not know it before, that he will not take less than the whole."

Fifteenth Sunday after Pentecost.

EPISTLE. *Gal. v.* 25; *vi.* 10. Brethren: If we live in the Spirit, let us also walk in the Spirit. Let us not become desirous of vainglory, provoking one another, envying one another. And if a man can be overtaken in any fault, you, who are spiritual, instruct such a one in the spirit of mildness, considering thyself, lest thou also be tempted. Bear ye one another's burdens, and so shall you fulfil the law of Christ. For if any man think himself to be something, whereas he is nothing, he deceiveth himself. But let every one prove his own work, and so he shall have glory in himself only, and not in another. For every one shall bear his own burden. And let him who is instructed in the word communicate to him that instructeth him, in all good things. Be not deceived, God is not mocked. For what things a man shall sow, those also shall he reap. For he that soweth in the flesh, of the flesh also shall reap corruption. But he that soweth in the Spirit, of the Spirit shall reap life everlasting. And in doing good, let us not fail. For in due time we shall reap, not failing. Therefore, whilst we have time, let us do good to all men, but especially to those who are of the household of the faith.

GOSPEL. *St. Luke vii.* 11–16. At that time: Jesus went into a city called Nain: and there went with him his disciples, and a great multitude. And when he came nigh to the gate of the city, behold a dead man was carried out, the only son of his mother; and she was a widow: and much people of the city was with her. And when the Lord saw her, he had compassion on her, and said to her: Weep not. And he came near and touched the bier. (And they that carried it stood still.) And he said: Young man, I say to thee, Arise. And he that was dead sat up and began to speak. And he delivered him to his mother. And there came a fear on them all: and they glorified God, saying: That a great prophet is risen up among us: and God hath visited his people.

SERMON CXXI.

Behold a dead man was carried out.—St. Luke vii. 12.

The sight which our Lord saw, and which is recorded in to-day's Gospel, we have often seen. We can scarcely walk a mile or two in a great city without seeing a dead man carried out. The hearse, the funeral procession, the pall, the coffin, the sabled mourners, are all familiar and every-day objects. Again, we read of death every day. We find in the newspapers, the hospital reports, and so forth, death in a thousand shapes. We see that death waits for us at every corner of the street, that it lurks in the river, hovers in the atmosphere, hides in our very bodies, is concealed even in our pleasures. Again and again we have heard the beating of its heavy wings and seen the clutch of its clammy fingers—sometimes in our own houses, sometimes in our neighbors', sometimes on the sea, sometimes on land, sometimes in the busy street, sometimes in the silent chamber.

Strange to say, however, although nothing is better known than death, nothing is more forgotten. We hear people saying every day, " How shall we live ? " but seldom do they ever think of adding, " and how shall we die ? "

My brethren, every one of you here this morning *must* die.

There will come an hour when your heart will cease to beat, when you will close your eyes and fold your hands in death, and when, like the dead man in the Gospel, you will "be carried out."

O brethren! how are you preparing for that supreme moment?

Are you ready *now*, at this moment, to die? If you are not you ought to be. Let us, then, see how we should prepare ourselves.

Above all things you should never forget death. When you see other men die, when you read of death, when you see the priest in black vestments, and hear the sweet tones of the choristers chanting the solemn requiem, then you should say to yourselves, "It may be my turn next."

Keep death always before your eyes; then when it comes you will not shrink from its touch. Again, keep your conscience clear, and make every confession and Communion as if it were to be your last. How many have come to their duties on Saturday and Sunday, and on Monday have departed for ever from this world!

The earth, dearly beloved, is a vast field, and Death with his sharp scythe toils in it every day. Blade after blade, flower after flower, tender plant and fragrant herb, fall beneath his sweeping blows every hour, every second. You may now be as the grass that is the most distant from the steel: there may be acres upon acres between you and the severing blade, but the strong, patient mower is nearing you slowly but surely. Listen! listen! and you will catch the sharp hiss of his scythe and hear the **murmur of the** falling grass. Oh! then be ready, with girded loins and burning lamp. Be ready, for you know not when death shall come. Be ready, with clear conscience and well-cared-for soul, for the last great hour.

Lastly, pray to St. Joseph that you may obtain the grace of a happy death. Go to his altar; kneel at his feet and say, "O dear spouse of our Lady and foster-father of Jesus Christ! obtain for me to die, as thou didst, in the arms of Jesus and Mary, and to remain with them and thee in the paradise of God."

Beloved, death is nearing, death is coming. Oh! then, I beseech you, neglect not these words of warning and advice. " Here we have not an abiding city, but seek one to come," even the heavenly Jerusalem, the City of God, which shines above. The gate of that city is a good and Christian death. God grant, then, that through that blessed portal we all may pass, lest we be left cold and shivering in the black night of the outer darkness! B.

SERMON CXXII.

If we live in the spirit, let us also walk in the spirit.—GAL. v. 25.

THERE is a saying which, in Latin, runs as follows: "*Dum vivimus, vivamus.*" Put into English, it is: "While we live let us live"; or, to bring out the idea more clearly: "While we live let us make the most of life."

It is a saying which has always been very popular with infidels. We have this life, they say—it is our own; but we do not know what is coming after it, or, indeed, if anything at all is; so, while we have it, let us use it; there is not much of it, and it will soon be gone, but it is ours now. A bird in the hand is worth two in the bush; so, then, "*Dum vivimus, vivamus*"—while we live let us make the most of life.

Now, the Christian idea of life and the way to use it is somewhat different from that of the infidel. A Christian does know what is coming after this life; he knows that this short life is only a preparation for the next, which is eternal; he knows that pursuing the pleasure of this world, after the infidel fashion, will endanger his salvation; and if he values his salvation—that is to say, if he has common sense—he looks out for the life of his soul rather than that of his body, so that he may always be ready for death when it shall come. And he has a fear of pleasure, rather than a desire of it, on account of its danger; he crucifies the flesh, with its vices and concupiscences, as St. Paul says in the conclusion of the Epistle of last Sunday, that it may be subject to the soul, instead of subjecting the soul to itself.

He makes up his mind, in short, to live in the spirit instead of the flesh; and in that, as I have said, he shows his common sense. But when he has got as far as that his common sense seems too often to fail him. He ought then to come back to the maxim of the infidel; for it is a very sensible one in itself, the only trouble with it being that the infidel has the wrong idea of life. It would be all right for the Christian.

The Christian ought to say—you and I, my dear brethren, ought to say: "*Dum vivimus, vivamus.*" Or, in the words of St. Paul in the beginning of to-day's Epistle, which immediately follows that of last

Sunday, we ought to say: "If we live in the spirit, let us also walk in the spirit." That is, if we are going to live in the spirit rather than in the flesh, let us make the most of our spiritual life. Let us enjoy it, advance in it, and get all out of it that we can. We have, indeed, much more reason to say so than the man of the world; for not only shall we have more of it in the next world for all that we get out of it now, but there is much more to be got out of it even here than out of the life of the body.

And yet many, perhaps most, good Christians content themselves with simply keeping in the state of grace and avoiding sin. They just keep themselves spiritually alive, and that is all. They are like misers, who starve in the midst of their gold. There are pleasures for them, even in this world, far above what it can itself give, and they do little or nothing to obtain them.

Something has to be done to obtain them, of course. It is the same, however, with bodily pleasure, and those who seek it know that. Many a man has made a slave of himself all his life to get a few years of ease and comfort at the end of it. Why should not we do the same for the comfort of our souls?

Something has to be done, but not so much after all. A little more earnestness in prayer; a little more fidelity in meditation and spiritual reading; a little more care to uproot our evil habits; a little more charity and spirit of sacrifice for our brethren; and, last but not least, a little mortification beyond what is forced on us, or what is necessary to avoid sin, and the reward would soon come. Temptations would be lighter; the struggle would be easier; God would come nearer to us; and that dawn would rise in our hearts which is brighter than the lights which earthly hands can kindle, and which is the sure forerunner of the eternal day.

SERMON CXXIII.

Let us not become desirous of vainglory.—GAL. v. 26.

THESE words, my dear brethren, are from the Epistle of the Mass of this Sunday. I feel quite sure that the advice which St. Paul gives us in them is a very sensible one, and one which we all need to take very much to heart.

What is this vainglory of which he speaks? It is the vain and false glory which comes from the admiration of others. It is what, in the more important matters of life, the world calls glory, and does not call vain. It is what many great geniuses have spent their lives to acquire, and have even been admired for doing so. But it is what in smaller matters the world calls it vanity to seek; and the world generally laughs, at least in its sleeve, at those who do so.

The girl whose great desire it is to have her hat acknowledged to be the prettiest one in church is called vain and made fun of, perhaps, even by her rivals, who wish in their hearts that they had a nicer one, if it was only to take the conceit out of her; but the man whose ambition it is to have the brain that his hat covers acknowledged to be the smartest one in the country is not laughed at, but very much respected, if the brain be really a fine one. And yet the desire is really all the same thing in both of them.

Now, my brethren, we are all more or less vain or desirous of this vainglory; rather more, in fact, than less. It will not do for us to laugh very hard at each other for it, for we are all in the same boat. It is a passion which is almost universal. Some people who are quite proud may fancy that they do not care a straw for what others think of them; but I fancy that they do, though perhaps the reason may be that the praise of others will help them to admire themselves.

So you see that I was right in saying that St. Paul's advice was one which we all need to take very much to heart—all of us, not only girls with the new styles of hats, but young men at college or in business, eminent merchants and professional men, including those whom God has called to serve him at the altar. We have all got to look out for this snare of vainglory.

And how? By despising it? Yes, in a certain way, but not in the way of pride. By resolving to value nothing according to the opinion that men have of it, but according to that which Almighty God has of it.

He values nothing much but what is, like himself, eternal. He does not care so very much more for your cleverness than for your beauty. He could spoil either one of them in an instant, if he chose. But what he does care for, and what he himself cannot spoil, though of course he could not wish to, are the merits which he has given you this life to acquire and to bring before the throne of his judgment, to be transformed into your immortal crown. Those are the only things which are worth your caring for, because they are the only things which he cares for.

And they are what all can have, however low in worldly station they may be.

Yes, my dear Christians, that is the glory for us to seek—the glory of God ; that which comes from him. Try to have him think well of you. It is not vain to wish to be praised and admired, only let him be the one whom you want to have praise and admire you. **He will do it,** if you want him to and will give him a chance. He, your Creator, desires to honor and glorify you for ever. When you think of this can you care for other praise ?

Sixteenth Sunday after Pentecost.

EPISTLE. *Eph. iii.* 13–21. Brethren: I beseech you not to be disheartened at my tribulations for you, which is your glory. For this cause I bow my knees to the Father of our Lord Jesus Christ, of whom all paternity in heaven and earth is named, that he would grant you, according to the riches of his glory, to be strengthened with power by his Spirit unto the inward man. That Christ may dwell by faith in your hearts: that being rooted and founded in charity, you may be able to comprehend, with all the saints, what is the breadth, and length, and height, and depth. To know also the charity of Christ, which surpasseth knowledge, that you may be filled unto all the fulness of God. Now to him who is able to do all things more abundantly than we ask or understand, according to the power which worketh in us: to him be glory in the church, and in Christ Jesus, throughout all generations, world without end. Amen.

GOSPEL. *St. Luke xiv.* 1–11. At that time: When Jesus went into the house of a certain prince of the Pharisees, on the Sabbath day, to eat bread, and they were watching him. And behold, there was a certain man before him that had the dropsy. And Jesus answering, spoke to the lawyers and Pharisees, saying: Is it lawful to heal on the Sabbath day? But they held their peace. But he, taking him, healed him, and sent him away. And answering them, he said: Which of you whose ass or his ox shall fall into a pit, and will not immediately draw him out on the Sabbath day? And they could not answer him to these things. And he spoke a parable also to them that were invited, marking how they chose the first seats at the table, saying to them: When thou art invited to a wedding, sit not down in the highest place, lest perhaps one more honorable than thou be invited by him: and he who invited thee and him, come and say to thee: Give place to this man; and then thou begin with blushing to take the lowest place. But when thou art invited, go, sit down in the lowest place: that when he who invited thee cometh, he may say to thee: Friend, go up higher. Then shalt thou have glory before them that sit at table with thee. Because every one that exalteth himself shall be humbled: and he that humbleth himself shall be exalted.

SERMON CXXIV.

They were watching him.—St. Luke xiv. 1.

How condescending and kind, brethren, was the spirit of our Lord when he entered into the house of the Pharisee to eat bread; how base and ungracious, on the other hand, the conduct of the latter and his friends, who, as the Gospel says, "were watching him"!

They watched him that they might catch him breaking the laws of the Sabbath.

They envied him because his reputation was great with the people.

They watched him because "he had a daily beauty in his life which made theirs ugly," and tried to find something to carp at, something to find fault with.

He was their guest; they were bound to treat him with respect and kindness; yet they violated the rules of hospitality, deceitfully making the banquet a cover for their plan to catch him.

He was their Saviour and the benefactor of their

people; one who, as they well knew, had healed the sick, given speech to the dumb, and made the blind to see. The knowledge of his goodness and power only moved them to envy. He was greater than they, and so they watched him that they might find something in his conduct which would lessen his reputation and good name.

Are there not found some in our own day who imitate the conduct of the Pharisee and his friends?

Jesus is often near you; you often meet him in your every-day life, often have him in your house in the person of one of his pious servants—I mean any one of your neighbors whose life is better than your own.

There are many who watch such an one with the spirit of envy and criticism, and they try to find out worldly motives for their neighbor's piety. Such persons say, as Satan did of old, "Does Job serve God for naught?" Often they exclaim, "I see my neighbor frequently at Communion, but she only goes for show; I should like to see some change in her life"; or "What does she run to church so much for? It would be a great deal better for her if she stayed at home and minded her family."

Again, many watch the prosperity of their neighbor with an envious eye; they hate to see their neighbor in a better house than their own, don't like him to have more money than themselves, and so forth. All this is watching Jesus as the Pharisee did.

There are many, too, whose consciences must accuse them of watching Jesus in the persons of his priests, who envy the priest's position, envy his authority over them, and such like. These people try to pick a hole in the priest's ways, to pass their opinion on his manner, his judgments, his actions. They watch him in his words, at table in their own houses, to see if perchance they can find something to make a dish of scandal out of. Yes, brethren, there are many such watchers as these, and Pharisees are they all.

Envy, which prompts this horrible spirit of unchristian criticism, is one of the worst offences against the great and fundamental virtue of charity.

Envy has inspired the hearts of men with the most wicked crimes. Envy delivered the innocent Lamb of God to a cruel death. Envy, therefore, is a grievous sin.

Envy and the spirit of criticism spring from pride. Envy makes us watch others, and such watching is from pride.

Watch yourselves rather than your neighbor and your superiors.

"Brethren," says St. Paul, "if a man be overtaken in any fault, you, who are spiritual, instruct such an one, in the spirit of meekness, considering thyself lest thou also be tempted."

Walk and pray lest ye enter into temptation. Watch Jesus and his servants, if you will, but do so to be edified, do so to learn something good. Watch Jesus, who is meek and humble of heart, that you may learn the lesson which he tried to teach the proud and envious Pharisees: "Every one that exalteth himself shall be humbled, and he that humbleth himself shall be exalted." **B.**

SERMON CXXV.

Every one that exalteth himself shall be humbled.—St. Luke xiv. 11.

That was an unlucky guest who sat down in the first place and was sent to take the lowest. No wonder he was covered with shame; served him right. To be humbled in the very act of exalting ourselves is indeed hard punishment, sharp and painful as a pang in a tenderly sore spot. It is like being caught in a theft or a lie. For, truly, pride is theft. We have no right to be proud, because we own as our property nothing that we may be proud of. All that we have that is good is God's; to pride ourselves on that is to rob God of his due and appropriate what does not belong to us. And pride is a lie, a deceit; "for if thou hast received," says St. Paul, "why dost thou glory as if thou hadst not received?" A vain boast is simply lying.

To lie and to steal are very mean things to do. To be caught lying and stealing makes us feel very mean in the eyes of others; and that is what comes to us when our pride is evident and is found out by our fellow-men, and then we are humbled as was the poor guest spoken of in the Gospel. Truth is the badge of honor among men. Humility is truth, because humility is to know our place and keep it; in this is truthfulness and comfort also. We feel at ease when we are where we ought to be. A bone dislocated is a torture; anything out of place is an offence and a nuisance, whether it be a misshapen limb or a stovepipe that doesn't fit and smokes. You remember in the fable the fate of the foolish frog who wanted to be as big as the ox—he blew until he burst and collapsed.

Now, is there not a great deal of that kind of work among us—I mean getting too big, reaching above us, exalting ourselves—in a word, not knowing our place? Let me instance: The poor will pass for rich: fine dress and flashy jewels in broad daylight on the street; at home, dirt, wretchedness, almost starvation. The ignorant will know more than they have learned, and so stretch themselves all out of shape, and wed in the most repulsive manner pretentious speech to gross ignorance. Not only is one man as good as another, but a great deal better. The layman will teach theology and canon law to the priest. The ward politician, who buys votes at five cents a glass, and trades them off for street contracts or other valuable consideration, can run the world, the Holy See not excepted. Our American boy of twelve thinks the old folks not a circumstance to him, and shows it in his behavior. The school girl who can do a sum and thump an "easy exercise" on the piano scorns domestic work, leaves the kitchen to "ma," and cultivates the fine arts in the parlor. Our talk, our press even, is full of unreality, inflated bombast and buncombe. We have no degrees of comparison but the superlative. God help us for a vain, boastful set! What is it all but untruthfulness, want of humility, strutting up to the head of the table in one way or another? Our conversations are full of ourselves; we threaten horrors or we promise wonders; and it all issues, like the mountain in travail, in ridiculous failures. Let us know our place, or humiliation will teach it us. Adam and Eve were well off, and might have been till this day had they known their place and been satisfied; but they wanted to go up, to become as God—and they came down to all the miseries of fallen nature. Simon the Magician started, with the help of the devil, to ascend into heaven like our Saviour; but God brought him down before he got very far. "He that exalteth himself shall be humbled." Moreover, pride finds its punishment in the very ridiculousness of itself. The fool imagines himself to be other than he is; the insane insists on taking to himself a character which is not his. Well, brethren, the mock-king and queen of the asylum are not more foolish and insane, because not more untruthful, than the proud man.

The lesson, then, is this: Keep to the place God has given you, don't put yourself forward in conversation, acknowledge your nothingness before your Creator, be true and real to your fellow-men; thus you will escape shameful humiliation and deserve to be exalted in the esteem of others and in the kingdom of heaven.

Seventeenth Sunday after Pentecost.

Epistle. *Eph. iv.* 1–6. Brethren: As a prisoner in the Lord, I beseech you that you walk worthy of the vocation in which you are called, with all humility and mildness, with patience, supporting one another in charity, careful to keep the unity of the Spirit in the bond of peace. One body and one Spirit: as you are called in one hope of your vocation. One Lord, one faith, one baptism, one God and Father of all, who is above all, and through all, and in us all, who is blessed for ever and ever.

Gospel. *St. Matt. xxii.* 35–46. At that time: the Pharisees came nigh to Jesus: and one of them, a doctor of the law, asked him, tempting him: Master, which is the great commandment in the law? Jesus said to him: Thou shalt love the Lord thy God with thy whole heart, and with thy whole soul, and with thy whole mind. This is the greatest and the first commandment. And the second is like to this: Thou shalt love thy neighbor as thyself. On these two commandments dependeth the whole law and the prophets. And the Pharisees being gathered together, Jesus asked them saying: What think you of Christ? Whose son is he? They say to him: David's. He saith to them: How then doth David in spirit call him Lord, saying: "The Lord said to my Lord: Sit on my right hand, until I make thy enemies thy footstool"? If David then call him Lord, how is he his son? And no man was able to answer him a word: neither durst any man from that day forth ask him any more questions.

SERMON CXXVI.

Thou shalt love thy neighbor as thyself.—St. Matt. xxii. 39.

Nothing can be plainer than the fact that we must love God, and it is equally plain that we must love our neighbor. Our Lord declares that on these two precepts depend the whole law and the prophets. Yet we see people who make very little of them both. The precept to love our neighbor is perhaps the least regarded. Let us, therefore, reflect upon this commandment to-day. In the first place, there is no doubt about the obligation. Jesus says plainly, and with authority: "Thou shalt love thy neighbor"; and again, in another place, he says: "A new *commandment* I give unto you, that you love one another. By this shall all men know that you are my disciples, if you have love for one another."

So, then, if you want to keep the commandment of Jesus Christ, if you want to be known as his disciples, you *must* love your neighbors. The obligation is clear and plain.

But our Lord not only gives a *commandment*, but also explains the *method* of fulfilling it. He not only says, "Thou shalt love thy neighbor," but also adds "as thyself." He does not say as much as thyself, because, of course, the orders of nature and charity both require that we should love ourselves better than our neighbor. We must save our own soul first. We must not peril our own salvation in order to benefit our neighbor. Our Lord says "as thyself"—that is, in the *same manner*, not in the *same degree.* We must love our neighbor for his own sake, just as we love ourselves for our own sake. If we only love our neighbor on account of the use he can be to us, the pleasure he can give us, or the positions he can obtain for us, then that is really no love at all. That is nothing more or less than loving ourselves. We must love him as Jesus Christ has loved us—with a supernatural love, with a love which is founded on a desire to save our neighbor's soul.

And now in every-day life how must we treat our neighbor in order to fulfil the command of Jesus Christ, "Thou shalt love thy neighbor as thyself"? First, do your neighbor no wrong, either by thought, word, or deed. You don't like any one to think evil of you. Very well, don't think evil of your neighbor. You don't like any one to speak ill of yourself; you don't like to be insulted; can't bear to be abused. Ah! then be careful that you don't visit such things upon your neighbor.

You don't like to be defrauded or cheated; you don't like to have your property or your reputation injured, or to be wronged in any way. Why? Because you love yourself. Very well, then, "love thy neighbor *as* thyself," and don't do to him what you are unwilling should be done to you.

Again, not only refrain from doing your neighbor wrong, but wish him well and do him good. Try to have his name on your lips when you are at prayer. Say: "O God! prosper my neighbor, even as thou hast prospered me." Endeavor to show your fellow-Christian that you are interested in his well-being, and heartily glad when he succeeds in life. Have that spirit in your heart which makes you as glad to hear that your neighbor has gained five hundred dollars as if you had made the sum yourself. Then, when you can do your friend a good turn, do it with a hearty good-will; give him a helping hand; try to encourage him in his business. Don't say, "Every man for himself and God for us all, and the devil take the hindermost"; but say, "Do unto others as you would they should do unto you."

And, lastly, you want God to forgive your sins? You want men to condone your offences and look over your shortcomings and defects? Then love your neighbor as yourself. If he has injured you, pardon him; if he has done wrong, overlook it; if he has got defects, bear with them. "All things," says one of the saints, "are easy to him who loves." So, then, love God, love your neighbor, and all things will be easy to *you*. This life will pass away all the more pleasantly, and the life to come will be all the more bright and its reward all the more precious, if you will only remember and act upon this great commandment: "Thou shalt *love* thy neighbor *as thyself*." B.

SERMON CXXVII.

With patience, supporting one another in charity.—EPHES. iv. 2.

WE hear a great deal nowadays, my dear brethren, about toleration. It is a thing which the nineteenth century takes a special pride in. It seems to imagine that it is really a great deal more charitable and patient than any previous one, and that, in fact, the apostles themselves might learn a lesson of Christian virtue from it, if they could come back to the earth.

I wish that such were actually the case; but if we examine this pretended toleration and charity we shall has to confess that it is simply a sham, having nothing whatever in it to make it deserve the name it takes. You would not say of any man that he was of a tolerant and patient disposition because he was quite willing that some stranger should be interfered with, provided he himself was let alone. Well, that is precisely the tolerance of the nineteenth century. The world is now tolerant about all things in which the rights of Almighty God are concerned, because it has made him a stranger to itself; but it resents interference with itself, and insists on being let alone in its own enjoyments as much as, or more than, ever

The world, then, has not yet learned to be tolerant, patient, or charitable in any true sense of those words, in spite of all its boasting ; and it is much to be feared that it never will. After all, it is not much wonder that it has not ; for this is a very difficult lesson, and one which one must have the help of God to learn. True tolerance or patience, bearing with others when they interfere, not with somebody else, but with ourselves, is a fruit of grace rather than of nature. It cannot be expected from those who have rejected the grace of God as a needless encumbrance in the journey of life. If they have the appearance of it, it is only an outside finish of what is called politeness, put on merely to save trouble and make things more comfortable on the whole.

But it is not for Christians who are trying to live by the light of grace, not of nature; who believe in God and are trying to keep his commandments; who wish to imitate Christ, and are receiving the sacraments which should enable them to do so, to follow the example of such.

We ought to try to be really tolerant with our

brethren, whatever their faults or defects may be or however much they may put us out or interfere with our comfort consciously or unconsciously, " with patience, supporting one another in charity," as St. Paul says in the Epistle of to-day. And yet must we not confess that too often we do not even make an attempt to practise this virtue? Your neighbor offends you in some trifling way, perhaps without really meaning to do so or knowing that he does; it may be even by some peculiarity which is not really his fault at all. Do you put up with it; do you say: "Oh! that is not much; I must take people as I find them and as God made them, not as I would like to have them; we all have plenty of defects, and perhaps I myself am the worst of all"? Do you not rather say: "Oh! there is no getting along with such a person; I will keep out of his way; I cannot bear the sight of him; it will be better for us to avoid speaking," and the like?

This intolerance, which is so common, is simply avoiding a cross which we ought to carry, not only for the love of God, like all others, but for the love of our neighbor also; and especially when it comes from those who are our brethren not only by a common humanity but by a common faith, who have with us, as St. Paul goes on to remind us, "one Lord, one faith, one baptism, one God and Father of all, who is above all, and through all, and in us all." Try, then, to bear this cross cheerfully, and show, by so doing, that you really are aiming to fulfil the great commandments given in to-day's Gospel, by loving God, from whom it comes, with your whole heart and soul and mind, and your neighbor, by whom it comes, as yourself.

Eighteenth Sunday after Pentecost.

EPISTLE. 1 *Cor. i.* 4–8. Brethren: I give thanks to my God always for you, for the grace of God that is given you in Christ Jesus, that in all things you are made rich in him, in every word, and in all knowledge: as the testimony of Christ was confirmed in you: so that nothing is wanting to you in any grace, waiting for the manifestation of our Lord Jesus Christ, who also will confirm you unto the end without crime, in the day of the coming of our Lord Jesus Christ.

GOSPEL. *St. Matt. ix.* 1–8. At that time: Jesus entering into a boat, passed over the water and came into his own city. And behold they brought to him a man sick of the palsy lying on a bed. And Jesus, seeing their faith, said to the man sick of the palsy: Son, be of good heart, thy sins are forgiven thee. And behold some of the Scribes said within themselves: This man blasphemeth. And Jesus seeing their thoughts, said: Why do you think evil in your hearts? Which is easier, to say, Thy sins are forgiven thee; or to say, Rise up and walk? But that you may know that the Son of man hath power on earth to forgive sins (then saith he to the man sick of the palsy), Rise up: take thy bed and go into thy house. And he rose up, and went into his house. And the multitude seeing it, feared, and glorified God who had given such power to men.

SERMON CXXVIII.

Why do you think evil in your hearts ?—St. Matt. ix. 4.

ALL those, dear brethren, who are trying to lead a holy life have a great horror of *external* sins. They will not lie, steal, murder, or be guilty of adultery or intemperance. Still, I am afraid a great many of us are awfully careless about *internal* sins. We forget that not only the sins which we openly commit, but those also which we secretly assent to in our own minds, are offences against God.

You can see this in to-day's Gospel. When our Lord said to the sick man, "Thy sins are forgiven thee," the Scribes directly said *"within themselves,* He blasphemeth"; and although they did not shape this sentence in words, it was accounted to them for sin, as we can see from the reply of Jesus Christ contained in the text.

You see, then, brethren, if you want to keep your conscience clear, you must not only avoid external but even internal sins. Indeed, I think the sins which we commit internally are even more deadly than the external ones. First, because they always precede the open offence; as our Lord says in another place, "From the heart come forth evil thoughts, murders, adulteries, fornications, thefts, false testimonies, blasphemies." Now, you will see at once that "evil thoughts" come first on the list, by which I think our Lord wishes to intimate that they are the root of all the others.

Again, evil thoughts, whether they are against charity, or against chastity, or against faith—whether they are thoughts of pride, of hatred, or envy, or avaricious thoughts—insomuch as they are concealed from the sight of others, do not cause the same shame to the guilty person as an overt act would. Thus, being the more easily committed, they are the more frequent and the more deadly.

Lastly, dear friends, evil thoughts pollute the mind and heart, and in proportion as they and their darkness enter God and his brightness leave. To indulge in evil thoughts is to defile the stream at its fountain-head and poison all the river below.

Be on your guard, then, dear brethren, against this insidious enemy.

Perhaps evil thoughts against faith may assail you. Cast them out before they have time to enter fully into the mind. Many, better perhaps and holier than you, have in times past become heretics, apostates, enemies of God's church because they did not trample at once upon these beginnings of evil. You may be assaulted by imaginations against holy purity. Stifle them, I beseech you, at once, or they will grow in strength and gain in frequency till they have buried the grace of God, peace of mind, and strength of intellect in one common and unhallowed grave. You have all doubtless heard of the avalanche which happens in regions where the mountains which rise from the great valley and tower above the nestling valleys are covered with perpetual snow. Perhaps it is a slight puff of air, or the light tread of the mountain goat, or it may be nothing but the brushing of a bird's wing that detaches the ball of snow; but be that as it may, the particle, once started, rushes down the mountain-side, gathering strength as it hurries on, leaping from one precipice to another, till finally, having swept everything before it, the enormous heap falls upon the peaceful village and buries everything in "a chaos of indistinguishable death." Yet in the beginning that avalanche was but a ball of snow. So it is with evil thoughts against faith, chastity, charity, humility, and all the other virtues. Once let them start and you can never tell in what awful ruin they will end.

Nip evil thoughts, then, in the bud; and as chief remedies I would say: 1. Fill your mind with good thoughts. A vessel cannot be full of two liquids at the same time. Think of heaven; think of God, of Jesus, of Mary and her pure spouse, St. Joseph. 2. Remember the eye that sees the secrets of all hearts, and Him who saw the thoughts of the Scribes in the Gospel of to-day. 3. Remember that you can commit a mortal sin by thought as well as by deed. Lastly, picture to yourself One ever standing by your side, with wounded hands and pierced heart, "whose name is faithful and true, whose eyes are as a flame of fire, and on his head many diadems; who is clothed with a garment of blood," and who cries to you night and day, "Why do ye think evil in your hearts?"

B.

SERMON CXXIX.

And Jesus seeing their faith, said to the man sick of the palsy: Son, be of good heart, thy sins are forgiven thee.—St. Matt. ix. 2.

THESE words of our Lord must have been something of a surprise to the paralytic and his friends; welcome they must have been, but still unexpected, and to some extent disappointing. For the sick man had not been brought to Christ to have his sins forgiven; and that favor had not been asked, at least no request had been made for it in words. The paralytic himself must have wished it, it is true, for God never forgives our sins unless we desire forgiveness ; but he did not say so, and his mind, like those of his bearers, was probably more occupied with his bodily than with his spiritual cure.

It will be worth our while to see why our Saviour chose to give them this surprise ; why he did not cure the sick man first and forgive him afterwards. That might seem to be the more natural way: to restore him first to bodily health, and then to move him by gratitude to repentance and conversion. Still, when we come to consider it I think we shall hit upon two very good reasons for his course, and that without very much reflection. The first reason, then, for our Lord doing as he did, was to show us that the health of the soul is more important in his sight than that of the body, and hence requires our first attention. The second follows from the first: it was to remind us that, such being the case, we cannot reasonably expect bodily health or any other temporal blessing if we neglect to reconcile ourselves to God.

Now, these are two things that all of us, my dear brethren, must certainly know very well, otherwise they would not occur to our minds so readily. But in spite of this we too often fail to give our knowledge a practical application.

How few there are, strange to say, who really act as if the health of their souls were of more importance than that of their bodies ! Take, for instance, in proof of this, a fact which we have often seen recorded lately in the daily papers. The yellow fever, you will hear, has appeared in some Southern town, and what has been the result? All the inhabitants who could leave the place immediately did so, perhaps taking the very next train, and, it may be, leaving their property in the hands of strangers. Well, we may think this a little cowardly and foolish, considering that, after all, there would not have been, perhaps, more than one chance in ten even of sickness, if they had stayed; but still we cannot blame them, for we feel that we should very likely have done the same ourselves. But how many would act in this way in the presence of a spiritual danger, though it were much more certain and imminent than that of the body in this terrible Southern plague? Ask yourselves the question, you who remain contentedly in unnecessary occasions of sin, with much more than one chance in ten, nay, with an absolute certainty, that your soul will be not only sick but dead as long as you remain there; ask yourselves if you value the health of your soul more than that of the body; see if you practise what you must believe if you are a Christian—that it is better to die even to-day in a state of grace than live for a moment in that of sin.

Well, whether you act on this belief or not, Almighty God does. He shows you that, as I have said, in this Gospel of to-day. And it follows that you cannot please him or be in his grace as long as you do not do for your soul what you would do for your body; that is, as long as you do not remove it from needless dangers. That is the first practical lesson to be learned from our Lord's action in the cure of the paralytic.

And the second is that, if we hope to obtain from God temporal favors out of the natural order of his providence, we must first provide for our souls, which come first in his estimation. And yet many people seem to expect him to reverse the order which he has established. They promise conversion if they obtain the temporal blessing which they want. They may succeed through his abundant mercy; but the better and the surer course would be to think of the soul first and the body afterward. "Seek first," as he says, "the kingdom of God and his justice, and all things shall be added unto you."

And remember that this must be the real disposition of your souls, if you would be saved. The catechism tells you that the only contrition which will obtain forgiveness, even in the sacrament of Penance, must be what is called " sovereign "; that is, " we should be more grieved for having offended God than for all the other evils that could happen to us." Think well of this, and you will be able to add a good deal to what I have had time to say.

Nineteenth Sunday after Pentecost.

Epistle. *Eph. iv.* 23-28. Brethren: Be ye renewed in the spirit of your mind: and put on the new man, who, according to God, is created in justice, and holiness of truth. Wherefore, putting away lying, speak ye the truth every man with his neighbor: for we are members one of another. Be angry, and sin not. Let not the sun go down upon your anger: Give not place to the devil. Let him that stole, steal now no more, but rather let him labor, working with his hands that which is good, that he may have to give to him who is in need.

Gospel. *St. Matt. xxii.* 2-14. At that time: Jesus spoke to the chief priests and Pharisees in parables, saying: The kingdom of heaven is like to a man being a king, who made a marriage for his son. And he sent his servants to call them that were invited to the marriage: and they would not come. Again he sent other servants, saying: Tell them that were invited: Behold, I have prepared my dinner; my beeves and fatlings are killed, and all things are ready: come ye to the wedding. But they neglected, and went their ways, one to his farm, and another to his merchandise. And the rest laid hands on his servants, and, having treated them contumeliously, put them to death. But when the king heard of it he was angry, and, sending his armies, he destroyed those murderers and burnt their city. Then he saith to his servants: The wedding indeed is ready: but they that were invited were not worthy. Go ye therefore into the highways, and as many as you shall find, invite to the wedding. And his servants going out into the highways, gathered together all that they found, both bad and good: and the wedding was filled with guests. And the king went in to see the guests, and he saw there a man who had not on a wedding garment. And he saith to him: Friend, how camest thou in hither not having a wedding garment? But he was silent. Then the king said to the waiters: Having bound his hands and feet, cast him into the exterior darkness: there shall be weeping and gnashing of teeth. For many are called, but few are chosen.

SERMON CXXX.

Let him that stole, steal now no more—EPHES. iv. 28.

THESE words, dear friends, are taken from the Epistle appointed to be read to-day, and contain a most useful lesson.

Now, I know the words "steal, stealing, thief, etc.," have a very ugly sound.

People have a horror of them. The worst insult you can give to any one is to say, "You are a thief." Still, in spite of this feeling, we know that sins against justice are very often committed.

Public men steal from public moneys. Employees rob their employers, children steal from their parents, servants from their masters, trustees from those whose affairs they have under control, and so on. From the time that Judas put his hand into the bag and filched from the scanty funds of his Master and his brethren, down to this present day, there have been Catholics who have so far forgotten themselves and "the vocation to which they are called" as to steal. Do you doubt this? Take up the first daily paper that comes to hand, and you will have evidence in black and white.

Now, there are three ways in which we can commit the sin of stealing: first, by taking that which does not belong to us; secondly, by unjustly retaining what does not belong to us; and, thirdly, by injuring what is not our own. First, then, we must not take what is not our own. Now, this you all know so well that I need only say a few words about it. Brethren, the man, woman, or child who takes money, articles, clothing, or what not from another, without their consent and knowledge, is a thief!

When such persons creep to the till, the box, the desk of their neighbors, with stealthy tread and bated breath, to take what does not belong to them, God sees them, God's angel sees them; and, could they but hear it, they would be aware of a hundred voices crying aloud, "Thou shalt not steal." You are a thief! You are a thief!

If you steal you must restore. Having stolen, you will find it very difficult to restore even when you have the money. If you do not restore (being able) you will go to that "outer darkness where there is weeping and gnashing of teeth." Oh! then, "he that stole, let him now steal no more."

Again, we must not retain what is not our own, for this also is a species of stealing. First under this head comes paying our just debts. "Brethren, owe no man anything," says St. Paul. Now, my friends, if you contract debts, and then when the time comes you do not pay them, but use the money for other purposes, you are unjustly retaining what is not your own, and thereby commit a sin against justice. There are some people who "want" (as the saying is) "to have their cake and eat it." They run in debt, they enjoy the things obtained on credit, and then when the time comes to pay they want the money also. Brethren, the motto of every Catholic ought to be, "Pay your way." When we leave our debts long without liquidation we not only destroy our credit, but we practically steal from our neighbor.

Then we must be careful also to pay our debts to God by supporting our pastors and our churches. It is a solemn command of God that we should give to the support of church and priest. It is our duty. It is a debt *owing* to God. If you do not give of your means to this holy purpose you rob God—you steal from the Almighty by retaining what belongs *by right* to church and pastor. Ah! then, "he that stole, let him now steal no more."

Lastly, we can sin against justice by injuring property or goods which belong to our neighbor. Now, my friends, if we hire a house or lands, or if we take some official charge of our fellow-Christian's goods, we ought to be as careful of these things as if they were our own. If we, through our carelessness, our neglect, allow another's property to be damaged, lost, lessened in any way in value, we steal from him just that much. Be careful, then, of these sins against justice. Do not rob your fellow-men. Do not retain what is their due; do not injure their goods or property. Remember the great God who sees you. He is not only perfect charity; he is also perfect justice, and with his justice will he one day judge.

B.

SERMON CXXXI.

And he sent his servants, to call them that were invited to the marriage: and they would not come.—St. Matt. xxii. 3.

We cannot for a moment hesitate, my dear brethren, as to who is represented, in this parable of our Lord, by the king who made a marriage for his son. It is God the Father; and it is his Divine Son for whom he has made the marriage. And that marriage is the union of our human nature with his divinity; it is what we call the Incarnation. And those who were first invited to this marriage, to partake of its benefits, are the Jews, who were first called to the church, to whom alone our Lord himself preached, and who were the first objects of the labors of his apostles; but who would not answer the invitation, even persecuting and putting to death those who gave it, and thus causing it to be given to others—that is, to ourselves—the city of Jerusalem being at the same time destroyed, together with the national existence of the Jewish people, as a punishment for their rejection of the Gospel invitation.

We Gentiles have accepted what they, his chosen people, refused. We have come by faith and holy baptism to this marriage of the King's Son, for we are within the fold of his Holy Catholic Church. But having done so, we are now all invited to sit down at the marriage feast. It does not satisfy his love for us that we should simply be within the four walls of his house; he wishes that we should also partake of the good things which he has prepared in it for the refreshment of our soul—that is to say, the special graces which come to us only by means of the church, and which are not found outside: particularly the sacraments, and, most of all, the great and wonderful Sacrament of the Altar, in which he has given us his Precious Body and Blood for the food of our souls.

This, then, is pre-eminently the marriage feast of which he has invited us to partake, now that we are within his house. It is the Holy Communion. One would think we would be only too glad to do so. You would not expect to find wedding guests insulting their host by refusing to taste of the refreshment prepared for them.

But how is it in fact? As he has had to send all over the world by his messengers, the apostles and their successors, through its highways and byways, to find people, not rich and great, as he might expect, but poor, humble, and despised, to fill up his house, so he has to send round among those guests whom he has secured, to beg them to eat at his table. He has been obliged not only to ask them but to entreat them, and even to command them, under penalty of being turned out of his doors by excommunication, if they refuse. And in spite of all this, there are so many that do refuse that he does not carry out this threat, lest even his house should be deserted.

Is not this a shame? Is it not too bad that we, his miserable and unworthy guests, who have no right to be in his church at all, should have to be compelled to receive the food which he has prepared for us in it? More especially when we remember what that food is; that it is himself, his own Body and Blood; for such is his love that nothing else seemed to him good enough for us.

Here it is, this royal banquet, waiting for us all. Every day we are allowed to receive it. And yet how few there are who do so! If any one should go to Holy Communion once a month he is regarded rather as presumptuous than obedient. In spite of our Lord's repeated request, his people do not seem to believe that it is his will that not only a few but all of them should frequently come to receive him in this sacrament of his love.

Of course, if you are to do his will in this matter, you must in others too. This feast is not for those who continually and obstinately break his laws. But how often you can approach it is a question for those to whom it has been entrusted to decide. Let the responsibility rest on your confessor, not on yourself. Do not let it be said that you, who are invited, will not come. Let not our Lord have to reproach you with ingratitude. Let not his table be deserted through your fault. The communion-rail is the place for all, not for a few. Come, then, often to it, if not for your own sakes, at least for the sake of Him who so longs to see you there and who has done so much for you.

Twentieth Sunday after Pentecost.

EPISTLE. *Eph. v.* 15-21. See, brethren, how you walk circumspectly: not as unwise, but as wise: redeeming the time, for the days are evil. Wherefore become not unwise, but understanding what is the will of God. And be not drunk with wine, wherein is luxury, but be ye filled with the Holy Spirit. Speaking to yourselves in psalms and hymns, and spiritual canticles, singing and making melody in your hearts to the Lord: giving thanks always for all things, in the name of our Lord Jesus Christ, to God and the Father: being subject one to another in the fear of Christ.

GOSPEL. *St. John iv.* 46-53. At that time: There was a certain ruler whose son was sick at Capharnaum. He having heard that Jesus was come from Judea into Galilee, went to him, and prayed him to come down and heal his son, for he was at the point of death. Then Jesus said to him: Unless you see signs and wonders, you believe not. The ruler saith to him: Sir, come down before that my son die. Jesus saith to him: Go thy way, thy son liveth. The man believed the word which Jesus said to him, and went his way. And as he was going down, his servants met him: and they brought word, saying that his son lived. He asked therefore of them the hour wherein he grew better. And they said to him: Yesterday at the seventh hour the fever left him. The father therefore knew that it was at the same hour that Jesus said to him, Thy son liveth; and himself believed, and his whole house.

SERMON CXXXII.

Sir, come down before that my son die.—ST. JOHN iv. 49.

THERE are many useful lessons to be learnt from the ruler in to-day's Gospel. We can admire his confidence in Jesus Christ, his perseverance in prayer, his ready and speedy conversion to the faith. There is, however, another lesson to be learnt from him which is contained in the above words: "Lord, come down before that my son die." Now, disease, sickness, fever, etc., is, as you know, dear friends, the symbol of sin, while death is the symbol of mortal sin and eternal perdition. Now, you will notice that the ruler did not wait till his son was dead before coming to Christ; he came when his child was at the point of death, or when (according to the exact meaning of the Latin text) "he began to die." The ruler, then, is a model for parents. He teaches you what care you ought to take of your children's souls. Many of your children, dear brethren, are sick. They are sinful, disobedient, careless, and so forth. Now, do you correct them *in the beginning?* Ah! I know a great many of you do not. You let them go on till the fever of sin rises higher and higher and burns fiercer and fiercer. You let them go on till they die and are buried in habits of mortal sin, and not till then do you call upon God and his church.

Brethren, of all things you should watch your children when they are young. A husbandman does not try to force the well-grown wood to grow as he wishes; he trains the young and tender shoots. How often we see in the streets of our city a tribe of swaggering boys and wanton, frivolous girls, who have upon their faces the very mark of premature age and sinful precocity! We see young boys and girls at beer-gardens, at variety theatres, in billiard-saloons; and, alas! if they are there, there is every reason to fear that the grace of God does not adorn their souls.

These poor children are spiritually dead. Ah! but there must have been a time when they "began to die." There must have been a moment when they first took to these scandalous habits. Then why did you not see that they went to confession, to Mass, to Holy Communion? Why did you not insist upon their morning and evening prayers being said? Why did you not keep them at home after dark? Brethren, soon we shall come to this pass: that none will be considered a child after five years of age. Our children of this age and country are "at the point of death." They are growing up with ideas of false independence, false liberality, and false religious principles. You parents, then, must call upon Christ. Jesus is represented on earth by his church and his priests. You must go, then, to church and priest, if you want your children to be saved before they die the death of sin. You must cut them off from the beginning of evil as soon as you see the least sign of the fever of sin upon them. Go yourself to Jesus Christ. Kneel down and pray for them. Lift up your voices and cry: "Lord, come down before that my child shall die." Send them to the sacraments; send them to Sunday-school; send them to Vespers and Benediction. Above all, interest yourself in your children. Go to Jesus, as the ruler did. Pray for your children every time you go to Mass and Communion, and every night and morning. Do not let them form evil companions and low associates. Insist upon their obeying the parental authority, and above all, teach them that boys and girls of fifteen or sixteen are not men and women. Lastly, let us all, priests and people, lift up our hands and cry to Jesus: "Lord, come down before that these children die; come down with thy lessons of obedience; come down in Holy Communion; come down with thy grace and with thy quickening Spirit." Then, if we do these things—if we attend to our solemn duties as parents and pastors—we may each expect to hear from our dear Master's lips: "Go thy way, thy son liveth." B.

SERMON CXXXIII.

Giving thanks always for all things.—EPHES. v. 20.

IF we stop a moment, my dear brethren, to consider the meaning of these words, which we find in the Epistle of to-day, they will, I think, seem to us rather surprising; and if we did not believe in the inspiration of their author we should be inclined to say that he rather exaggerated the truth, and that we cannot be expected to take the lesson which he here teaches us quite literally. "Surely," we might say, "St. Paul must have meant that we should give thanks for all things which are really fit subjects for thanksgiving; that we should not neglect our duty of gratitude to God for his benefits. And when he tells us to give thanks for all things it was a little slip of his pen; we must understand not all things, but all good things."

We might talk in this way, I say, if we did not

know that St. Paul was inspired; but knowing that, we must drop the idea that there can be any mistake or exaggeration. It must really be that we ought to give thanks for all things that happen to us, without exception. If our plans succeed we must give thanks; but we must do the same if they fail. Whether our wishes are gratified or not, we must give thanks. If we have riches, good health, plenty of friends, or if, on the other hand, we are poor, sick, and without a friend in the world, we must thank God, in adversity the same as in prosperity.

"Well," you may say, "it must be so, since we have the word of the Holy Ghost for it; but, for my part, I cannot see how it can be. I should be very willing to thank God for all these bad things, but I do not see what there is in them to thank him for. I acknowledge that I deserve punishment for my sins, and I will try to take it with as good a grace as I can; but as to giving thanks for it, that is a little too much for me. It seems to me that I should only be a hypocrite if I should pretend to do so."

Some of you, I am pretty sure, feel like talking in this way, at least at times when trouble has come upon you. Let us see if we cannot find the reason that your faith is so much tried.

It seems to me that it is because it seems to you that you are required to believe that evil is really good; and of course that is as hard to believe as that black is really white. You think that our Lord means evil to you; that he is acting with you as the authorities of the state might act. If any one breaks the laws he is shut up in prison or has to pay a fine. Well, that may do him good, but it is not meant for that. It is meant to do harm to him, that others may profit by his example and that the good order of society may be maintained. So a criminal cannot personally thank the judge, if he sentences him to hard labor for five years. It would not be reasonable for him to do so, and the judge does not want him to do it, for he does not mean to give him a favor.

So you think, when our Lord punishes you in any way, that he really means to do you harm, for some wise end in his providence, to be sure, but still really harm as far as you yourself are concerned. You regard it simply as the satisfaction of his justice on you, or perhaps for some good purpose in which you are not concerned; and so it is as hard for you personally to thank him for it as to say that black is white.

But this is just where you are mistaken; for there is a great difference between the punishments of God and those of man. If our Lord sends you any misfortune or cross it is principally for your own good. He always has that in view; he is not like a human judge. He would not allow a hair of your head to be touched, were it not really for your good; for he loves you more dearly than your best friend in the world can possibly do.

This, then, my dear brethren, is the right exercise for our faith: not to believe that evil is good, but to believe that God is good and does not mean evil to us, and that when he gives what seems to be evil it is really a blessing in disguise. Though it is plain that it must be so, instead of being contrary to reason, still it is an exercise of faith for all that; but an easy one, if we will only try it. Try it, then, when you are tempted to murmur against God's providence, and you will be able to give thanks for all things, whether they seem to be bad or good ; and you will see that after all it is only good things which you are told to thank him for, because all things which he sends you really are good.

Twenty-first Sunday after Pentecost.

EPISTLE. *Eph. vi.* 10–17. Brethren : Be strengthened in the Lord, and in the might of his power. Put you on the armor of God, that you may be able to stand against the snares of the devil. For our wrestling is not against flesh and blood : but against principalities and powers, against the rulers of the world of this darkness, against the spirits of wickedness in the high places. Wherefore take unto you the armor of God, that you may be able to resist in the evil day, and to stand in all things perfect. Stand, therefore, having your loins girt about with truth, and having on the breastplate of justice : and your feet shod with the preparation of the gospel of peace: in all things taking the shield of faith, wherewith you may be able to extinguish all the fiery darts of the most wicked one. And take unto you the helmet of salvation ; and the sword of the Spirit (which is the word of God).

GOSPEL. *St. Matt. xviii.* 23–35. At that time: Jesus spoke to his disciples this parable : The kingdom of heaven is likened to a king, who would take an account of his servants. And when he had begun to take the account, one was brought to him that owed him ten thousand talents. And as he had not wherewith to pay it, his lord commanded that he should be sold, and his wife and children and all that he had, and payment to be made. But that servant, falling down, besought him, saying : Have patience with me, and I will pay thee all. And the lord of that servant being moved with compassion, let him go, and forgave him the debt. But when that servant was gone out, he found one of his fellow-servants that owed him a hundred pence; and laying hold of him, he throttled him, saying: Pay what thou owest. And his fellow-servant, falling down, besought him saying: Have patience with me, and I will pay thee all. And he would not: but went and cast him into prison, till he should pay the debt. Now his fellow-servants, seeing what was done, were very much grieved, and they came and told their lord all that was done. Then his lord called him, and said to him: Thou wicked servant! I forgave thee all the debt, because thou besoughtest me: shouldst not thou then have had compassion also on thy fellow-servant, even as I had compassion on thee? And his lord being angry, delivered him to the torturers until he should pay all the debt. So also shall my heavenly Father do to you, if you forgive not every one his brother from your hearts.

SERMON CXXXIV.

Our wrestling is not against flesh and blood: but against principalities and powers.—Ephes. vi. 12.

It is a most important truth, my brethren, and a very practical one for all of us, which is contained in these words of St. Paul; and it is the subject of the whole Epistle of this Sunday, from which this passage is taken.

This truth is that we have a host of enemies to contend with in the battle which we must fight to win the kingdom of heaven, who are much more powerful than flesh and blood—that is, than any human foes; much more formidable than any others which attack us, from within or from without.

Who are these enemies? They are Satan and all his army of fallen angels. That these are what the apostle means by "principalities and powers" is plain from these very words, which are the names, as you know, of two of the nine angelic choirs. It is plain also, from what he says immediately before, that we should put on the armor of God, in order to be able to stand against the deceits of the devil.

Who can doubt that these lost spirits are terrible enemies to our salvation? They desire nothing more earnestly than our eternal ruin, and labor most persistently to bring it about. They have a malicious hatred and envy for us, and spare no effort to induce us to sin, as that is the greatest evil which can happen to us. As there is joy before the angels of God upon one sinner who repents, so there is exultation among these fallen angels over every one who does not, and especially over every one who repents of his repentance and turns to sin again.

And besides the will which they have to injure us, they have an immense power to do so. They are superior to us in the order of creation; they have much more intelligence, knowledge, and strength than we. If they were permitted they could easily make us all subject to them, and reign over us with a more cruel tyranny than the world has ever seen.

"Well, father," you may say to me, "of course this must be true; but then they are not permitted to trample on us in this way. God holds them in check, so that they cannot do us the harm which they wish, and would otherwise be able to accomplish."

I grant you this. They certainly are not allowed to do us all the harm they might do and would like to do; but they are allowed to do a great part of it—so much that, without the help of God on our side, they would, even as it is, destroy us, soul and body.

By our own strength we cannot possibly escape

these terrible and merciless enemies, but only by the power of God. Without that we should be as helpless before them as a child among lions and tigers. If we would escape them it can only be, then, by calling upon God, and getting from him the strength and protection which he alone can give.

This is what St. Paul tells us in this Epistle. "Put on the armor of God," he says; and again, "Take unto you the armor of God." If you do not you will fall. Our Lord has allowed the devils to have the power which they still have to injure us, that we may learn in our dire extremity to have recourse to him.

And yet so far are we from realizing our danger, and seeking the only protection which can save us, that many Christians seem almost to doubt, like infidels, the very existence of the devil and his angels. There is nothing which Satan likes better than this, or which puts us more completely in his power. He does not care that we should know, just now at least, who does us the harm, so long as the harm is done; and he knows that if we do not believe in him we shall not look out for him, and that if we do not look out for him we shall certainly fall into his snares.

Rouse yourselves, then, my brethren, from this indifference to your greatest peril. Believe, with a real and practical belief, in the existence and the tremendous power of these enemies who are hunting down your souls. Know that you cannot resist them of your own strength, and act on that knowledge. Pray to God to protect you, to keep them from you, and you from them. Ask Our Blessed Lady, who is their terror, to drive them away, and your guardian angel to keep them from your side. Avoid the **occasions**

of sin which they prepare for you. Flee from them
if you can; if not, resist them, and they will flee
from you; but when you resist them, let it be in the
name of Him who has conquered them, or they will
conquer you.

Twenty-second Sunday after Pentecost.

EPISTLE. *Phil. i.* 6–11. Brethren: We are confident of this very thing, that he, who hath begun a good work in you, will perfect it unto the day of Christ Jesus. As it is meet for me to think this for you all: because I have you in my heart; and that in my bonds, and in the defence, and confirmation of the gospel, you all are partakers of my joy. For God is my witness, how I long after you all in the bowels of Jesus Christ. And this I pray, that your charity may more and more abound in knowledge, and in all understanding: that you may approve the better things, that you may be sincere and without offence unto the day of Christ. Replenished with the fruit of justice through Jesus Christ, unto the glory and praise of God.

GOSPEL. *St. Matt. xxii.* 15-21. At that time: The Pharisees going away, consulted among themselves how to ensnare Jesus in his speech. And they sent to him their disciples with the Herodians, saying: Master, we know that thou art a true speaker, and teachest the way of God in truth, neither carest thou for any man; for thou dost not regard the person of men. Tell us, therefore, what dost thou think, Is it lawful to give tribute to Cæsar, or not? But Jesus, knowing their wickedness, said: Why do you tempt me, ye hypocrites? Show me the coin of the tribute. And they offered him a penny. And Jesus saith to them: Whose image and inscription is this? They say unto him: Cæsar's. Then he saith to them: Render, therefore, to Cæsar the things that are Cæsar's, and to God the things that are God's.

SERMON CXXXV.

The Pharisees going away, consulted among themselves how to ensnare him in his speech.—St. Matt. xxii. 15.

It is needless to say, brethren, that they waited in vain. Our dear Lord never uttered anything but words of wisdom, justice, and piety. Is it so with us? We have enemies, strong and powerful, who have consulted among themselves how to ensnare us in our speech. Satan and his demons, evil companions, enemies of the holy faith—all these are watching to see if they cannot destroy us by means of our tongue. What, then, must we do to control *it*, of which St. James says: "The tongue is a fire, a world of iniquity; the tongue is placed among our members which defileth the whole body, being set on fire by hell"? We must watch it carefully, watch it jealously, watch it constantly.

Some of the older writers have said that nature herself has taught us how careful we ought to be of our tongue. First, because we have only one. We have two eyes, two ears, two hands, two feet, but only one tongue.

Again, the tongue is placed in the centre of the head, to show (as they say) that it ought to be under the absolute control of our reason; again, because nature places it behind two barriers, the lips and teeth, so as to keep it prisoner; and, lastly (says an old writer in his quaint way), because it is chained in the mouth.

But there are other more solid reasons than these for watching our tongue.

There is nothing so poisonous as a bitter word, an uncharitable remark, an offensive observation,

Words such as these have ruined families, have caused murders, have damned souls. How often has a bitter word rankled so deeply in our neighbor's mind and heart that he curses us, refuses to speak to us, and thus is driven by us into mortal sin! What then? The devil, who is on the watch, has ensnared us in our speech; he has got one more sin recorded against us. Had we watched our tongues he would not have caught us; we should not have sinned; our neighbor would not have been scandalized. How common it is for us to hear God's name taken in vain and spoken lightly; how frequently, alas! do we hear the sweet name of Jesus used for a curse; how often that holy name, "which is above every name," is bandied about as though it were as the name of the lowest of creatures! Blasphemer! reviler of the Holy One! Satan has ensnared you in your speech. You have cursed, blasphemed, *sinned!* Had you watched your tongue you had not done so.

And what horrible mutterings are these that we hear coming up from dark corners, from workshops, from factories, from lodging-houses, from streets? What whisperings are these, hot and burning with the fire of hell? They are words of impurity and bad conversations. They are accents that slay living souls, that pollute both the lips of the speaker and the ears of the listener; and, alas! the tongue, the unguarded, unwatched tongue, is the offender again. Ah! you are ensnared once more in your speech. Watch your tongue, then, lest you die the death of mortal sin. There is an every-day expression, brethren, which contains, I think, the best advice that can be given you; and that is, "Hold your tongue." Yes, *hold* it under control of reason; chain it by prayer and the sacraments. If it wants to run into bitter words and unkind speeches, hold it back. If it wants to blaspheme, hold it; hold it, or you are lost! If it wants to utter words contrary to Christian modesty, hold it for Christ's sake, or you are undone. Take care lest Satan ensnare you in your speech; if he does he will condemn you to a cruel death in hell. Speech is silver and silence is gold. Few, if any, have been saved by much speaking; many have been lost by it. Oh! then, watch your tongue lest it destroy you. B.

SERMON CXXXVI.

Render, therefore, to Cæsar the things that are Cæsar's, and to God the things that are God's.—St. Matt. xxii. 21.

WHAT does our Lord mean by this, my brethren? He seems to say that there are some things which do not belong to God, but to some one else; that God has only a partial right in this world which he has created. It would appear to belong partly to Cæsar; and who can this Cæsar be, who shares the earth with its Creator?

Cæsar was the name of the Roman emperor, and our Lord means by Cæsar the temporal authority of the state. Now, it must seem absurd to any Catholic, and indeed to any one who believes in God at all, to say that this authority has any right in the world other than that which God has lent to it; so we cannot imagine that our Lord meant anything like that. Nevertheless, there are plenty of people, who do not profess to be atheists, who really maintain not only that the state has rights against him, but even that its right always prevails over his. They say that we must render everything to Cæsar, whether God wants it or not; that the law of the state must be obeyed, even against the law of God as shown to us by conscience.

These people are really atheists, whether they profess to be or not. The only true God, in whom we believe, will not and cannot resign his right to our obedience or give up his eternal laws. Nay, more, he will and must reserve to himself the right of making new laws if he pleases, and annulling laws of the state which are contrary to them. Besides all this, he has also only given to the state a limited sphere in which it can work, and in which only its laws can have any force—that is, he will only allow it to make laws providing for the temporal well-being of its subjects.

This, then, is what belongs to Cæsar—that is, to the state. It has the right to claim and enforce our obedience to laws intended for the temporal welfare of its subjects, and to these only as far as they are not contrary to the eternal law of God, or to others which he may choose to make. And that is all.

When it does not exceed its rights we must give our obedience to it; and we must presume that it does not exceed them unless it is clear that it does. This is what we must render to Cæsar.

But how shall we tell that it does exceed its rights? First, by the voice of conscience, when that voice is clear and certain; secondly, by our knowledge of the laws which God himself has made; lastly, by the voice of that other authority which he has put in the world to provide for our spiritual welfare—that is, the Catholic Church. When God speaks to us in either of these ways we must obey him.

whether it interferes with Cæsar or not; this is what we must render to him.

If the state makes a law commanding us to blaspheme, deny our faith, or commit impurity, we will not obey. Conscience annuls such a law. If the state commands us to do servile work on Sunday its law has no force. We know that God's law is against it. And, lastly, if the state goes outside its sphere, and makes laws regarding things not belonging to its jurisdiction, as the sacraments, we are not bound by such laws. It has no power, for instance, to declare marriage among Christians valid or invalid. The church has told us this plainly. It is here specially where the state goes out of its province, that it is subject to correction by the church; though it may be in other matters also.

Our Lord, then, means that we should render to Cæsar the things that belong to him, not because of any right that he has in himself, but because God has lent it to him; but that we should render to God the things that he has not lent to Cæsar, whether Cæsar consents or not. Obedience must always be given to God. Give it to him through the state in those things about which he has given the state authority, and in other things without regard to the state; thus shall you render to Cæsar the things which are Cæsar's, and to God the things that are God's.

Twenty-third Sunday after Pentecost.

EPISTLE. *Phil. iii.* 17; *iv.* 3. Be followers of me, brethren, and observe them who walk so as you have our model. For many walk, of whom I have told you often (and now tell you weeping) that they are enemies of the cross of Christ: whose end is destruction, whose God is their belly, and whose glory is in their shame: who mind earthly things. But our conversation is in heaven: from whence also we wait for the Saviour, our Lord Jesus Christ, who will reform the body of our lowness, made like to the body of his glory, according to the operation whereby also he is able to subdue all things unto himself. Therefore, my dearly beloved brethren, and most desired, my joy and my crown: so stand fast in the Lord, my most dearly beloved. I beg of Euodia, and I beseech Syntyche to be of one mind in the Lord. And I entreat thee, my sincere companion, help those women who have labored with me in the Gospel, with Clement and the rest of my fellow-laborers, whose names are in the book of life.

GOSPEL. *St. Matt. ix.* 18–26. At that time: As Jesus was speaking these things unto them, behold a certain ruler came, and adored him, saying: Lord, my daughter is just now dead; but come, lay thy hand upon her, and she shall live. And Jesus, rising up, followed him, with his disciples. And behold a woman who was troubled with an issue of blood twelve years, came behind him, and touched the hem of his garment. For she said within herself: If I shall but touch his garment I shall be healed. But Jesus, turning about and seeing her, said: Take courage, daughter, thy faith hath made thee whole. And the woman was made whole from that hour. And when Jesus came into the house of the ruler, and saw the minstrels and the crowd making a rout, he said : Give place, for the girl is not dead, but sleepeth. And they laughed at him. And when the crowd was turned out he went in, and took her by the hand. And the girl arose. And the fame hereof went abroad into all that country.

SERMON CXXXVII.

My daughter is just now dead ; but come, lay thy hand upon her, and she shall live.—St. Matt. ix. 18.

Such was the entreaty made by the ruler to our Lord in to-day's Gospel, and such are the words that the Lord says to us during the month of November, in behalf of the poor souls in purgatory. These souls have been saved by the Precious Blood, they have been judged by Jesus Christ with a favorable judgment, they are his spouses, his sons and daughters, his children. He cries to us, "*My children* are even now dead; but come, lay your hands upon them, and they shall live." What hand is that which our Lord wants us to lay upon his dead children? Brethren, it is the hand of prayer. Now, it seems to me that there are three classes of persons who ought to be in an especial manner the friends of God's dead children, three classes who ought always to be extending a helping hand to the souls in purgatory. First, the poor, because the holy souls are poor like yourselves. They have no work—that is to say, the day for them is past in which they could work and gain indulgences and merit, the money with which the debt of temporal punishment is paid; for them the "night has come when no man can work." They are willing to work, they are willing to pay for themselves, but they cannot; they are out of work, they are poor, they cannot help themselves. They are suffering, as the poor suffer in this world from the heats of summer and the frosts of winter. They have no food; they are hungry and thirsty; they are longing for the sweets of heaven. They are in exile; they have no home; they know there is abundance of food and raiment around them which they cannot themselves buy. It seems to them that the winter will never pass, that the spring will never come; in a word they *are poor*. They are poor as many of you are poor. They are in worse need than the most destitute among you. Oh! then, ye that are poor, help the holy souls by your prayers. Secondly, the rich ought to be the special friends of those who are in purgatory, and among the rich we wish to include those who are what people call "comfortably off." God has given you charge of the poor; you can help them by your alms in this world, so you can in the next. You can have Masses said for them; you can say lots of prayers for them, because you have plenty of time on your hands. Again remember, many of those who were your equals in this world, who like yourselves had a good supply of this world's goods, have gone to purgatory because those riches were a snare to them. Riches, my dear friends, have sent many a soul to the place of purification. Oh! then, those of you who are well off, have pity upon the poor souls in purgatory. Offer up a good share of your wealth to have Masses said for them. Do some act of charity, and offer the merit of it for some soul who was ensnared by riches and who is now paying the penalty in suffering; and spend some considerable portion of your spare time in praying for the souls of the faithful departed.

And lastly, the sinners and those who have been converted from a very sinful life ought to be the friends of God's dear children. Why? Because although the souls in purgatory cannot pray for themselves, they can pray for others, and these prayers are most acceptable to God. Because, too, they are full of gratitude, and they will not forget those who helped them when they shall come before the throne of God. Because sinners, having saddened the Sacred Heart of Jesus by their sins, cannot make a better reparation to it than to hasten the time when he shall embrace these souls that he loves so dearly and has wished for so long. Because sinners have almost always been the means of the sins of others. They have, by their bad example, sent others to purgatory. Ah! then, if they have helped them in they should help them out.

You, then, that are poor, you that are rich, you that have been great sinners, listen to the voice of Jesus; listen to the plaint of Mary during this month of November: "My children are now dead; come lay thy prayers up for them, and they shall live." Hear Mass for the poor souls; say your beads for them; supplicate Jesus and Mary and Joseph in their behalf. Fly to St. Catherine of Genoa and beg her to help them, and many and many a time during the month say with great fervor: "May the souls of the faithful departed, through the mercy of God, rest in peace!"

B.

SERMON CXXXVIII.

When Jesus was come into the house of the ruler, and saw the minstrels and the crowd making a rout, he said, "Give place."—St. Matt. ix. 23.

ONE of the great difficulties against which God's church has to contend to-day is the spirit of worldliness which has crept in to a very serious extent among the faithful. There are many dear brethren among us who (as St. Paul says to-day in the Epistle) "mind earthly things"; Catholics who try as far as they can to conform themselves to this world and the fashions thereof. We can see this worldly spirit in the manner in which many Catholics dress, the style with which they decorate their houses, the way in which they speak and act. But there is another way by which this tendency is indicated. I mean the manner in which we bury our dead.

Now, certainly, there is nothing more beautiful to the eye of faith than a dead Christian body. What is it that lies there still, and motionless, and cold? A corpse? Yes; but something more than that. Brethren, that poor dead thing is beautiful, it is holy. Its head has been touched by the cleansing waters of baptism and anointed with holy chrism, its tongue has touched the Body and Blood of Christ. Its eyes, ears, and hands, all its senses have been anointed with holy oil. That poor body has been the temple of the Holy Ghost.

More than this: that cold clay is a germ, a seed from which one day shall rise a fairer flower than earth hath ever seen; for, as St. Paul says, "That which thou sowest is not quickened except it die first. And that which thou sowest thou sowest not the body that shall be, but bare grain, as of wheat or of some of the rest." Yes, brethren, this dead thing is the "bare grain," but in the eternal spring-time it shall bud forth into the full ear, for it is the seed of a body glorified by the power of God.

Oh! then, seeing how holy the dead body of a Christian is, no wonder that the church should surround the burial of it with a certain holy pomp.

She burns lights by its side, she carries it in procession, she sprinkles it with holy water, she censes it with incense. Not only does she pray for the soul, she also respects the body.

So then, dear friends, to show respect for the dead, to surround them with that pomp which the church wishes, is well and good; but to make a dead body an object about which to display earthly vanity and pride is to defile that which is holy and outrage that which is decent. Yet this is often done. In place of the simple shroud or the holy habit which used to be considered the proper raiment of the departed, we now see them arrayed in garments which vie in extravagance and fashion with those of the theatre and the ball-room. Oh! brethren, when I think of our dear Master's body, in Bethlehem's manger, wrapped up in swathing bands, in the holy garden enveloped in linen cloths, and even to this day reposing upon our altars on the fair white linen corporal, it shocks me to think of those Christian dead who go down to the tomb decked out in silks and lace, and satins and trinkets, as though they were rather the votaries of earth than the heirs of the kingdom of heaven. I seem to see the Master standing by, and saying, "Give place."

Again, what an abuse it is to see a body followed to the grave by a train of carriages which would often be more than enough for the funeral of a cardinal or a pope. What some one has called "the eternal fitness of things" requires that something of public display should be made over those whom God has set in authority. But to make such display over any ordinary Christian is simply absurd. Oh! my dear friends, far better spend your money to have Masses said for the soul than for a hundred vehicles to follow the body. Alas! I fear those hundred carriages and two hundred horses soothe your pride far more than they comfort the poor soul in purgatory who is panting and longing for the possession of God.

Let me end with a slight paraphrase of the text, such as we may imagine our Lord, were he now on earth, might use: "And when Jesus was come into the house of death, and saw the silks and the satins, and the worldly display, and the multitude making a tumult, and the horses and the carriages, and the garlands and the wreaths, and the feasting, he said: 'Give place, give place to me and to my church; and may the souls of the faithful departed rest in peace. Amen."
B.

SERMON CXXXIX.

Many walk, of whom I have told you often (and now tell you weeping) that they are enemies of the cross of Christ: whose end is destruction, whose God is their belly, and whose glory is in their shame: who mind earthly things.—PHIL. iii. 18, 19.

HERE St. Paul gives us, dear brethren, a rule by

which we may know, by their manner of living, the difference between the bad and the good anywhere in the world. This rule, however, shows us also who is a bad Christian and who is a good one. For it is too true that we can find many, calling themselves Catholics, who hate the cross, who find their happiness in sensuality, who love this world more than they love God, and who make a boast of their sins and crimes. The end of these is indeed destruction and eternal ruin.

Now, who are they? One need not go far to find them. They are those who are boasting about how much they can eat and drink more than another. They are those who try to drink others drunk, and then brag about it. They even make a laughing-stock of the poor, wretched man or woman who can't stand as much as they can. Neither are they to be found only among the men who almost live around and in grog-shops. Young men of great respectability and old gray-headed parents, of high position in society, do these things. They even look with contempt upon him who can't sin as much and as boldly as they do. More than all, the poor man feels ashamed and blushes because he is not superior to them in this kind of wickedness.

In the same way do some boast of their impurities, and their lying and swindling, in a business way, as they call it. These indeed glory in that which is a shame to the heathen. How much more, indeed, then, is this a shame to him who calls himself a Christian.

But these are not the only crimes in which they glory who are enemies of the cross of Jesus Christ. There are those who cannot bear to be outdone in malice or revenge. Often do we hear them say, "I paid him off for it," or again, "She got as good as she sent." This generally means that by malice, spite, revenge, the one who did the first wrong was punished more severely than justice required. It means that the devil and one's evil passions were listened to, their promptings followed, and all made a boast of afterwards. A beautiful Christian example! Two immortal souls trying to see which can insult the crucified Redeemer the most! How can such an one ever kiss the crucifix? How dare to press those lips there represented, from which blessings were always returned for cursing?

Again, those who glory in their shame are those who boast of their careless lives, of never going to Mass, to confession, or to their Easter-duty, and of never observing the light law of the church by keeping the fasts of Lent and other days.

Others, again, boast of spending their money freely, not heeding the cries of wife and children for food. They neglect those who have been entrusted to them by God. They let the poor wife work herself to death merely because they love the praise of a world which calls their folly openheartedness. These are really the meanest of men, but they believe the world when it calls them good, generous, noble.

All of these are, indeed, truly enemies of the cross which all Christians are bound to love. They are its enemies because the cross saves mankind, whereas they try to ruin souls. By their example and false teaching they make others like themselves. They help souls to hell while our crucified Lord is trying to save them. They take the part of the devil against **their God.**

Easter being a movable *Feast* which can occur **on any day** from the 22d of March to the 25th of April, the number of Sundays between *Epiphany* and *Septuagesima*, and between *Pentecost* and *Advent*, varies according to the situation of *Easter*. There are always at least two Sundays, unless *Epiphany* falls on a Sunday, and never more than six, between *Epiphany* and *Septuagesima*. Likewise, there are never fewer than twenty-three Sundays after *Pentecost*, or more than twenty-eight. The Gospel and Epistle for the last Sunday after *Pentecost* are always the same. When there are twenty-three Sundays, the Gospel and Epistle for the last Sunday are substituted for those of the twenty-third. When there are twenty-five Sundays, the Gospel and Epistle for the sixth Sunday after *Epiphany* are taken; when there are twenty-six, those also of the fifth after *Epiphany*; when there are twenty-seven, those of the fourth, and when there are twenty-eight those of the third, in order to fill up the interval which occurs. In any year, in which there are more than twenty-four Sundays after *Pentecost*, proper sermons for these Sundays are to be found among those which are arranged for the Sundays following the Feast of the *Epiphany*. If one sermon is wanting, it is taken from the sixth Sunday after *Epiphany*; if two, three, or four are needed, the last two or three or four sermons which precede *Septuagesima* are to be taken, in their order.

Twenty-Fourth or Last Sunday after Pentecost.

Epistle. *Col. i.* 9–14. Brethren: We cease not to pray for you, and to beg that you may be filled with the knowledge of his will in all wisdom and spiritual understanding: that you may walk worthy of God, in all things pleasing: being fruitful in every good work, and increasing in the knowledge of God: strengthened with all might according to the power of his glory, in all patience and long-suffering with joy, giving thanks to God the Father, who hath made us worthy to be partakers of the lot of the saints in light: who hath delivered us from the power of darkness, and hath translated us into the kingdom of the Son of his love: in whom we have redemption through his blood, the remission of sins.

Gospel. *St. Matt. xxiv.* 15–35. At that time: Jesus said to his disciples: When you shall see "the abomination of desolation," which was spoken of by Daniel the prophet, standing in the holy place.: he that readeth, let him understand. Then let those that are in Judea flee to the mountains. And he that is on the house-top, let him not come down to take anything out of his house: and he that is in the field, let him not go back to take his coat. And woe to them that are with child, and that give suck in those days. But pray that your flight be not in the winter or on the Sabbath. For there shall be then great tribulation, such as hath not been from the beginning of the world until now, neither shall be. And unless those days had been shortened, no flesh should be saved: but for the sake of the elect those days shall be shortened. Then, if any man shall say to you: Lo, here is Christ, or there, do not believe him. For there shall arise false christs and false prophets, and shall show great signs and wonders, insomuch as to deceive (if possible) even the elect. Behold I have told it to you beforehand. If therefore they shall say to you: Behold he is in the desert; go ye not out: Behold he is in the closets; believe it not. For as lightning cometh out of the east, and appeareth even unto the west, so shall also the coming of the Son of Man be. Wheresoever the body shall be, there shall the eagles also be gathered together. And immediately after the tribulation of those days, the sun shall be darkened, and the moon shall not give her light, and the stars shall fall from heaven, and the powers of the heavens shall be moved. And then shall appear the sign of the Son of Man in heaven: and then shall all the tribes of the earth mourn: and they shall see the Son of Man coming in the clouds of heaven with great power and majesty. And he shall send his angels with a trumpet, and a great voice: and they shall gather together his elect from the four winds, from the farthest parts of the heavens to the uttermost bounds of them. Now learn a parable from the fig-tree: when its branch is now tender, and the leaves come forth, you know that summer is nigh. So also you, when you shall see all these things, know that it is near, even at the doors. Amen I say to you, this generation shall not pass till all these things be done. Heaven and earth shall pass away, but my words shall not pass away.

SERMON CXL.

Behold I have told it to you beforehand.—St. Matt. xxiv. 25.

Once in a venerable manor-house, at the head of the carved oak stairway, stood an old clock. About half a minute before it struck it made a curious, buzzing, whirring sound. Then all the children of the house said, "Ah! the old clock is *warning*"; and upstairs they ran to see the clock strike. The clock told them beforehand what it was going to do.

Now, brethren, there is a clock that has gone on warning and striking for many a century, and that clock is called "the Church's Year." It was wound up last Advent, and since then it has struck Christmas, it has struck Epiphany, it has struck St. Paul's Day, it has struck Easter, Pentecost, Assumption, All Saints and All Souls. To-day it has nearly run down; it is *warning* for next Sunday, when it will strike Advent again.

The Church, next Sunday, will bring you face to face with judgment. To-day she *warns* you that the great season of Advent is coming once more; that the old year is passing, that the new one is about to begin. So, then, brethren, before the clock strikes for judgment, before time is dead, while life and grace and opportunities still remain, take up your stand before the old clock; look at the hours depicted on the dial, and ask yourself how you spent last year, how you would be prepared if judgment should come to you a week hence.

Listen! How merrily that chime rings. You heard it about a year ago. It was the Church clock striking Christmas. Where were you then? Some of you, we know, were where you should be—at holy Mass, receiving Holy Communion at the altar-rail. You heard the organ pealing and the choir singing *Adeste fideles;* you saw the little Infant Jesus in the crib, and the bright evergreens decking the church, and felt in your hearts that indeed there was peace on earth. Happy you if it was thus. But, alas! was it so? Were you not away from Mass last Christmas? Were you not neglecting your religion? Were you not in mortal sin? Were you not revelling, getting drunk, thinking rather of feasting and enjoying yourselves than of devotion and thanksgiving?

Then the hour of Epiphany struck! What gifts had you to bring to the manger-bed? Had you the gold of Christian charity to present? Had you the incense of faith and the myrrh of sweet and fragrant hope? Ah! it is to be feared that some knelt not at the manger-bed of Jesus, but on the brink of hell: forgetting God, scandalizing their neighbor, damning their own souls. On the "Feast of Light" (as the Epiphany is sometimes called) some were kneeling at the shrine of the world and "holding the candle to the devil." Didn't you hear the pendulum of the old clock ticking, ticking, and seeming to say. as it swung: "Behold! I have told you beforehand! Behold! I have told you beforehand!" Why, then, did you not do penance?

Then came Lent; and on the first Sunday of that holy time the clock warned loud and clear for Easter. A voice almost seemed to be heard shouting in your ears: "Easter-duty! Easter-duty! 'Time and tide wait for no man!'" And so at last the clock struck. Easter had passed. You had been "told beforehand." You did not heed, and thus, oh! listen heaven, and listen hell, another Easter-duty was missed, and another mortal sin committed.

To-day, dear friends, the Church clock warns you again. The Church herself cries to you to cast "off the works of darkness and put on the armor of light." Give ear, then, while there is yet life and hope. Have you been negligent? "Better late than never";

now is the time to mend. Have you been a drunkard ? Now "be sober and watch." Have you neglected your children? Begin to care for them as you should. Have you neglected the sacraments? Come, prepare at once to receive them worthily. Whatever your state may be, remember—judgment is coming; death is at hand! Maybe God's clock in heaven already points, for you, at the last hour; maybe this is the last time that you will be *warned*, and then the clock will *strike* and you will be in eternity. Time and tide are rushing on. Every tick of the clock brings you nearer heaven or nearer hell. Oh! then prepare yourself for the great day, that so when time *is* dead and gone; when the great clock strikes for the *last* time, you may be found ready, and go in with Jesus to his marriage feast. B.

SERMON CXLI.

That you may walk worthy of God.—Col. i. 10.

"Brethren," says St. Paul, in the Epistle of this Sunday, "we cease not to pray for you, . . . that you may walk worthy of God." These words may, no doubt, be understood to mean that we should live in such a way as to be worthy to receive God in his Real Presence at the time of Holy Communion, and by his grace at all times; and, finally, to receive him, and to be received by him, in his eternal kingdom of glory. But there is another sense, perhaps a more natural one, and certainly a more special one, in which we may understand them.

This sense is, that we should live in a way worthy of, and suitable to, the dignity and the favor which he has conferred upon us, in making or considering us worthy, as the apostle goes on to say, " to be partakers of the lot of the saints in light "—that is in bringing us into, and making us members of, his one, true, and Holy Catholic Church. In other words, that we should behave in such a way as to be creditable to him and to his holy church, to which we belong.

Now, this is a point the importance of which cannot be overrated, and which we are too apt to forget. We lose sight of the fact that the honor of God and of his church has been placed in our hands, and confided to our charge; so that every sin which we commit, besides its own proper malice, has the malice of an indignity to the holy state to which we have been called. For this reason, a sin committed by a Catholic is always greater than the same sin committed by any one else; not only on account of the greater grace and clearer light which he has received, but also because God is more specially robbed of his honor by it.

You all see this plainly enough when it is a question of a sin committed by one who has been called to the ecclesiastical or religious state. If a priest or a religious is guilty of any offence, though it be but a small one, you are scandalized by it, not only because he ought to have been better able to avoid it, but also because it dishonors God's choice of him to be a special image in this world of his divine goodness.

But you forget that you also, merely because you are Catholics, dishonor God, and bring him and his holy religion into contempt by the sins which you commit. It is plain enough, however, that you do, though in a somewhat less degree than those whom he has more specially chosen.

And other people do not forget it, though you may. "Look at those Catholics," the world outside is continually saying; "they may belong to the true church, but they do not do much honor to it. See how they drink, lie, and swear. If that is all the good it does one to be a Catholic, I would rather take my chance of saving my soul somewhere else than be reckoned among such people."

Now, it is all very true that such talk as this is unjust and unfair, and that the very persons who say such things may really be much worse, at least considering their temptations, than those whom they find fault with. But still they have a right to find fault that those whom God has brought into the true church are not evidently as much better as they ought to be, than those whom he has not; and you cannot altogether blame them for finding fault with him rather than with yourselves, and saying that this Catholic Church of his is rather a poor instrument to save the world with.

Remember then, my brethren, that a bad Catholic is a disgrace to his church, and a dishonor to Almighty God, who founded it. A story is told of a man who, when drunk, would deny that he was a Catholic; he had the right feeling on this point, though he committed a greater sin to save a less one. Imitate him, not in denying your faith, but in taking care not to disgrace it; for God will surely require of you an account, not only of your sins, but also of the dishonor which they have brought on the holy name by which you are called.

SERMON CXLII.

As lightning cometh out of the east, and appeareth even unto the west: so shall also the coming of the Son of Man be.
—St. Matt. xxiv. 27.

These words of our Lord, my dear brethren, refer principally to the general judgment, which will come suddenly upon all, at least all of those who shall be alive at the time when it shall occur. And he could not have used a more striking comparison to show how sudden it will be; how it will take every one unawares, even of those who will be expecting it. You know that when you watch the flashes of lightning in a thunder-storm, though you are expecting them all the time, yet each one takes you by surprise; you hardly know that it has come till it has gone; you do not so much see it as remember it. So it will be at the last and awful day; all at once, without any warning, the heavens will open, and God will come suddenly, not this time in mercy, but in justice; not to save the world, but to judge it; there will be no time even for an act of contrition, but as every one is then found, so will he be for all eternity.

Probably you and I will not be in this world at the time of the general judgment; it is most likely that we shall die before it comes. We shall rise from our graves and be present at it, but we shall have been already judged; so that it will not be by it that we shall be saved or lost. But that judgment which we shall have gone through will perhaps also have come on us suddenly; as suddenly as the one on the last day. For it will come on us the instant that our souls leave the body; the moment after we die we shall appear before the throne of God to receive the sentence of eternal salvation or condemnation. So it may surprise us at any moment; for we may suddenly die.

There is not one of us here who has any certainty that he may not before to-day's sun sets, nay, even this very hour or minute, even before he can draw another breath, be standing before that terrible judgment seat and receiving that sentence from which there is no appeal.

How often do we hear of people suddenly struck down by death without a moment's warning; people who were promising themselves, as you no doubt are promising yourselves, many more days to live. They did not do anything, so far as we can see, to deserve such a sudden blow; they were living lives no worse and no better than those of others around them. "Those eighteen," says our Lord, "upon whom the tower fell in Siloe, and slew them; think you that they also were debtors—that is to say, sinners—above all the men that dwelt in Jerusalem?" No, God calls us suddenly in this way to show that he is the owner of our lives, that he has made no promise to give any one of us a single moment beyond those which he has already given.

But sudden death is not, we may say, any special visitation of God. It is natural, not wonderful. If you could see the way in which your own bodies are made, you would wonder not so much that people die suddenly, but rather that they should die in any other way. It is not more surprising that one should die suddenly than that a watch should suddenly stop. The body is in many ways a more delicate thing than a watch; and in its most delicate parts the slightest thing out of order may be fatal. So we continue to live rather by the special care which our Lord takes to preserve our lives, than by any hold which our souls have on our bodies.

But you will say, "After all, father, very few really do die suddenly, compared to those who have time to prepare." Well, it is true that there are not many who pass instantly from full health into the shadow of death; but if there were only one in a million, is it not a terrible risk for one who is not prepared? And, besides, in another way it is not true. For almost all die sooner than they expect. All think, even when they have some fatal illness, that they will have more time than is really to be given them. Death, when it actually comes, is a surprise; for every one, perhaps, the coming of the Son of Man is at the last like the lightning; every one expects it, but not just then; every one looks for a few moments more.

When you think of these things, my dear brethren, there is only one reasonable resolution for you to make. It is to live in such a way that you may be ready to die at any instant; to be like those wise virgins of whom the Gospel of to-day's feast, the feast of the glorious martyr St. Catherine, tells us, who had oil in their lamps when the cry came at midnight: "Behold the bridegroom cometh, go ye forth to meet him." To have the grace of God, which is represented by that oil, always in the lamp of your soul; to be always in the state of grace, never in that of sin; for most assuredly that cry will come to each one of you, and sooner than you think; and woe be to you if you are not prepared when it shall sound in your ears!

www.ingramcontent.com/pod-product-compliance
Lightning Source LLC
Chambersburg PA
CBHW051857300426
44117CB00006B/436